The Dilemma of "Double-Consciousness"

Denise Heinze

The Dilemma of

"Double-Consciousness"

Toni Morrison's Novels

The University of Georgia Press
Athens and London

© 1993 by the University of Georgia Press
Athens, Georgia 30602
All rights reserved
Designed by Louise OFarrell
Set in 10/14 Linotype Walbaum
   by Tseng Information Systems, Inc.
Printed and bound by Thomson Shore Inc.
The paper in this book meets the guidelines for
permanence and durability of the Committee on
Production Guidelines for Book Longevity of the
Council on Library Resources.

Printed in the United States of America
97 96 95 94 93   C   5 4 3 2 1

Library of Congress Cataloging in Publication Data
Heinze, Denise.
The dilemma of double-consciousness :
Toni Morrison's novels / Denise Heinze.
p. cm.
Based on the author's thesis (Ph.D.)—Duke
University.
Includes bibliographical references and index.
ISBN 0-8203-1523-0 (alk. paper)
1. Morrison, Toni—Political and social views.
2. Literature and society—United States
—History—20th century.   3. Afro-Americans in
literature.   4. Race relations in literature.
5. Polarity in literature.   I. Title.
PS3563.08749Z68   1993
813'.54—dc20

92-21425

British Library Cataloging in Publication Data available

To my mother, Miriam Gorton Heinze,
who, with the certainty of a prophet
and the conviction of mother love,
said, "One day you will be a writer."

Contents

Acknowledgments

This book was just a glimmer in my eye while I was completing my master's degree at North Carolina Central University. It later grew into a doctoral dissertation at Duke University. These professors provided guidance, encouragement, and, most important, consistency: John Sekora, Patsy Perry, and Muriel Mellown of North Carolina Central University; Victor Strandberg and Cathy Davidson of Duke University; and Linda Wagner-Martin of UNC–Chapel Hill. Since graduate school, this book has undergone extensive revision and might never have reached fruition had it not been for the expertise of Karla Holloway and Nellie McKay.

Most instrumental in providing support were my family and friends: the Heinze family (bloods and nonbloods alike); D. J. Maniace and family; my colleagues at Western Carolina University, especially Gayle Miller, Brian Railsback, and Elizabeth Addison; Donna Lee Frega, Cathy West, Wendy Cravens, Elizabeth Evans, and the principal members of my feminist reading group at Duke University, Pat Kalayjian and Mary Gillian. I also thank Nancy Norgaard for her technical assistance.

The Dilemma of "Double-Consciousness"

Introduction

When Toni Morrison attended a book
signing at the Smithsonian Institution for *Beloved*, her readers—
"most of them women—[held] the volume close to their chests like
a treasured object,"[1] an act of reverence matched in intensity by
the majority of reviewers—most of them men—who in an unusually effusive outpouring of praise called her novel "intense," "formidable," "dazzling," and "extraordinary."[2] Meeting the criteria for
greatness in many arenas, *Beloved* was considered by one reviewer
"a milestone in the chronicling of the black experience in America,"[3]
and by another "a stunning book and lasting achievement [which]
transforms the sorrows of history into the luminous truth of art."[4] As
if ethnic and universal applicability were not enough, John Leonard
elevates *Beloved* to the status of spiritual healer; without *Beloved*,
he says, "our imagination of the nation's self has a hole in it big
enough to die from." Consequently, he feels *Beloved* "belongs on the
highest shelf of American literature, even if half a dozen canonized
white boys have to be elbowed off." Walter Clemons agrees and in
a single sentence announces the White Election: "I think we have a
masterpiece on our hands here."[5]

Such spectacular praise represents not just a hallmark in Toni
Morrison's career, but quite possibly in the history of African-American writers in American literature. In the reviewers' unabashed
endorsement of Morrison is not only the acknowledgment of her
combined greatness as a voice for black people and as a master crafts-
person of the dominant literary artistic form—a feat several other
African-American writers (Toomer, Hurston, Wright, Baldwin, Elli-

son, and Walker, to name a few) have also been recognized for—but what appears to be the assertion that Morrison as a black woman writer has moved from the fringe of the literary establishment to become a dominant articulating vision of current and future literary culture. Joanne Braxton makes this claim for contemporary black women writers in general who, she says, have placed "the Black woman at the center of human experience, art, and consciousness, instead of at the periphery."[6]

But Morrison is more than just a member of that elite group; she quite possibly is its major figure. Before readers had caught their breath from *Beloved*, Morrison launched *Jazz* (1992), her sixth novel, which met with generally positive, sometimes breathless, reviews and solidified her prominence as "one of the finest contemporary writers in America."[7] Released simultaneously with *Jazz* was Morrison's *Playing in the Dark* (a scholarly work based on three lectures Morrison gave at Harvard). The publisher, Harvard University Press, decided to run twenty-five thousand initial copies of this book, instead of the traditional number of fifteen hundred.[8] While Harvard Press's confidence in a scholarly work is not without precedence— Eudora Welty's Harvard lectures produced a best-seller for the press in 1984.[9]—it is clearly indicative of Morrison's stature as a great American novelist.

As if cognizant of the possibility that they may be witnessing an evolution of literary culture, the reviewers of *Beloved* and *Jazz* appear to grope for the appropriate superlative, the illuminating phrase, even to wax poetic in an endeavor to articulate the cultural phenomenon that Morrison represents. Indeed, John Leonard wants to get rid of an infield of canonized white male writers in deference to the power of Morrison's writings. David Gates, in a review of *Jazz*, calls Morrison "the last classic American writer, squarely in the tradition of Poe, Melville, Twain and Faulkner."[10] Though she fits few preexisting categories of authorship and will indeed be a strange addition to the Kiwanis Club of American literature— Irving, Cooper, Hawthorne, Poe, Melville, James, Twain, Faulkner, Fitzgerald, and Hemingway—her inclusion in this group is now axiomatic, not arbitrary, and to a great extent, a challenge to the

superstructure of which she is now a predominant part. Her readership has clutched her to the American breast in spite of the fact that
she is a woman and a black and in spite of the fact that her books
are often a slap in the face to an America suffering from moral and
intellectual lethargy.

One wonders if Morrison's novels function in the same way that
the ghost Beloved does—to haunt and torment a guilty conscience
in need of absolution and redemption, for in each of her works
Morrison launders one American ideal after another, while a huge
contingency of Americans—male and female, black and white, rich
and poor—wildly cheer her on. She is a mythbasher in a country
where writers have been canonized for creating and perpetuating
the myths that form the foundation of the American way of thinking: the cult of domesticity and true womanhood, romantic love and
ideal standards of beauty, capitalism and the Protestant work ethic,
western culture and its obsession with modern technology, Christianity and science, and the collective notion of reality. Morrison
even challenges the very literature she generates, debunking the
tendency of society to elevate writers to mythic status. But Morrison
is also a mythmaker whose ontology, though nebulous, finds meaning in nature, primitivism, the past, the supernatural, and spiritual
love—certainly the stuff that dreams are made of, but not likely to be
the equation to satisfy an increasingly hardheaded, advanced, and
sophisticated society.

Her popularity, then, appears to run counter to what at least one
critic, W. Lawrence Hogue, sees as the dominant culture's attempt
at "repression of nonconformist literary texts." [11] Hogue states that
the dominant literary establishment, "editors, publishers, critics and
reviewers," tend to publish only those texts that reinforce the prevailing attitudes and values of the status quo. Nonconformist texts
that do not reflect the dominant values are judged against a literary criterion and found wanting: "In short, [the establishment]
determine[s] what is a 'good' or 'bad' literary text in accordance
with the degree to which it effectively reproduces certain values and
codes of the dominant society. The entire mode of literary production is society's social ideologies." [12] Hogue implies that the success

of African-American texts like those written by Morrison are functions of how they "reproduce many of the dominant establishments'
values" [13] and thus can be appropriated to perpetuate the system.

> Literature is one of the social institutions within society, or even
> within oppressed social groups within society. Its function is to gen-
> erate a group's world views or ideologies. It is to provide indices or
> coherent myths for social subjects as they seek equilibrium. But, when
> a group is not in control of its literary productions, as is the case for
> Afro-Americans, it must become aware of the ways in which the group
> which is controlling Afro-American literary productions is using them.
> It must be concerned with the question of whose interests those produc-
> tions serve.[14]

If Hogue is correct in assuming that Morrison's novels are being
used by the literary establishment (keeping in mind that, as a former
editor, Morrison could be considered part of that establishment), the
question begs why, if Morrison consistently undermines and challenges those values and codes that Hogue claims are so diligently
guarded by the dominant society?

Certainly, her popularity is not unanimous and she has been subject to the reproof of at least a few critics including a trouncing by
Stanley Crouch, who saw *Beloved* as "the failure of feeling that is
sentimentality." [15] Invoking the tried and true charge of excess sentiment that buried the reputation of many respected female writers of
the nineteenth century, Crouch accuses Morrison of "almost always
[losing] control" and of not resisting "the temptation of the trite
or the sentimental." [16] Crouch characterizes Morrison's affinity for
ghosts and the fantastic as a typically female proclivity that "fails to
rise to tragedy because it shows no sense of the timeless and unpre-
dictable manifestations of evil that preceded and followed American
slavery." [17] Such traditional valorization of intellect over feeling and
general/timeless over specific/timely events has done damage to the
careers of no less personages than Jane Austen and Virginia Woolf,
literary luminaries whose female otherness clings to them in spite
of recent efforts to integrate them into a more comprehensive perspective of literary history. Crouch attempts to diminish Morrison's
reputation and stature by trivializing her genius at moving the heart

and at stretching the limits of the imagination. What Crouch perceives as a weakness is exactly what thousands of Morrison's readers see as a strength: her ability to re-create the lives of ordinary citizens at the mercy of extraordinary events. In addition, in Morrison's novels, emotionality, rather than a hindrance, is often a precursor to intellectual awakening.

Crouch's criticisms, certainly reflective of the literary establishment, are muted by the overwhelmingly positive response of the majority of reviewers. Returning to Hogue's charge that successful African-American literature like Morrison's novels somehow serve the interests of the dominant ideology, the question remains in what way and for what purpose?

The answer to the issue Hogue has raised may reside in terms of Du Bois's double-consciousness, a state of affairs in which an individual is both representative of and immersed in two distinct ways of life. Patricia Collins calls it the "outsider within status" in which "outsider allegiances may militate against [black women] choosing full insider status, and they may be more apt to remain outsiders within."[18] Michael Awkward, in his study of the literary tradition of African-American women writers, agrees with anthropologist Victor Turner that double-consciousness can often become a permanent condition with no resolution: "Certainly one way to conceive of the Afro-American's attempt to resolve double consciousness is as a struggle to be initiated into the larger American society. Such a struggle does not necessarily conclude in acceptance by that society (what Turner terms 'aggregation'), to be sure. In other words, Afro-American double consciousness is not always resolved."[19]

Morrison's acceptance as a great American novelist constitutes, if not a resolution, a rare accommodation of two often competing literary selves. Indeed, her very success as a writer may be a testimony to the power of irresolution as a motivating factor in the psychic and spiritual struggle for wholeness. In many respects her novels reproduce the recognizable elements of the traditional literature: plot, characters, themes, and symbols; and deftly and eloquently appropriate the language of Standard English. This is hardly surprising since, as Henry Louis Gates Jr. says, "black writers, like critics of black literature, learn to write by reading literature, especially the canonical texts of the Western tradition. Consequently, black texts resemble other, Western, texts. These black texts employ many of the conventions of literacy form that comprise the Western tradition. Black literature shares much with, far more than it differs from, the Western textual tradition. . . . But black formal repetition always repeats with a difference, a black difference that manifests itself in specific language use." [20]

Gates explains this language use in terms of Mikhail Bakhtin's "double-voiced words," "a word or utterance . . . decolonized for the black's purposes 'by inserting a new semantic orientation into a word which already has—and retains—its own orientation.' " [21] The double-voiced words in this case are those found in the black vernacular that frequently decolonizes Standard English. Gates calls this play on Standard English "Signification," an "obscuring of apparent meaning," [22] capitalized in difference to the white term signification or apparent meaning "because it always entails formal revision and an intertextual relation." [23] The identical spelling illustrates "first, that a simultaneous, but negated parallel discursive (ontological, political) universe exists within the larger white discursive universe." [24] Rather than argue that conformist and nonconformist texts are independently contrived, in this case novels written by blacks within the constraints of the white establishment, Gates speaks of a symbiotic relationship in which both products of black and white culture are to a great extent dependent on and imitative of each other. "Ironically, rather than a proclamation of emancipation from the white person's standard English, the symbiotic relationship between the black and white, between the syntagmatic and paradigmatic axes, between black vernacular discourse and standard English discourse, is underscored here, and signified, by the vertiginous relationship between the terms *signification* and *Signification*, each of which is dependent on the other." [25]

Morrison's novels reveal a relationship with a preexisting text that she at once appropriates and repudiates. Her novels do not submit solely to traditional expectations, but transform, as Terence Hawkes says, the whole system that they embody and that has produced them: they do "not merely rehearse preordained categories and combine them in novel ways." Instead they modify what they consist of.[26]

Morrison defamiliarizes not only by extending and modifying the language[27] (or allowing the signifier to slip over the signified infusing names, nursery rhymes, and human acts with meaning); but also by shifting the voice of the narrator, if not displacing it altogether; by refusing to demystify her characters; by constructing a plot that defies presupposition; and by declining to distinguish realism from allegory.

Extending beyond the Signification of semantic and literacy form, Toni Morrison Signifies thematically on the very values and ideals the literary establishment expounds. Her double-voicedness is one manifestation of her double vision for she employs both the black vernacular and Standard English to challenge the established value system. Complicating this state of affairs is the fact that Morrison herself was, and is, the beneficiary of many of the values she attacks. She belonged to a family in which the father worked very hard and the mother stayed home and ran household affairs. Probably very much as a result of this traditional arrangement, she went to college and later landed a good job. In addition, she was a beauty queen who eventually fell in love and got married. She is a perfectionist in her own work as was her father in his ship welding and thus a shining example of the efficacy of the Protestant work ethic that is the engine behind capitalism. Now a faculty member at Princeton University, she has achieved the highest level of professional success. If anything, Morrison is the quintessential success story, a modern-day Horatio Alger who remains unconvinced of the validity of the system that may have contributed to her success.

But if Morrison is a product of her times, she is more so a visionary capable of shelving her personal accomplishments to uncover the ashes behind the glitter. As a child she experienced enough poverty, hatred, and racism to last a lifetime. Certainly watching her father toil at three jobs simultaneously for seventeen years left a shadow on her own brilliant success. Howard University was not a mecca for intellectual stimulation: "It was about getting married, buying clothes, and going to parties."[28] Her marriage ended and she refuses to talk about it. Surrounding her disappointments and failures is the suffering of vast numbers of black people, a condition she cannot forget or forgive in spite of the fact that she has achieved success. Her own success is only partial compensation for her primary desire to effect change in American culture, a goal that becomes her albatross by virtue of her membership in the black community, an affiliation of race, history, and culture that cannot be dissolved by wealth and fame.

Morrison, however, is an artist, not a sociologist or historian; she writes fiction and thus acts as a mediator of the real world rather than its mimic. Hogue contends that the writer cannot mirror "Afro-American social reality" but can only present "an ideological representation of the Afro-American social reality."[29] Houston Baker explains this idea in terms of the blues: "The singer and his production are always at this intersection, this crossing, codifying force, providing resonance for experience's multiplicities. Singer and song never arrest transience—fix it in 'transcendent form.' Instead, they provide expressive equivalence for the juncture's ceaseless flux. Hence, they may be conceived of as translators."[30]

As an artist, Morrison negotiates a very complex matrix of reality in which she is both despised and revered, absent and present, ignored and sought after. The result is a double-visionary canon, a symbiosis of novel-writing in which Morrison has complete mastery over the fictive reality she creates. And by her creative mediation between the real and fictive worlds, she generates possibilities rather than records continued frustration and oppression. Morrison may not write from a stance of art as life, but she may be a psychological and spiritual Wizard of Oz for life as art.

If Morrison can Signify upon traditional American values, apparently without alienating her white readership, she does so because she employs traditional, recognizable, often comfortable modes of storytelling, and because much of what she does write eventually leads back to the universal condition of being human. But for her, having witnessed the corruption of human values in the dominant society, that leading back or rediscovery of those values is best effected in black culture. Morrison's work becomes an articulation of Black Cultural Nationalism (BCN), which, according to Harry Reed, "contends that black people possess a culture, style of life, world view, and aesthetic values different from white Americans."[31] As a Black Cultural Nationalist, Morrison "validate[s] black culture and reaffirm[s] adaptive survival power, its creativity amidst oppression, life-affirming qualities, as well as its ancient wisdom and humanity and its capacity for survival."[32] But, Reed claims, Morrison's, and other black women writers', attempts to equate cultural with political survival have largely been ignored by the predominantly male political activists of the BCN movement: "Generally, the writers who have taken a holistic approach to BCN have been drowned out by their more political opponents."[33] According to Norris Clark, Morrison, rather than using art for strictly political purposes like other black artists of her ilk—Gwendolyn Brooks, Clarence Major, Albert Yound—"realized that political persuasion (propaganda), rhetorical inanities, 'Black English,' or a strict adherence to a political dogma would be insufficient to promote the aesthetic qualities of art."[34] Black Cultural Nationalists like Morrison chose to subordinate the political in order to "establish a positive black identity and to reorder racial consciousness through serious exploration and rediscovery of the black community's unique cultural heritage: its own particular beauty, its rich and varied oral tradition, its private joys and agonies, as well as its communal 'trials and tribulations.' "[35] Though she validates the aesthetic qualities of the black community, Morrison is anything but apolitical. She says, "The work must be political. It must have that as its thrust. . . . The best art is political and you ought to be able to make it unquestionably political and irrevocably beautiful at the same time."[36]

By combining political consciousness with aesthetic sensibility, Morrison achieves a very delicate balance: without directly denouncing white society, she illustrates the demise of blacks who have adopted the corrupting influence of the white community. By indirection Morrison avoids the polarization of black and white humanity—one as inherently good, the other irrevocably corrupt—and thus allows all people to vicariously experience a rebirth through the black community. While her intent may be to valorize the black community and ignite both blacks and whites into political action, what she also wishes is to elevate through art the beautiful—and hence reclaimable—in the human condition.

Perhaps therein lies her appeal, for in denouncing the dominant culture she presents to an aging America alternatives that have always existed and are now emerging, but which have long been suppressed by the rhetoric of an entrenched ideology. Morrison's success as a great American writer is perhaps a function of two factors: (1) her ability to manipulate her insider/outsider status, for she both subverts and maintains, is exploited by and exploits the literary establishment, and (2) her recognition that her double-consciousness can never be, perhaps never should be, integrated into a single vision. Indeed, she is in the truly remarkable position of being able to articulate with near impunity two cultures—one black, the other white American. By orchestrating this sense of connectedness between cultures rather than attempting to dissolve the differences, Morrison's successful career appears to have transcended the "permanent condition"[37] of double-consciousness that afflicts her fictional characters.

But the issue of Morrison's double-consciousness cannot ultimately be explained in terms of her relationship to the dominant culture. Placing Morrison's work in the tradition of African-American literature, as Michael Awkward does in his analysis of *The Bluest Eye*, provides an understanding of the shared history of double-consciousness as it is manifested in the writings of black Americans. Awkward contends that the splitting of Pecola's voice as she goes insane and "the double-voiced narration of the novel" (Claudia and the omniscient narrator) are "coded intertexts of W. E. B. Du Bois's discussion of a Black 'double-consciousness.' "[38] He says:

> Morrison's double-voiced narration in *The Bluest Eye* encodes not the
> anger of the author as Hedin argues, but her employment and refigu-
> ration of this Black cultural code. Pecola's means of achieving peace—
> double voicedness—is Morrison's means, through the complexity of
> her narrative structure, of positioning her novel in relationship to other
> Afro-American texts that explicitly explore *structural* means of merg-
> ing two almost antithetical "selves." *The Bluest Eye* resonates in the
> company of Du Bois' *Souls* and Zora Neale Hurston's *Their Eyes Were
> Watching God.*[39]

Awkward admits that Morrison's positioning is not always conscious or intentional—she says she never read Hurston—nevertheless, he illustrates that her works are a refiguration of preexisting

African-American texts, especially those written by black women concerned with double-consciousness. Her writing, Awkward states, is a quest she shares with her female literary ancestors "for (psychic and narrative) unity and community."[40]

Perhaps more compelling than the fact that Morrison writes in reaction to or in sympathy with preexisting white and black texts is that she refigures her own texts in such a fashion that she is the literary father of her subsequent works. Morrison exhibits at times a dissatisfaction with aspects of her earlier works, often revisioning or expanding previous familial structures—her trinity of women; communities—Lorain and Bottom, alone constituting difference; and spatial and temporal considerations—her characters increasingly become participants in a larger geography and history. She even goes so far as to question the methodology of her own literary production and the validity of her role as author, revealing the extent she will go to break the sound barrier of double-consciousness.

By virtue of the fact that she challenges not only western values, but even the constraints and limitations of her own novels, all the while utilizing western literacy form, Morrison establishes a diverse readership that crosses racial, cultural, and class lines. What she attempts and achieves is identification. Theresa Enos, in her discussion of writer, subject, and audience, explains that identification is a process by which the writer initially creates an imaginary audience that is allied to her values and ideals. By presenting this fictive audience to the reader and the ethical and moral ambience it generates, the writer in a sense invites the reader to become part of the audience. Enos explains that

> the writer creates the audience out of potentially shared perceptions of reality. Furthermore, instead of a real audience listening to the classical orator, the discourser's audience today is likely an interiorized one in the Vygotskian sense—that is, in "creating" our audience we're "inventing" what is already part of us. . . . Furthermore, and importantly, out of the writer's inventive universe comes a generative ethos that makes possible interlocking identification among writer, subject, and audience.[41]

By creating a fictive audience that essentially and initially shares her values and ideals, as Peter Elbow says, an "*inviting* audience of

trusted friends or allies,"[42] Morrison "project[s] a self that invites
the reader in, and, if readers identify with this self, they, in effect,
become part of that 'self,' become the audience, in the process of
reading."[43] To complete the identification, because the writer creates
an audience with a given set of values in a text, the writer "through
ethos . . . also becomes one with the audience that has been created."[44] Robert Roth states that given the nature of reader response
theory and the poststructuralist debunking of the notion that writers
send messages and readers decode them "it may not seem strange to
say that writers may be their own audiences or to think of audience
as a textual entity that writers create during composing and readers
create anew when they perform the text."[45] In essence, Morrison has
imagined the ideal audience into existence. Roth calls this the "end
of authorial dominance" in which "writers search for ways to bring
readers into their texts."[46]

In her novels Morrison begins her search by addressing what is
most intimate and meaningful to her—the black family—and then
broadens her scope to the black community, regions of the United
States, foreign lands and alien cultures, history, and reality. Each
novel moves forward to a new concern, but without having completely left behind previous ones; thus, the movement is both linear
and circular, a Yeatsian gyre that spins back on itself but inevitably
leads upward to new ways of seeing old systems of belief. In this
respect her novels are, to invoke Robert Stepto, an intratextual call
and response, a progressive troping of her own works.[47] Each novel
in progression is an increasingly bold and original revoicing of previous concerns. She characterizes the demise of the family organized
according to patriarchal principles; she exposes the demoralizing
and dehumanizing commodification of romantic love and standards
of beauty; she sees capitalism as a corrosive and insidious perverter
of human worth; modern technology, science, and religion become
a panacea for spiritual depravity; and reality is propaganda for the
bourgeoisie.

As an established member of the literati and a product of America's
underclass, Morrison brings to her writing a complicated perspective;
she employs rational and controlled methods to naturalize increasingly irrational responses to life. Morrison's successes necessitate an

investigation of what those values and ideals are that often stand in stark contrast to the status quo and how they manage to capture the imagination of a large and growing readership. Where Morrison has come from and what she stands for are embedded in her novels; what remains to be done is to place her in history and ultimately ourselves in herstory. In effect, Morrison invites her readership to come along with her in Du Bois's symbolic Jim Crow car,[48] a journey into double-consciousness in which the final destination—truth and understanding—is only the beginning.

Beauty and Love:

The Morrison

Aesthetic

In Morrison's endeavor to understand how self and identity are affected by society, she turns her double vision on the notion of aesthetics. Morrison confronts both the aesthetics of white culture, and the ever-evolving, often conflicting definition of aesthetics in the black community. The black aesthetic has undergone a series of revisions, moving in the sixties and seventies from an overtly political stance that disavowed "traditional assumptions of art" [1] to an attempt to re-create in art the beauty of the black experience. Norris Clark cites artists like Gwendolyn Brooks, Ishmael Reed, and Toni Morrison who felt that political rhetoric was "insufficient to promote the aesthetic qualities of art," [2] and who then challenged "the relationship between 'art and Politics' rather than 'politics and arts.' Their ideological emphasis was on art rather than on polemics or racial rhetoric." [3] Morrison and writers of her persuasion see the black aesthetic as not just the re-creation of the black experience, but the artistic rendering of that experience, which will necessarily have a political cast.

Perhaps even more significantly, Morrison and other black writers recognize that the black aesthetic in art "should, by definition, incorporate a sense of what it is like to face life's multitude of complexities as a person affected by racial values (Afrocentric and Eurocentric) pertaining to the black communities."[4] In a somewhat radical shift from a strictly indigenous concept of aesthetics, Toni Morrison's writings suggest that it is insufficient—indeed naive—to define a black aesthetic independent of white aesthetics. As Henry Louis Gates Jr., has discussed, "racial values" as a function of "race" are not a biological but a cultural phenomenon. "Race" as social construct, Gates says, "has become a trope of ultimate, irreducible difference between cultures, linguistic groups, or adherents of specific belief systems which—more often than not—also have fundamentally opposed economic interests."[5] Toni Morrison foregrounds the aesthetic values of a white race that sees blackness as a metaphor for lack, perhaps as a justification for disenfranchising blacks politically and economically. But rather than illustrate exclusively the victimizing power of decadent values, Morrison frequently alters, substitutes, or replaces the white aesthetic by presenting or creating a black aesthetic of difference.

In particular, and the focus of this chapter, Morrison Signifies upon the wholesale acceptance of the aesthetic of idealized beauty, one of the most dangerous of societal constructs because, by placing value on a very limited set of physical criteria, it can reduce human beings on sight to objects. Idealized beauty has the power to disenfranchise a child of mother love, to psychically splinter an entire race identity, and to imprison all human beings in static and stagnant relationships. It even shapes Morrison's image of herself. She once asked a reporter, "Are you really going to put a middle-aged, gray-haired colored lady on the cover of this magazine?"[6]

Her incredulity, though certainly somewhat feigned, reveals, nevertheless, a skepticism that informs the reality of being female, older, and black in a society that valorizes males, youth, and whiteness. Her question provides context for her denunciation of standardized beauty and its destructive force. Morrison, in her novels, focuses on the spurious criteria of beauty and its cause and effect relationship to love: if one is pretty, one is loved.[7] Morrison rejects those standards of beauty—perhaps even the possibly variant ones that once elected her beauty queen—that exclude and torment the majority of women torn between self-love and self-loathing. Idealized beauty can turn the uninitiated against themselves, their children, their lovers, even their culture. It affects the instinctive love of parents for children, the desire for a healthy, monogamous relationship, and the proclivity for racial and community pride. Because it manifests itself in self-hatred, inter- and intraracial hatred, it has the power to destroy the potential for love, and it is exactly that thwarted possibility that consistently haunts the characters in Morrison's world. She fine-tunes the fuzziness that, like the glow surrounding the movie heroine, deludes the observer into a false sense of reality. Her novels are an unrelenting reminder of the futility of imitating a discriminatory standard in hopes of attaining an even more unrealistic state of perfect love. But while Morrison tosses one icon of beauty into the incinerator, she also raises the edifice of another, thereby enriching and expanding the definition of beauty and, ultimately, its relationship to love.

Colorism

Best expressing Morrison's sentiments about ideal beauty is Claudia, the narrator in *The Bluest Eye*, who cannot understand the universal allure of the white baby doll.

> I had only one desire: to dismember it. To see of what it was made, to discover the dearness, to find the beauty, the desirability that had escaped me, but apparently only me. Adults, older girls, shops, magazines, newspapers, window signs—all the world had agreed that a blue-eyed, yellow-haired, pink-skinned doll was what every girl treasured. "Here," they said, "this is beautiful, and if you are on this day 'worthy' you may have it." . . . I could not love it. But I could see what it was that all the world said was lovable.[8]

Claudia's hatred is born of a painful childhood lesson that teaches her she can never be as beautiful or lovable as the standards of western culture dictate. Intensifying her bitterness and confusion is not only the unquestioning adoration of the doll but the fact that she, too, is forced—expected—to love the very iconoclastic reminder of her own unworthiness. Claudia's desire to dismember the doll is a deconstructive attempt to make sense of an incomprehensible aesthetic. Claudia refuses to accept the value that resides in the plastic representation until she understands how that meaning was produced. But she cannot "discover the dearness" or "find the beauty" because it is buried under layers of enculturation. While "all the world" may agree that blonde hair and blue eyes are beautiful, no one can explain to Claudia the origins of that belief system, for they have come to accept without question that western beauty is somehow natural.

The fact that western beauty is anything but natural for all people is partially addressed by Sander Gilman whose fascinating study of nineteenth-century European art, medicine, and literature traces the historical conspiracy to construct a sexual and aesthetic difference between black and white women, placing white women at the top of an imaginary hierarchy of beauty and sexual virtue while consistently relegating black women to the lowest order of female. Gilman says, "The antithesis of European sexual mores and beauty is embodied in the black, and the essential black, the lowest rung on the great chain of being, is the Hottentot. The physical appearance of the Hottentot is, indeed, the central nineteenth-century icon for sexual difference in sexual physiology which puzzled even early monogenetic theoreticians such as Johann Friedrich Blumenbach."[9] Black women came to represent sexual immorality and were compared to prostitutes. Not only was their sexuality reduced to pathology, but their skin color as well: "The favorite theory, which reappears with some frequency in the early nineteenth century, is that the skin color and attendant physiognomy of the black are the result of congenital leprosy."[10]

Divested of any knowledge of the social construction of beauty, Claudia is eventually enculturated to white ways, and repudiation gives way to acceptance: "I learned much later to worship [Shirley Temple], just as I learned to delight in cleanliness, knowing, even as I learned, that the change was adjustment without improvement" (p. 22). This initial step toward self-hatred is the first in the process leading to the black community identifying against itself. A massive assault on the black psyche, it not only creates a schism between races but is also responsible for colorism, an even more perplexing form of racism within the black community. Alice Walker defines colorism as "prejudicial or preferential treatment of same-race people based solely on their color." [11] Colorists will jockey for position on a color hierarchy with whiteness as either that which should be emulated or repudiated. Those blacks who are light-skinned often assume, or are perceived to assume, a superiority based solely on the relative absence of melanin from their skin, while dark-skinned people take such overblown pride in their African heritage as to label light-skinned blacks Uncle Toms.

Although not all blacks acknowledge the existence of colorism—on one fairly recent Phil Donahue broadcast the panel was hotly divided over whether it was a problem at all [12] and at least one black professor at Howard University claims colorism has never been proven [13]—most black writers and journalists support the notion that blacks have historically seen light skin as an avenue to greater equality. In fact, Alice Walker attempts to trace the very origins of colorism to nineteenth-century black men and women writers who, while more comfortable in portraying dark-skinned heroes, nevertheless created exclusively light-skinned heroines. Walker takes aim at William Wells Brown, Frances Ellen Watkins Harper, Emma Dunham Kelly, and Pauline Hopkins, all of whom used light-skinned heroines from the middle and upper-middle class. Says Walker, "The three black women novelists of the nineteenth century turned away from their own selves in depicting 'black womanhood,' and followed a black man's interpretation of white male writers' fantasies. Consequently, as late as 1929 it was unheard of for a very dark-skinned woman to appear in a novel unless it was clear she was to be recognized as a problem or a joke." [14] Walker concedes that these writers wrote for a predominantly white audience, but she laments that "their depictions of themselves and black people as whiter than we are has led to a crippling of the imagination and truth itself for which we pay dearly—in anger, hurt, envy, and misunderstanding—to this day." [15]

While Walker may be correct in her analysis of the effects of the prevalence of the light-skinned heroine, she oversimplifies the reasons why black writers in the nineteenth century chose to rely on the trope of passing and the tragic mulatto. Black women writers did not necessarily "turn away from themselves"; rather, as Hazel Carby suggests, they attempted to expose the reality of miscegenation to a white readership mired in denial. [16] In addition, Missy Dehn Kubitschek contends that "the trope of passing depicts more than a privileged individual's purely personal decisions; it investigates an individual's relationships with history." [17] If black women writers of the nineteenth century contributed to the legacy of colorism as Walker suggests, they did so unintentionally, and in an endeavor to contextualize themselves and their fictional heroines in a highly complex and confusing social matrix.

Also responsible for the problem of color were the black male leaders who were themselves light-skinned or who chose mulatto, or even white, spouses. Paula Giddings writes, "Black men themselves commented on the phenomenon of their attraction to fair-skinned women. 'It is generally the case,' said the editor T. Thomas Fortune during a debate about Black identity, 'that those Black men who clamor most luridly and persistently for the purity of Negro blood have taken themselves mulatto wives.' " [18] Based on this cultural influence and the fact that so many of the male leaders and writers were themselves light, Alice Walker emphasizes that we must contextualize their contributions: "We can continue to respect and love many of these writers, and treasure what they wrote because we understand *America*; but we must be wary of their depictions of black women because we understand ourselves." [19]

The perception of white as better, while diminishing in the last few decades, lingers in the minds and hearts of blacks. In his movie *School Daze*, director-producer Spike Lee addresses the dilemma of colorism. His drama created such a controversy that the United Negro College Fund broke off negotiations for a premier showing, and Lee's alma mater, Morehouse College, would not let him finish shooting.[20] In her article "The Bluest Eye?" Elsie Washington sees the trendiness of blue contact lenses in the black community as a disavowal of racial identity. She says that "the wish to acquire what we were not born with, to adopt the coloring that has for centuries been touted as prettier, finer, better, carries with it all the old baggage of racial inferiority and/or superiority based simply, and simplistically, on physical traits."[21] One sociologist, Harriette McAdoo, comments that while skin color is not now as important as it once was, "some light-skinned Blacks still feel superior and prefer to socialize with those of similar appearance, while others who are very dark continue to harbor feelings of group-imposed inferiority or insecurity."[22]

In an understandable if not justifiable reaction to the perception of lighter as better, dark-skinned blacks have resorted to their own brand of colorism in the last twenty years by touting blackness as beautiful. One light-skinned man tells of his painful experiences growing up. "I bumped into memories of the epithets of miscegenation that dogged my early childhood: red, high yella, sunshine, Casper-white boy."[23] Many light-skinned men, he says, struggle to throw off the notion that they take pride in their white attributes, especially since they are often made to feel less black, and masculine: "I felt like damaged goods as she, herself light-complected, explained how dark men, such as her husband, possessed a sultry exoticism, a primal power and an aura of full-blooded masculinity. In other words, only dark-skinned brothers were the real brothers."[24] One light-skinned woman took her grievance to court: "In Atlanta, Tracy Lynn Morrow, 27, a light-skinned black typist at the Internal Revenue Service, filed a lawsuit against her employer, contending that her supervisor, a dark-skinned black woman, had discriminated against her and later fired her because of her skin color."[25]

Morrison is no less conscious of colorism and appears to have a distaste for it no matter what shade the perpetrator. According to Norris Clark, Morrison does not advocate the black aesthetic of Black is Beautiful: "To Morrison, the obsession with establishing blackness and its beauty is a reaction to a white idea, which means it is a white idea turned inside out; and a white idea turned inside out is still a white idea."[26] Those who attempt to lord their blackness over lighter-skinned people, Morrison suggests, are no less guilty of adopting a racist attitude. In addition, although Morrison does not state explicitly, she seems to imply that assuming superiority based on skin color is more a sign of weakness than strength since skin color—a biological given—has very little to do with the much more difficult task of proving intrinsic worth.

Yet, while Morrison chastises those who set themselves off because of their skin color, she frequently parades for the reader's perusal a string of entirely unappealing light-skinned characters—Maureen Peal (Pecola's snobbish schoolmate), Helene Wright (Nel's mother), Jadine (Son's lover), and Ruth Foster (Milkman's mother). They approximate the characteristics of the nineteenth-century black heroine, which included, besides being mulatto, "fragile beauty as the norm; qualities of helplessness, chastity, and refinement rather than, say, strength, endurance, and intelligence."[27] Constituting a rejection of those values, Morrison's own heroines—Eva, Pilate, the lady in canary yellow, Baby Suggs—are black-black, physically powerful and imposing, independent, classless, asexual, primal, and perhaps godly. Morrison creates wonderfully unique, dynamic black heroines and implies the unlikelihood of a similar strength and purpose in lighter-skinned blacks, representing them with only two sympathetic portraits, the Creole whore Rochelle who is gone in an instant in *Sula*, and the teacher Lady Jones who appears belatedly in *Beloved*. Not until *Jazz* does Morrison minimize the significance of color in her portrayal of the creamy Dorcas and the black-black Violet, both of whom are deserving of our sympathy and condemnation for reasons that are not implicitly tied to their skin color.

Morrison's bout with colorism seems a necessary purgative in her attack on ideal standards of beauty, which in her experience, it appears, have been most abused by light-skinned blacks. Morrison spares no feelings; she feels no compunction, to mitigate her belief that the valorization of light-skinned beauty is the most disturbing and prevalent form of colorism and thus functions as one of the greatest barriers to the spiritual and psychic health of the black community. C. A. Davis explains this same race hatred in Sartrean terms as allying oneself "to the Third so as to look at the Other who is then transformed into our object."[28] Light-skinned blacks absorb white values and translate them into hatred of dark-skinned blacks. "In this world," Davis says, "light-skinned women can feel superior to dark ones, married women to whores, and on and on. The temptations to Bad Faith are enormously increased, since one's own reification can be 'escaped' in the interlocking hierarchies that allow most to feel superior to someone. Only the very unlucky, or the truly free, are outside the system." [29] Such is the world Morrison creates in her novels in which people of the same race can be embroiled in a civil war as subtle as a reproving glance or blatant as a verbal assault.

Apparently most disturbing to Morrison are those blacks who attain a certain level of power and financial security but who use it either to anesthetize or distance themselves from their black roots. Dr. Foster, Milkman's light-skinned grandfather in *Song of Solomon*, and Jadine in *Tar Baby* are in a position to empower their race but choose instead to ignore or scorn it. And it is the example they set that determines the responses of other aspiring blacks. In a trickle-down effect, the Dr. Fosters of the world are the standard bearers who affect the Helenes and Geraldines (Junior's mother in *The Bluest Eye*) who in turn affect their children. Dr. Foster was, according to Macon Dead, a "high-yellow nigger who loved ether and hated black skin" and who called Negroes in town "cannibals." [30] Jadine is essentially oblivious to skin color or its ramifications until she sees the tar-black woman in canary yellow. Before this climactic experience, she perceived herself, and was perceived to be, culturally more white than black. Son, in fact, calls her "white girl," [31] an epithet that enrages her, but that cannot jolt her into any sustained awareness or action. She continues relatively unchanged, mimicking the life-style of the rich WASP culture. She and Dr. Foster, then, are powerful symbols who establish a standard that is adverse to community and conducive to bitter competition.

Their example directly influences the burgeoning middle class best represented by Geraldine and Helene Wright. Both are light-skinned blacks bent on driving the blackness out of themselves and, more importantly, their children. Junior and Nel are brought up in the most rigid western tradition of good morals and cleanliness, though neither can be totally disabused of their blackness. Even when they embrace what are essentially universal human values, the mothers—and Morrison fairly consistently points the finger at the mother—cannot, try as they might, make their children's skin white. Nel grows up relatively unaffected, probably because she has not inherited her mother's "custard-colored skin,"[32] but other children, like Junior and Maureen Peal, inherit the prejudice of their mothers. Maureen in *The Bluest Eye* is an especially disturbing symbol of colorism because as a child, she unleashes a cruelty unmatched by adults. Maureen Peal is "a high-yellow dream" but with "lynch ropes" for hair. When she takes in an unwitting Pecola and then humiliates her, she represents the epitome of same-race hatred. The greatest insult she can hurl at Pecola and Claudia is "I am cute! And you ugly! Black and ugly black e mos. I am cute!" (p. 61). And while Claudia struggles to cast off the implications of one child's perspective, she "could not destroy the honey voices of parents and aunts, the obedience in the eyes of our peers, the slippery light in the eyes of our teachers when they encountered the Maureen Peals of the world" (p. 62).

But as drawn as the lines appear to be between light and dark, Morrison shows that colorism is a complicated problem; those who struggle to acquire a superiority based on the color of their skin often experience conflicting desires to attach themselves to those across the color line. Though Son, the primal black man, reprimands Jadine for her white ways, he nevertheless is irresistibly and profoundly attracted to her, as well as defensive when she is attacked. Gideon calls Jadine Son's "first yalla" to which Son retorts, "She's not a yalla. . . . Just a little light." Son "didn't want any discussion about shades of black folk" (p. 133), perhaps because such a conversation might reveal Son's own conflicts about race and color. The same dilemma afflicts Macon Dead whose hatred for Dr. Foster and his uppityness does not deter him from marrying his "lemony skinned daughter" (*Song of Solomon*, p. 139), thus marrying into the world that has rebuked him for his blackness. Helene Wright takes comfort in the fact that her daughter is not as light as she is and that she has inherited her father's "broad flat nose . . . and his generous lips . . . although [she] expected to improve [the nose] somewhat" (*Sula*, p. 18). Finally in *Beloved*, Lady Jones, a mulatto, "believed in her heart that, except for her husband, the whole world (including her children) despised her and her hair. She had been listening to 'all that yellow gone to waste' and 'white nigger' since she was a girl in a houseful of silt-black children, so she disliked everybody a little bit because she believed they hated her hair as much as she did."[33] In an attempt to deny her light skin, Lady Jones had married "the blackest man she could find" (p. 247).

Morrison's concern with colorism exposes the many sides of a problem that continues to assault the black community. Morrison herself appears to have softened her own hard-line position on light-skinned characters just by virtue of the sympathetic creation of Lady Jones. Having gone from such invectives as "the origins of a mule and a mulatto were one and the same" (*Beloved*, p. 52), to the positive portrayal of a much-maligned school teacher, Morrison begins an incorporation into her world of victims of both sides. She further collapses the polemic of intraracial skin color in *Jazz* by avoiding earlier tendencies to valorize the black-black woman over the light-skinned one. Both the high yaller Dorcas and the dark-skinned Violet are victims and victimizers. Though Dorcas's light skin is not to blame for Joe Trace's infidelity, Violet's own obsession with whiteness becomes a barrier to understanding her husband's more complex need for renewal, for remembering "the way it was when he and Violet were young,"[34] and for self-determination: "Just as he had decided on his name, the walnut tree he and Victory slept in, a piece of bottomland, and when to head for the City, he decided on Dorcas" (p. 30).

Black Women and White Beauty

In the majority of Morrison's novels, colorism functions as an addiction, alternately anesthetizing people to the reality of their cultural heritage and driving them to fits of rage and violent acts. A social disease in a sense, it is only one manifestation of the insidious and lethal standard of westernized beauty. Morrison looks at how western beauty devours the black anima and destroys the white Streets, the very constituents of that standard. By fictionalizing black and white pain alike, Morrison reveals the universally destructive power of textbook beauty. No human being is capable of physical perfection; thus, all are doomed to varying degrees of self-hatred. That

there is more darkness than light in Morrison's novels is testimony
to her inability to reconcile a corrosive ideology and the people who
embrace it. Most susceptible are black women and girls, who too
often anchor their identity on the slippery surface of physical beauty,
not realizing the sacrifice of self and family. Those women in Morrison's world who have made western beauty their raison d'être fail to
realize that what they strive to be in their search for physical beauty
is the object not necessarily of black male desire, but of white male
desire. Therein lies the confusion, frustration, and demise of many
of the male-female relationships in Morrison's novels, for she seems
to say that the way black men and women see each other is often
profoundly at odds. Several of Morrison's main male characters—
Cholly, Milkman, and Son—*do* see the Hottentot as the antithesis
of white beauty, but, for them, the hierarchy is reversed. In addition, Morrison suggests that black men do not see black women as
objects at all but as mirrors of their own subjective selves, a subjec-
tivity that resides in shared cultural values about the intrinsic worth
of human beings. While a strong case could be made that black
men have to a great extent ingested notions of western beauty or
practice their own form of objectification—and some of Morrison's
own male characters, Macon Dead, for example, bear this out—
Morrison fictionalizes those men who have not denied the physical/
intrinsic beauty of their own culture, but who are helpless to stop
the dehumanization of their women who have.

Her first novel epitomizes a community of all shades that has swal-
lowed whole a convoluted notion of beauty and worth and then spit
it out at each other and their children. The controlling metaphor for
this state of affairs is in the title, the bluest eye—the transparent
eyeball gone mad—that becomes a synecdoche for western beauty,
for schopophilia and objectification, appropriation and commodification, acquiescence and insanity. The point of view in the novel is
not Pecola's or Claudia's or Pauline's or Cholly's but the bluest eye,
which orchestrates, obliterates, or ultimately determines all other
points of view. It is a decidedly male point of view, a Lacanian Gaze
in which the appropriating gaze of the subject is male and the object
of that gaze is female. Epitomizing this point of view is the store-
keeper Yacobowski, who will not even cast his bleary blue eyes on

a little black girl like Pecola because "nothing in his life even suggested that the feat was possible, not to say desirable or necessary" (p. 42). Indeed, so tunneled is his vision that "he cannot see her view—the angle of his vision, the slant of her finger, makes it incomprehensible to him" (p. 42). Pecola, a bright child, arrives at the conclusion early on that point of view holds the answer to whether one is pretty and thus loved. When "trying to discover the secret of the ugliness, the ugliness that made her ignored or despised at school" (p. 39), she realizes that "if her eyes, those eyes that held the pictures, and knew the sights—if those eyes of hers were different, that is to say beautiful, she herself would be different" (p. 40). What Pecola is wishing for is to be in the position of both subject and object; to possess *the* point of view is to see herself into existence. But Pecola is doomed because the impossibility of empowering herself is cemented as much by the dominant culture's values as her mother's acceptance of those values. Had Pecola's perspective been tempered by an exceptionally strong mother or father, she might at least have endured the evil eye, but the tragedy of Pecola in *The Bluest Eye* begins initially when Pauline Breedlove accepts Cholly's gaze as a measure of her worth and becomes irreversible the moment Pauline Breedlove substitutes the gaze of her husband for that of the bluest eye.

Pauline's unlove of herself begins early in life. Afflicted by a slight limp, she attributes all subsequent neglect and indifference to this slight deformity. As Morrison explains, "One easiest thing to do would be to build a case out of her foot. That is what she did herself" (p. 88). Possessed of a vivid imagination, Pauline assimilates all external events vaguely related to her and translates them into an exaggerated tragic vision. Replete with a romanticized image of herself, she conjures an idealized lover so abstract she can conceptualize him only as a Presence "with gentle and penetrating eyes, who—with no exchange of words—understood; and before whose glance her foot straightened and her eyes dropped" (p. 90). Cholly's arrival fulfills her dreams by translating her deformity into an asset—so powerful is the Significant Other in Pauline's life. But in the process of becoming physically whole, Pauline's "eyes dropped" suggesting a relinquishing of her mind's eye and, hence, a loss of self-determination. She submits totally to the appropriating eye of the Presence—Cholly—"who would know what to do. She had only to lay her head on his chest and he would lead her away to the sea, to the city, to the woods . . . forever" (p. 90). Because Pauline is blinded by her idealization of Cholly, she cannot foresee that her dependence on him to make her whole will resurrect the emotional scars of his life and wreak havoc on their domestic bliss.

The turning point for Pauline—when the healthy values of her southern childhood dissolve into the inverted values of her adulthood—is symbolized in the loss of her tooth. At this juncture, Pauline, already a hopeless romantic, has added the toxic notion of idealized beauty. The combination becomes lethal, what Morrison calls "the most destructive ideas in the history of human thought": "Both originated in envy, thrived in insecurity, and ended in disillusion. In equating physical beauty with virtue, she stripped her mind, bound it, and collected self-contempt by the heap" (p. 97).

Improving her appearance becomes a major goal in life and signals the dissolution of her marriage. Bored with her life in a two-room apartment and alienated by black women who regard her as a country bumpkin, Pauline turns to clothes and makeup as a way to regain the affirming gaze: "She merely wanted other women to cast favorable glances her way" (p. 94). But her new-found obsession with clothes and the money to buy them leads to quarrels with Cholly who, initially irritated by her dependence on him, now senses an impending separation from him, and worse, a confusion of values. When Pauline becomes pregnant, she and Cholly are once again able to share a common bond, but Pauline's desire to fill the lonely void of her life drives her to the only school of worth she can find, the movie theater.

She retreats to the movie theater in hopes of escaping the gaze of white indifference, and worse, the judgmental appraisal of northern black women. She comes to know the standard of beauty by which she is judged, and, while bereft of her tooth she cannot approximate the flawless perfection of the movie goddesses, she can adopt the perspective of the very gaze that dehumanizes her: "She was never able, after her education in the movies, to look at a face and not assign it some category in the scale of absolute beauty, and the scale was one she absorbed in full from the silver screen" (p. 97). According to film theory, Pauline engages in "schopophilia, or sexual pleasure in looking," which "is activated by the very situation of cinema: the darkened room, the way the gaze of the spectator is controlled by the aperture of first, the camera and second, the projector, the fact that the spectator is watching moving images rather than either static ones (painting) or live actors (theater), all help to make the cinematic experience closer to the dream state than is possible in the other arts."[35] In the movie theater, Pauline can release her own romantic imagination and undergo "a kind of regression to the state of early childhood."[36] Though Pauline is not Harlow and her husband is not Gable, she indulges herself in the act of gazing, which consists in cinema of three looks: "(i) within the film text itself, men gaze at women, who become objects of the gaze; (ii) the spectator, in turn, is made to identify with this male gaze, and to objectify the women on the screen: and (iii) the camera's original 'gaze' comes into play in the very act of filming."[37] Rather than denounce an unrealistic standard of beauty, Pauline identifies with the male gaze and the representation of beauty on the screen; she succumbs to an external valuation of her life: "The master had said, 'You are ugly people.' They had looked about themselves and saw nothing to contradict the statement; saw, in fact, support for it leaning at them from every billboard, every movie, every glance. 'Yes,' they had said. 'You are right.' And they took the ugliness in their hands, threw it as a mantle over them, and went about the world with it" (p. 34).

Devoid of the necessary beauty to be visible, Pauline relies on her perceived ugliness as an avenue to martyrdom and redemption. Her relationship with Cholly, nothing but ashes of a former, tender love, rises like the phoenix in her fury to exorcise the ugliness and poverty of her family: "She needed Cholly's sins desperately. The lower he sank, the wilder and more irresponsible he became, the more splendid she and her task became. In the name of Jesus" (p. 37). Pauline's personal life becomes a constant battle and confrontation, a way of being seen if only in the red glare of hate and violence: "Cholly and Mrs. Breedlove fought each other with a darkly brutal formalism that was paralleled only by their lovemaking" (p. 37).

While Pauline succumbs to one-dimensional values, Cholly collapses under the weight of her condemnation. No match for the invasive representations of western beauty, Cholly no longer has the seminal power or authority to invest his own wife with self-worth. But Pauline becomes a "sight" for the dominant culture, not for Cholly now divested of even the power to empower.

Cholly's break with Pauline is inevitable given the conditions of his life. A waif and a victim of profound humiliation, Cholly knows only loneliness and separation, frustration and impotence. He has no father or mother love to instill in him any value system, and he is degraded and objectified in his very first sexual act. Cholly is divested of his maleness by an absent father and the voyeurism of his white oppressors. Considering the fact that Cholly has no ego center, it is no wonder that he was moved, not revolted, by Pauline's foot since his ability to make her finally love herself provides him with a sliver of self-esteem in a world that had already stripped him of his autonomy. His coupling with Pauline is a reprieve, but only a brief one since he is incapable of a sustained relationship in the context of a society that has so little use for him. When Pauline's self-worth becomes dependent on the society that abused him, his love alternates between rage and ennui.

As a last-ditch act of self-affirmation, he turns to Pecola, just as he did Pauline, in hopes of rescuing her from the dehumanizing glare of all white people and a subsequently loveless existence. Cholly's rape of Pecola could then be interpreted as a pathetic attempt to return to the heady days of first love when his very presence essentially created another human being. His tenderness and protectiveness, however, slip easily into lust and rage, which he directs at Pecola and all those like her "who bore witness to his failure, his impotence. The one whom he had not been able to protect, to spare, to cover from the round moon glow of the flashlight" (p. 119). Cholly's rage at his inability to shelter Darlene from the appropriating and humiliating gaze of the white male hunters releases itself years later on Pecola when Cholly realizes that he could not and cannot protect his women or even himself from the bluest eye.

Cholly's act and Pauline's obsession with beauty represent a failure of a man and woman, a marriage, a community, and a society.

The novel is an indictment of twisted values and tangled lives, and is Morrison's most blatant and harrowing testimony to the impossibility of love in a world that values looks at the expense of humanity.

The ultimate expression of total dependence on the validation of others is Hagar's graveyard love in *Song of Solomon*. Having existed in the magnified love of mother and grandmother and then of her barely pubescent cousin Milkman, Hagar crumbles when, in an older Milkman, that adoration dissolves. Hagar lacks a construct of self that is independent of external valuation, especially Milkman's. She simply does not exist except in his eyes. As Guitar says, "You think because he doesn't love you that you are worthless. You think because he doesn't want you anymore that he is right—that his judgment and opinion of you are correct. . . . You're turning your whole life over to him. . . . And if it means so little to you that you can just give it away, hand it to him, then why should it mean any more to him? He can't value you more than you value yourself" (pp. 309–10). Hagar, immature in her understanding of identity, fails to comprehend or act on Guitar's advice. The child becomes a monster.

When Milkman withdraws his love, Hagar has no internal reserve to fortify her until the pain of rejection dissolves. Her only recourse, like a child who has been spoiled then slighted, is to throw a temper tantrum. Love turns to rage (a reversal of Cholly's attempt to transform hate into love) and Hagar embarks on a murderous rampage, content to be feared if not loved. When she can no longer effect even this response, she lapses into a comatose state, as near self-effacement as possible.

But there is no epiphany for Hagar or near-death revelation that is not attached to external valuation. When she is presented with a compact mirror, she grasps at a false hope that signals her imminent demise: "From the moment she looked into the mirror in the little pink compact she could not stop" (p. 37). The mirror serves the same function as Milkman, to provide her with a view of herself, to affirm her existence. That Hagar equates the mirror and Milkman is testimony to the importance she places on her physical self—the only component that she sees as worthy of being loved. Her desperate attempt to imitate commercialized beauty is a last-ditch effort at reconciliation with Milkman, and by extension, with herself. The final disillusionment comes when her plasticized beauty melts before the shocked gaze of her mother and grandmother. "And it was in their eyes that she saw what she had not seen before in the mirror: the wet ripped hose, the soiled white dress, the sticky, bumpy face powder, the streaked rouge, and the wild wet shoals of hair. All this she saw in their eyes, and the sight filled her own with water warmer and much older than the rain" (p. 318).

Hagar's death is the inevitability of her own objectification, the result of a highly flawed ontology. She lives by two enormously errant theorems: (1) Milkman loves me; therefore I am; (2) Milkman will love me if I possess perfect beauty. But what Milkman likes and wants is a total mystification to Hagar. She believes that he desires the approximation of ideal white beauty:

> He loves silky hair.
> Hush, Hagar.
> Penny-colored hair.
> Please, honey.
> And lemon-colored skin.
> Shhh.
> And gray-blue eyes.
> Hush now, hush.
> And thin nose.
> Hush, girl, hush.
> He's never going to like my hair. (pp. 319–20)

What Hagar does not realize is that it is not so much her looks that are so undesirable to Milkman—after all, he fell in love with her at first sight—but her inability to sustain the interest of a spoiled and bored man-child. As a result, Hagar, in incorrectly assigning disproportionate value to her external appearance and thus the bulk of responsibility in a failed relationship, neglects her own spiritual, emotional, and intellectual growth, a condition that is a function not just of her own internal weaknesses but of Pilate's, Reba's, and Milkman's as well. In assessing blame for Hagar's demise, Guitar points the finger at Pilate and Reba. He asks what Pilate has done to her and wonders if "anybody told her the things she ought to know"

(p. 310). He adds, "Neither Pilate nor Reba knew that Hagar was not like them. Not strong enough, like Pilate, nor simple enough, like Reba, to make up her life as they had" (p. 311).

Their inability to effectively translate sustaining values to Hagar is a pardonable offense given their unconditional love for her. Not so excusable is Milkman's treatment of Hagar. His selfishness first drives him to take Hagar and then to discard her. Given his treatment of her as a commodity, it is no wonder Hagar attaches her self-worth to her looks.

But Hagar's obsession with physical beauty is not necessarily shared by Milkman, just as Pauline's, Jadine's, and Violet's obsessions are not those of Cholly, Son, and Joe. Thus, Hagar errs in assessing the essential nature and worth of her being, and seals her fate. Milkman's disaffection with Hagar is rooted more in his own desire for adventure, change, and challenge: "There was no excitement, no galloping of blood in his neck or heart at the thought of her" (p. 91). Milkman's boredom is a function of his own desire for growth that is not shared by the pampered Hagar whose values, like Pauline's, Jadine's, and Violet's, are divorced from their African-American heritage. When Milkman goes south he distances himself from artificial white values and encounters a femininity that is inherently and aesthetically beautiful: "They sat on porches and walked in the road swaying their hips under cotton dresses, bare-legged, their unstraightened hair braided or pulled straight back into a ball. He wanted one of them bad. . . . That's the way Pilate must have looked as a girl, looked even now, but out of place in the big northern city she had come to" (p. 266). What Milkman perceives as effortless beauty—the unrepressed sexuality of bare legs and girdless hips—is in stark contrast to the tortured attempt by Hagar to purchase that beauty in the form of Mango Tango rouge and jungle red lipstick (p. 318). Milkman finds the real thing in the South and it is immune to reification.

But while Milkman enjoys a rare epiphany, Hagar is left to die. Though he has undergone a transcendence, a spiritual rebirth, he makes no attempt to rectify his earlier treatment of and attitude toward Hagar as a commodity. Indeed, he is not even aware of her death until, having been strong-armed in the cellar by Pilate, he recognizes the depth of his selfishness: "While he dreamt of flying, Hagar was dying" (p. 336).

The impossibility of love between Hagar and Milkman is the result of divergent ontologies, one that plunges Hagar into dementia and death and one that liberates Milkman from a corrupt value system that commodifies women and then makes men responsible for their lives. Such a burden is not only suffocating, but often tragically fatal.

The same confusion of values and identity nearly destroys the marriage of Joe and Violet Trace. Violet's obsession with light skin blinds her to the very different demons that drive her husband to commit adultery and then murder. But the epiphany—the illuminating moment—that eludes so many of Morrison's other characters is partially effected in Violet and Joe, who come to realize how their family histories, though having intersected at one point, influenced their marriage in very different, ultimately antagonistic and tragic ways. Both Violet's and Joe's fetishization of figures in their past directly accounts for their concept of self and provides explanation for their subsequent acts of adultery and violence.

For Violet, Golden Gray is that mythic figure, the cherished mulatto child her grandmother True Belle "made [Violet] crazy about . . . in the first place" (p. 97). Having lost her mother to suicide at the age of twelve, Violet transfers her love and sense of identity to the memory of Golden Gray, the epitome of western beauty with his golden skin and long, flowing locks. He comes to represent, in Violet's mind, miscegenation as the avenue to assimilation and acceptance. Though Violet is considered a very attractive woman, she admits her lifelong yearning to shed her dark skin for a lighter one. With no mother to help her establish a self-esteem that is not tied to whiteness, and raised by a grandmother who is mesmerized by it, Violet displaces intrinsic values for external ones. Her obsession with Golden Gray and his white skin—and the fact that both Joe as a cosmetics salesman and Violet as a hairdresser are to some degree invested in the perpetuation of that standard of beauty—leads her to assume incorrectly that Joe chose the creamy Dorcas because she possessed light skin and long hair. She asks what Joe saw in Dorcas: "A young me with high-yellow skin instead of black? A young me with long wavy hair instead of short? Or a not me at all" (p. 97). Violet eventually learns that she has mistaken her own motives for Joe's. She admits that she "loved [Golden Gray] better than anybody" and that perhaps she held on to Joe but "wish[ed] he was the golden boy I never saw either" (p. 97). But Violet, unlike the majority of Morrison's characters, is able to change her perception before her life and marriage are ruined. She explains to Felice that she messed up her life by forgetting who she was, by wishing she were somebody else. When Felice asks who, Violet answers: "Not who so much as what. White. Light. Young again" (p. 208). She attributes this to stories of Golden Gray who "lived inside [her] mind. Quiet as a mole. But I didn't know it till I got there. The two of us. Had to get rid of it" (p. 208).

For Joe, the mythic figure of his childhood and the motivating force in his treatment of Dorcas is his mother, a wild woman who deserted him because she was "too brain-blasted to do what the meanest sow managed: nurse what she birthed" (p. 179). When Joe discovers the secret of his birth, he experiences profound shame. He would have traded a whore, a drunk, even an abusive mother for "this indecent speechless lurking insanity" (p. 179). In spite of his humiliation, he tries on three separate occasions to find her, to hunt her down, but his failure to do so drives him from the woods he loves so dearly. Though he absents himself from the scene in which his wild mother is "everywhere and nowhere" (p. 179), he takes with him the rest of his life the sum of his emotional responses to her: "In Vienna he had lived first with the fear of her, then the joke of her, finally the obsession, followed by rejection of her" (p. 175).

Having once shared a moment in time (when Golden Gray rescues the pregnant wild woman), these mythic figures reemerge in the psyches of Joe and Violet and then converge on the unwitting Dorcas who becomes the catalyst for Joe and Violet's reconciliation with the past and with each other. Well before the appearance of Dorcas, in fact, the moment they decided to get married, the Trace marriage was in trouble: Joe and Violet were not so much embracing each other as they were running from their pasts. In both cases, Joe and Violet were abandoned by their mothers—the wild woman having disappeared in the woods never to speak to or even appear before

her son, while Rose Dear jumped to her death in a well. Joe marries
Violet not so much out of choice but because he could "escape all
the redwings [a symbol of his mother] in the county and the ripe
silence that accompanied them" (p. 30). Though the Traces enjoyed
a happy marriage initially, "twenty years after Joe and Violet train-
danced on into the City, they were still a couple but barely speaking
to each other, let alone laughing together or acting like the ground
was a dance-hall floor" (p. 36). Having never resolved or perhaps
even discussed their respective childhood sufferings and divested of
the youthful optimism so potent in staving off internal woes, Joe
and Violet lapse into their own coping mechanisms—first Violet in
silence, then Joe in adultery. Indeed, it is Violet's silence, not Dorcas's
skin color, that drives Joe to the younger woman, for Violet's silence
triggers his mother's rejection, her refusal to acknowledge Joe as her
son: "All [his mother] had to do was give him a sign, her hand thrust
through the leaves, the white flowers, would be enough to say that
she knew him to be the one, the son she had fourteen years ago, and
ran away from, but not too far" (p. 37). When Joe pursues Dorcas,
he does so to stave off the silence and emptiness. With Dorcas, he
"had somebody to tell it to" (p. 37).

Joe and Violet's separation into their own private worlds is short-
lived, terminated abruptly by Dorcas's death. When Joe takes after
Dorcas, who has left him for a younger man, he is simply reliving
his earlier failed attempts to hunt down and find his mother and the
rejection that her self-imposed exile symbolized. Violet, meanwhile,
reacting in ignorance of her husband's motives, tries to disfigure the
dead Dorcas, attacking what she thinks is the reason for Joe's abandonment—Dorcas's light skin—but in reality living out her own rage
against western values of beauty.

Once again in Morrison's fictional worlds, the legacy of whiteness
as the standard of beauty informs the characters' views of themselves
and each other. Though beauty is not the primary agent in the disintegration of the Trace marriage as much as their motherless past
is, it intensifies their marital dilemma and complicates resolution.
Violet's confusion about Joe's desire for Dorcas does not negate the
destructive influence of western beauty; indeed, Violet's obsession

with white beauty becomes an obstacle to full disclosure, to ultimate understanding. Violet must first come to grips with the "mole" inside her—her desire to be white—before she can begin to understand her hatred for Dorcas and the need for communion that drives Joe. Once Violet resolves her own conflict, she can join Joe under the covers, free from the appropriating Gaze of the dominant culture, where they no longer "have to look at themselves anymore; there is no stud's eye, no chippie glance to undo them. They are inward toward the other, bound and joined by carnival dolls and the steamers that sailed from ports they never saw" (p. 228). Under the covers they can re-vision their pasts, convert them into positive images of real beauty and love where the redwing bird is not an incomprehensible mother but a sunrise, and a well is not a repository of death but a reservoir of gifts, "(lead pencils, Bull Durham, Jap Rose Soap) to distribute to them all" (p. 225).

Culture and Conflict

The motif of beauty and its effects on male-female relationships is multifaceted and complex in *Tar Baby*, as Morrison offers many representations of beauty: the lady in canary yellow, Jadine, Margaret Street, and the Pie Ladies. All are signifiers of the different cultures they represent. Thus, while Morrison pursues her denunciation of idealized standards of beauty, she also creates images of beauty that are not destructive. Those images cannot save the dead-end Street marriage or even the culturally estranged Jadine and Son, but their appearance is at least an articulation of beauty that inspires hope.

Jadine and Son are a sociological study of two different cultures—the sophisticated, accomplished Jadine epitomizing the best of white culture; the primitive, sensual Son, the best of black culture. In many ways, they, as a pair, represent the schizophrenia—the double-vision—inherent in being black in a white America. She is the persona, the public mask struggling to gain acceptance. He is the soul, the anima keeping alive a culture threatened by extinction. That they cannot resolve their differences, indeed, that their relationship becomes violent, is a manifestation of the psychic fragmentation of the culture as a whole. Jadine can never go back to the nonmaterial, simple life of black folk because she has become addicted to the white world, and Son can never become a middle-class black accepting western definitions of value and meaning.

In her characterization of Jadine and Son, Morrison accentuates initially the extreme differences in their cultures. Son is primitive and smelly, "a baboon" to a woman so removed from the natural that she feeds her vanity at the expense of dozens of mutilated baby seals. Jadine, a reification herself, views everything else as an object for personal pleasure. When Son first sees Jadine he is awestruck by her beauty until he realizes how that beauty has been commercialized in the slick pages of beauty magazines. The "baboon" now only sees a prostitute. He asks, "How much?. . . Dick. That you had to suck, I mean to get all that gold and be in the movies. Or was it pussy?" (p. 103). The hostility that is generated in their confrontation is an ironical racial tension; Jadine and Son could be no further apart culturally and ideologically had they been of different races.

An amelioration begins, however, when Son washes away the semiotics of primitivism and consequently his frightening and alien Otherness. Son and Jadine cross the cultural barriers that polarized them and soon respond to a shared sexual attraction—probably the most powerful and least understood of all human bonds. Their bliss, nevertheless, is momentary and illusory since it necessitates total separation from the outside world. Son cannot ignore the psychic pain and enormous waste of black youth in New York whose desperation to be attractive, worthwhile, and wealthy leads to disfiguration, prostitution, and even transvestism. New York for Son epitomizes the graveyard of black culture:

> The black girls in New York City were crying and their men were look-
> ing neither to the right nor to the left. Not because they were heedless,
> or intent on what was before them, but they did not wish to see the
> crying, crying girls split into two parts by their tight jeans, screaming
> at the top of their high, high heels, straining against the pull of their
> braids and the fluorescent combs holding their hair. . . . The street was
> choked with beautiful males who had found the whole business of being

black and men at the same time too difficult and so they'd dumped it.
(pp. 185–86)

The women are splitting apart, torn in their desire to be viewed as
valuable against conflicting but interdependent value systems. The
men cannot look at the women because they are now insignificant,
powerless to reverse the dehumanization of black women. For these
black men there is not even a pleasure in looking since what they
now see is an objectification of white male desire. Son recognizes
this state of affairs and is consequently alienated from "a whole new
race of people he was once familiar with" (p. 187).

Jadine's estrangement from her culture and heritage is symbolized
by the woman in canary yellow. Her "unphotographable beauty"
cannot be appropriated as has Jadine's; thus, she represents "transcendent beauty" (p. 39), the authentic self who makes Jadine feel
"lonely and inauthentic" (p. 40). The woman informs the rest of
Jadine's experience with Son, and serves as a painful reminder of
how Jadine has sold out, become a bauble for the indolent western
culture. The same womanly women haunt Jadine when she travels
south to Eloe. The night women's sagging breasts and imperfections
are indicators of their womanliness and humanity, not their inferiority. Jadine feels unnatural because her sense of worth and beauty
are tied to artificial constructs rather than biological processes.

Son and Jadine's differences aside, their love affair, for a while at
least, is a genuine moment in their adult lives. To reach this point,
Jadine is forced to relinquish an ego center that saw men merely
as objects to be restrained and controlled for her private pleasures.
When she assesses that Son is unmanageable, she is admitting she
could lose control of her love, the only aspect of herself that can
remain inviolate, that can't be commodified. Son recognizes this
barrier to their relationship, and though he cannot put a name to it,
he essentially deconstructs her—strips her of the cultural baggage
that inhibits self-knowledge. She then is free to re-create herself as
a single star in the dark sky of creation: "Imagine yourself in that
dark, all alone in the sky at night. Nobody is around you. You are
by yourself just shining there" (p. 184). Jadine's ego center dissolves
and she becomes an autonomous being capable of falling in love, a

state of total selflessness and total fulfillment: "Together they could not concentrate on the given world. They reinvented it, remembered it through the other" (p. 198).

Eventually their love crumbles under the weight of the outside world. Jadine and Son cannot disavow their upbringings: their cultural and geographical preferences, their outlooks on money and financial security, their aspirations for the future all invade the makeshift reality of their fragile love. The persona and anima cannot integrate, and the shadow of frustration, hate, and violence is the final, ugly manifestation.

After Morrison looks at how western beauty devours the black anima she then records the demise of the white Streets, the very constituents of that standard. By fictionalizing black and white pain alike, Morrison reveals the universally destructive power of institutionalized beauty. The white Streets exemplify the extent to which beauty becomes a fetish, a thing that must be possessed and preserved. Unlike Son and Jadine, Valerian and Margaret never loved each other. Valerian chose her as he did other valuable objects—for her aesthetic beauty. When Margaret asks if beauty is enough, Valerian responds, "Beauty is never enough. . . . But you are" (p. 71). This comment suggests that Valerian sees something in Margaret that is akin to the transcendent beauty in the woman in yellow; however, that potential never reaches fruition because of Valerian and Margaret's inability to effect such a transformation. She becomes "faceless" and "silent," a living Grecian urn whose beauty is susceptible to cracking, fading, and aging. Threatened with losing her most valuable asset, the middle-aged Margaret takes desperate measures to preserve her flawless beauty. She uses "frownies" to erase any suggestion of maturity, wisdom, and sentience. "I don't want to frown. Frownies don't make you frown. They erase the consequences of frowning" (p. 18). Instead of ridiculing her for this obsessive preoccupation, Valerian silently acquiesces, then remarks, "But why don't you just stop frowning? Then you won't need to paste your face with little pieces of tape" (p. 18). The underlying assumption, even if it was meant tongue in cheek, is that Valerian is a coconspirator in Margaret's quest for external beauty even at the expense of her inner growth.

Indeed, so complete is Valerian's assault on Margaret's selfhood that he even finds her eating intolerable since it exposes her imperfections; he desires her only as a vision of loveliness, a vision that apparently is shattered when she eats, a basic human need. This reminder of her biological reality is a disappointment; it means she is incapable of providing pure, sustained pleasure. The subject-object relationship Valerian orchestrates completely dissolves as Margaret resorts to real transgressions in an effort to assert herself. When she tortures her son, she finally creates a self, but one at odds, indeed a total reversal, of her external one. Intent on destroying the beauty that has become her albatross, she rebels against Valerian by abusing his son in a scarification ritual. She had been obsessed with disfiguring her son's creamy skin. When Valerian finds out, his awakening and abrupt lapse into silence is Margaret's coming out. Denied a complete childhood herself and snatched out of the home by an abusive father figure, Margaret grows up to him in stages of adoration, fear, rebellion, hatred, and finally individuated self. She divorces herself from a father rather than a husband: "She seemed strong to him. He was wasting away, filed to nothing by grief, and she was strong, stronger" (p. 204). She is no longer his beautiful object, and she becomes differentiated from him. "She looked real. Not like a piece of Valerian candy, but like a person on a bus, already formed, fleshed, thick with a life which is not yours and not accessible to you" (p. 206). But rather than find succor in a truly adult relationship, they create it in static tension. Valerian has no idea how to love a real woman because his love has been reserved for things that cannot love back.

The Beautiful Thing

Adult love, Morrison shows, cannot flourish in a society that values external qualities at the expense of internal ones. That recognition, she hopes, will lead to a new, more sophisticated awareness of beauty that will transcend the one-dimensional mania that is so reductive. Ideal beauty for Morrison is best summed up toward the end of *Tar Baby*. This passage, placed after the emotional upheaval of the Street household, is an apocalyptic moment, long in coming in Morrison's work:

> At some point in life the world's beauty becomes enough. You don't need to photograph or even remember it. It is enough. No record of it needs to be kept and you don't need someone to share it with or tell it to. When that happens—that letting go—you let go because you can. . . . A dead hydrangea is as intricate and lovely as one in bloom. Bleak sky is as seductive as sunshine, miniature orange trees without blossom or fruit are not defective; they are that. So the windows of the greenhouse can be opened and the weather let in. The catch on the door can be left unhooked, the muslin removed, for the soldier ants are beautiful too and whatever they do will be part of it. (p. 208)

Morrison's theory of beauty is akin to the Kantian notion of free beauty and pure judgment.[38] Kant divides beauty into categories, free and dependent. Beauty is free if it "presupposes no concept of what the object ought to be"; it is dependent, or adherent, if it "does presuppose such a concept and the perfection of the object in accordance therewith."[39] For example, a horse's beauty is adherent if the person judging looks at the horse in terms of, say, how many races it will win. Its beauty is free, however, if the person judging is unconcerned with a horse's production or performance, and instead derives pleasure from form. Devoid of interest, judgment becomes pure. Thus, Morrison's soldier ants can be beautiful in the free sense if the person judging (in this case Valerian) does not rationalize that ants will destroy his flowers. Freed from an invested interest in his possessions, Valerian can appreciate the ants for playing their part in the universal scheme of things: "Whatever they do will be part of it" (p. 208). What Morrison hopes for is pure judgment of beauty. As Kant says, "A judgment of taste, then, in respect of an object with a definite internal purpose, can only be pure if either the person judging has no concept of this purpose or else abstracts from it in his judgment."[40]

An avowal of disinterestedness, while perhaps improbable if not impossible, has, nevertheless, been shared by a number of proto-modernist and modernist poets who saw beauty in form, as Dickinson did in the evanescent quality of the hummingbird, Whitman in his blades of grass, and William Carlos Williams in a shard of green glass. Morrison suggests that this level of consciousness and contemplation of beauty will lead to Kant's sublime in which an object "may bring a satisfaction with it that is universally communicable. . . . This is not indeed a satisfaction in the object (because it may be formless), as in the case of the beautiful . . . but a satisfaction in the extension of the imagination by itself."[41]

Especially pertinent to a discussion of Morrison's notions of beauty is William Carlos Williams's search for the Beautiful Thing in *Paterson*. The Beautiful Thing engenders a complexity of meaning and is as illusive and mysterious as the imagination with which it is associated. In Williams's articulation of the Beautiful Thing, he uses metaphors strikingly similar to Morrison's. At once ephemeral and perpetual, it is often a woman, sometimes nature, primitive tribal rites, or art; the Beautiful Thing is whatever occurs in the present and the local and is available to the poet if he or she is imaginative enough to perceive it. The imagination, in inventing the Beautiful Thing, is the essence, the radiant gist, that the poet must return to in order to resurrect language from the dead. Consequently, Williams would include Morrison's dead hydrangeas, bleak sky, fruitless miniature orange trees, and soldier ants as an extension of his own catalogue of simple but vivid images: a mouse, red slipper, star, geranium, a cat's tongue or

> thought, thought
> that is a leaf, a
> pebble, an old man
> out of a story by
> Pushkin.[42]

Williams does not rely exclusively on image to convey the Beautiful Thing; he employs other literary devices in *Paterson* that are also used by Morrison. Most importantly, a comparison of Morrison's and Williams's ideas about beauty will illustrate simultaneously a shared tradition in American writing, and cultural and racial distinctions that inform their interpretation of, and experience with, beauty.

Morrison's notion of beauty is a liberation into the sublime, an

altered state of consciousness that engenders selflessness and understanding. A person who does not look at objects in terms of what they
can do for a bank balance or even self-esteem, but in what ways they
are pleasurable in and of themselves can liberate the imagination,
the precursor to communal and spiritual love. Morrison exhorts Valerian to open the windows and unlatch the doors of the greenhouse, a
symbol of Valerian's need to possess perfection. While Valerian may
appreciate the beauty of the flowery form, his endeavor to separate
that beauty into a category of perceived perfection and then to covet
it in an artificial world is the converse of universality and the obstacle
to communal love and understanding. Similar to Valerian Street are
Williams's arrogant scholars who, because they adhere rigidly to a
stagnant ideology, fail to invent the Beautiful Thing:

> How strange you are, you idiot!
> So you think because the rose
> is red that you shall have the mastery?
> The rose is green and will bloom,
> overtopping you, green, livid
> green when you shall no more speak, or
> taste, or even be. (p. 30)

To undo this process of covetousness is certainly no easy task for
a society that thrives on competition and individual ownership, and
thus tends automatically to view reality as a transaction. Morrison's
exhortation to relinquish self-interest, lost on the Streets of the world,
is Dickinsonian in its evocation of evanescence—the fleeting quality
of beauty that renders possession impossible and perhaps undesirable. It is also Whitmanesque and modernist in its celebration of
the seemingly insignificant object. But Morrison stretches beyond
the appreciation of form, an act Kant sees as a more individuated
intellectual process, to the sublime, or "deep feeling."[43] Valerian's
greenhouse is anathema to the "absolutely great" that defines the
sublime; thus, he is doomed to lovelessness, loneliness, and isolation,
a condition Morrison sees as endemic to the western world.

Williams, too, recognized isolation as a major obstacle to the perception of beauty and the sublime. At one point in *Paterson*, the
persona, also named Paterson, enters a park in search of beauty and

encounters people "devoted to pleasure: devoted to grasshoppers!" (p. 51). The crowd exudes an energy and vulgarity, but is unable to articulate its own vitality. The lovers are like the grasshoppers, but their Gay Wings of thought lead them not to insight but to sleep. The male, though asleep, feels his lover's sensuality "until there moves in his sleep/a music that is whole, unequivocal." Because he lacks Paterson's imagination, however, he labors against sleep but "does not waken" (p. 60). They are "blocked" (p. 62) by a desire to earn material riches, to exploit the local rather than to apprehend it aesthetically. Walter Peterson calls it the "appropriative view of life" in which "there is an underlying assumption that the pursuit of what is not immediately and pragmatically useful is necessarily contemptible and vain."[44] This appropriation infiltrates all aspects of life, even, as is suggested by the sleeping lover, sexual love.

In an industrialized setting, beauty and perfection become tangled up with standardized production. Perfect sameness becomes the singular goal of the producer and the consumer. The restrictive and artificial nature of this ideology is evident, though no less palatable, to a society that has become otherwise anesthetized to contemplation, imagination, sense, and deep feeling. By way of deconstruction, Morrison forces on her readership human images of *imperfection* and by extension, then, beauty becomes not the mirroring of a standard, but a standard in and of itself. Morrison asks us to perceive the other as valuable in difference, not similarity. Her most beautiful and lovable characters are those whose imperfections strengthen rather than weaken character. Those characters with flaws who are not as strong or appealing—Sula, Pauline, Sethe, and Dorcas—have accepted external labels of evil, inferiority, or shame. Incapable of translating, transforming, or transcending these imperfections, they leave interpretation to others and thus relinquish control of their identities. Consequently, love becomes an impossibility in which the imperfect searches for perfection in the loved one—quite a burden for someone struggling with his or her own insecurities.

Morrison's images of beauty are often fleeting but remarkably impressionistic. She says, "The genuine article only has to appear for a moment to become memorable. It would be anticlimactic to have a conversation with her, because that person is invested with all the hopes and views of the person who observes her. She is the original self."[45]

As Morrison's use of "she" suggests, her articulation of beauty is almost always a woman. Once again the parallels between Morrison and Williams are apparent. Williams's most successful creation of the Beautiful Thing in *Paterson* is a woman, and like Morrison's image, the woman is black. For Williams, the Beautiful Thing appears at times in the shape of two girls at Easter, as an African wife, and as a black woman. Indeed, Williams's affinity for black women bordered on the perverse fantasy that so riles black women writers. Williams recalls "once as a medical student falling in love with the corpse of a young negress, a 'high yaller,' lying stripped on the dissecting table before me."[46] Another real-life black woman, Mable Watts, appears in *Paterson* in the shape of the Beautiful Thing. According to Paul Mariani:

> His black Kore owed much to his memories of Mable Watts, the seductive patient from his early days as a doctor, a woman who had had as much sexual success with white men as with black. . . . She, too, like Beautiful Thing, had worn her hair up in a convoluted fashion topped by "a maid's cap, pure white and crisply starched." Beautiful Thing, living right there in his world, despised, invisible, desired, radiant, like so many of the black women to whom he was attracted. No Artemis, no European goddess, she nevertheless represented for Williams the black plush, the New World beauty, the radiant strain that would illuminate the dirty white sheets of Paterson.[47]

Implied in this description of the virginal New World and the sullied Old is the guilt of western imperialist's conquest of America. The black woman becomes the metaphor for the exploitation and appropriation of America, the Africanist presence, which Morrison speaks of in *Playing in the Dark*, that has informed American literature: "The fabrication of an Africanist persona is reflexive; an extraordinary meditation on the self; a powerful exploration of the fears and desires that reside in the writerly conscious."[48]

For Morrison, the quintessential image of beauty, the authentic self, is the woman in canary yellow, but unlike Williams's fictionalized Mable Watts, she is neither despised nor invisible, even to those riddled with guilt or bereft of an imagination. She is the essence, and, thus, need not be defined by any other. Though she is irregular in every aspect—she's too tall, too busty, too black—she induces the sublime, "bring[s] a satisfaction with it that is universally communicable."[49] Jadine and "everybody else in the store [was] transfixed" (p. 38). Their awareness of her becomes pure contemplation, free of interest; thus, they can watch her "with full glances instead of sly ones" (p. 38). In Jadine's eyes, she is a vision possessed of "transcendent beauty" (p. 39). What Morrison presents, mostly in the juxtaposition of the colors—the pitch-tar quality of the skin, the canary yellow, the white eggs, the gold track—is a formless, objectless image of beauty capable of lifting people out of the corporeal into the spiritual.

Other images of beauty are not always as mystical or ethereal. Morrison particularly delights in showcasing the prostitute, a morally imperfect being whose transgressions have perhaps deepened and enriched her humanity, a Morrisonian prerequisite for beauty. Here, Morrison and Williams again employ the same device, though for very different reasons. Williams is ambivalent about his seductive Mable Watts, recognizing her vitality and spontaneity but simultaneously condemning her vulgarity and foulness. "You smell/like a whore," he says to the Beautiful Thing. "I ask you to bathe in my/ opinions, the astonishing virtue of your lost body (I said)" (p. 105). He cannot, however, transform the whore into the virgin, an apparently male dilemma that wants both purity and carnality in a woman. Williams's attempt to force the Beautiful Thing into conforming to the traditional notion of what women (and by extension, poetry and reality) should be, constitutes a rape. Realizing this, he backs off from her to reevaluate his own motives for wanting the Beautiful Thing. Later, after an apocalyptic moment in the poem when the Old World is purged, Paterson/Williams returns to the Beautiful Thing no longer in need of possessing her. She is to Paterson "the most important aspect of the new world, she is the subject-matter and the language of poetry that are for Williams' poetry itself if they can be allowed to live free on their own terms—not locked in, and not raped."[50]

Morrison does not share Williams's ambivalence toward the pros-

titute, though she does recognize that confusion exists. Her decision
to valorize the whore represents a collapse of the virgin/whore dichotomy. Rochelle, also in canary yellow, is the authentic self. Her
authenticity, however, is less of an abstraction than the woman in
the supermarket. She is a Creole whore who, in her spontaneous
laughter and affection, epitomizes self-expression and freedom from
restraint. She possesses the transcendent but more tangible beauty
of nature. In contrast to the morbidity of a funeral replete with a
dead body, sputtering candles, and plaster virgins, Rochelle is the
light and the life, possibly even the way. That she is beautiful to the
little Nel is no wonder since her love of self flows over so freely and
unconditionally into the truly Christian love of life and others.

While Rochelle is hardly perfection in the conventional self, the
prostitute Marie is simply grotesque. But Morrison pushes us to
see beyond the jaded vision of our enculturation to the "satisfaction in the extension of the imagination by itself."[51] Indeed, no
less than a sensibility of Emersonian proportions could extend itself
beyond this description: "Tiny baby toes at the tip of puffy feet;
swollen ankles smoothed and tightened the skin; massive legs like
tree stumps parted wide at the knees, over which spread two roads
of soft flabby inner thigh that kissed each other deep in the shade
of her dress and closed" (p. 82). In this passage, Morrison elides the
grotesque and the beautiful—"puffy feet" and "baby toes," flabby
thighs kissing—in order to defamiliarize our notions of beauty so
that we can see beyond or into the "mountain of flesh" (p. 82).
What she is suggesting is that we return to the childlike vision of a
Claudia who responds to the essence of a person's life rather than
its accidents. Claudia employs nature imagery, in particular water,
to convey Marie's spirituality and life-sustaining qualities. Claudia
sees a waterfall in her eyes and compares her laughter to "the sound
of many rivers, freely, deeply, muddily, heading for the room of an
open sea" (p. 44). Marie's external self is merely a container of the
inner beauty that is as boundless as an ocean. The tension that Morrison creates by the apparent contradiction of the physical and the
spiritual is her attempt to dissolve the logical fallacy that idealized
beauty is spiritual beauty.

Morrison celebrates this dissolution; Williams agonizes over it in

Paterson. For both writers, beauty is best exemplified in female form, though their ways of understanding that beauty reveal very different levels of experience. Williams's tendency to represent the Beautiful Thing as a despised black woman is a metaphor for his own guilt about the treatment of blacks in America. By representing the Beautiful Thing as a black woman, he puts himself in a position to raise her from the basement of oppression. He becomes the liberator, the translator, the hero. However, in his earnest desire to tap into and then elevate this poetic and spiritual resource, he risks defiling her by virtue of his own Old World enculturation and the restraints it has placed on women, blacks, and as Williams sees it, the language. For Morrison this dilemma simply does not exist because she is free from the burden of guilt that beguiles Williams. Indeed, Morrison would suggest that the guilt experienced by Williams is his realization that the relative freedom he enjoys is intensified by the very absence of freedom that confronts him: "Freedom . . . can be relished more deeply in a cheek-by-jowl existence with the bound and unfree, the economically oppressed, the marginalized, the silenced."[52] Morrison, herself, is Williams's fetishized notion of the despised, the fecund potential of the untamed New World. But Morrison does not need a mediator or translator. In her expression of beauty, she is the New World, the *langage* that is so illusive to Williams, as well as a manipulator of the American *langue* in which she was educated, and the producer of a unique *parole.* Morrison's encounter with beauty is not wrested from feverish, nightmarish mania, but from a lifelong struggle with pain and bitterness made bearable by virtue of those infrequent novas of beauty. Beauty for Morrison constitutes survival; thus, she speaks for a culture in contradistinction to a society whose own search for beauty has been lost in the roar of Williams's Falls.

Spiritual Beauty and Love

Morrison does not restrict her notion of beauty to the female form. She recognizes it in many shapes and guises, in the least likely of circumstances, thus, expanding and enriching the potential for an encounter with the beautiful. In male images of beauty, Morrison's women are generally struck by the transcendent beauty in their men.

In fact, the men are very rarely described in any great physical detail, emphasizing the importance of an emotional and spiritual response to beauty. When Sula sees Ajax she is not impressed by bulging muscles or handsome features but by "two quarts of milk tucked into his arms like marble statues" (p. 124). Ajax asks, "Ain't they pretty?" knowing that she is taken by how "precious and clean and permanent" (p. 124) they look. When he drinks the milk in her presence he swallows the purity Sula assigns it and that action initiates her falling in love. In *Song of Solomon* Hagar, in a fit of murderous passion, is momentarily arrested by the beauty in Milkman's vulnerability. " 'Oh,' she thought, when she saw his face, 'I had forgotten how beautiful he is' " (p. 130).

In her men, Morrison also invokes nature and Africa to suggest expansiveness, freedom, and independence. Cholly "came big, he came strong, he came with yellow eyes, flaring nostrils, and he came with his own music" (p. 91). Pauline's memory of her first meeting with Cholly is marked by all the pleasant and natural colors of her adolescence: "It was like them berries, that lemonade, them streaks of green the june bugs made, all come together" (p. 92). Jadine, who would not allow herself to look past Son's initially filthy appearance, turns the artist's eye on a freshly cleaned Son: "But he was bathed now, clipped and beautiful with spacious tender eyes and a woodsy voice. His smile was always a surprise like a sudden rustle of wind across the savanna of his face" (p. 155). Paul D is described in scant but vivid detail: "Peachstone skin; straight-backed" (p. 7). Violet claimed on sight her "Virginia Joe Trace who carried a light inside him, whose shoulders were razor sharp and who looked at [her] with two-color eyes and never saw anybody else" (p. 96).

Epitomizing Morrison's masculine notion of beauty is Ajax. When Sula makes love to him she envisions the layers, the very essence of his maleness. Underneath his skin there is gold, then alabaster, and finally "loam, fertile, free of pebbles and twigs" (p. 131). In Ajax, then, Sula sees precious and enduring metal, a translucent and pure mineral, and most importantly, the very soil of creation. Ajax is the earth itself and Sula sees herself, in a reversal of a traditional metaphor, as the rain that will fertilize the earth and "make mud" (p. 131).

Images of beauty are not always as fleeting as an appearance or a look. Often, it is manifest in a major character's physical imperfections; Morrison Signifies on the Greek notion of beauty as regularity. Eva's and Pilate's disfigurements become their marks of superior beauty, while Pauline Breedlove, Sula, Sethe, and Dorcas are made to feel beautiful by sensitive lovers who recognize the pain and suffering inherent in their imperfections and consequently find them endearing.

Eva's remaining leg is rendered more beautiful by the absence of its partner: "Whatever the fate of her lost leg, the remaining one was magnificent" (p. 31). Eva appears bigger than life by virtue of her lost leg and the mysterious circumstance surrounding its disappearance. Her oddity inspires awe. Men flock around her not to gawk at her leglessness but to revel in the spirit and energy that inform the rest of her body: "The men wanted to see her lovely calf, that neat shoe, and watch the focusing that sometimes swept down out of the distances in her eyes" (p. 41). Eva's physical imperfection negates traditional gender roles so that men do not judge her by her physical beauty but by her character. They can appreciate her beauty, which is divorced from external definitions and consists instead of her unconditional love for the poor, orphaned, diseased, and sick. She gathers all who hurt and are in need of family and takes them into a house that grows according to its tenants' needs. What Eva creates with her Deweys and Pretty Johnnie is an extended family, a microcosm of the ideal community in which love is not stingily reserved for a chosen few. Eva, unmarried and probably celibate, is a Christ/Madonna figure capable of dispensing endless love since it is not invested exclusively in an exacting husband or in her own children. When she sets Plum on fire, she commits an almost incomprehensible act of love, for she has relinquished her own selfish love of her son in order to relieve him of a near animallike existence. But her act carries with it a burden of responsibility made unbearable by the accusations and recriminations of people incapable of understanding the magnitude of her love. When she is placed in a home by her own granddaughter, she is sealed off from ministering to a community sorely in need of spiritual healing.

Pilate possesses the same radiant beauty that draws people to

Eva. And like Eva, her source of fascination is a physical omission. Though her return to Southside is less than cause for celebration, she quickly becomes a figure of considerable power and influence. Without a belly button, Pilate is outside normal expectations of human appearance and behavior. Allowed or expected to develop a personality independent of societal constraints, she matures into a dynamic human being. In both appearance and personality, Pilate is a formidable character. "And when she stood up, he all but gasped. She was as tall as his father, head and shoulders taller than himself" (p. 38). Pilate, the narrator says, is not pretty in the conventional sense but Morrison's description of her redefines beauty: "They found her on the front steps sitting wide-legged in long-sleeved, long-skirted black dress. Her hair was wrapped in black too, and from a distance, all they could really see beneath her face was the bright orange she was peeling. She was all angles, he remembered later, knees, mostly, and elbows. One foot pointed east and one pointed west" (p. 36). As imagistically striking as Jadine's woman in canary yellow, Pilate is an obfuscation of traditional expectations of beauty. Her body is almost completely covered in black and is thus safe from the appropriative eye of the beholder. Wide-legged and all angles, she is neither ladylike nor soft. Her beauty defies but also reshapes reader expectation of what is beautiful: her geometric strength (all angles), expansiveness (feet pointed east and west), mystery (draped in black), and consummate power. Unlike the lady in yellow, however, Pilate does not disappear from the novel; she becomes instead the spiritual force that her physical power and beauty promise. Not surprisingly, Pilate resurrects the Dead family. Pilate, like Eva, is unmarried and celibate, her smooth belly an inducer of impotence. She too is free to spread nonsexual love generously. She transforms Milkman from a selfish spoiled brat into a man prepared to take her place as the life force of his family and community. Her death is not as tragic as Eva's internment because she has bequeathed her spiritual beauty to her nephew; in a Christlike way, Pilate dies so others may live.

While Eva and Pilate transcend their disabilities, Pauline Breedlove, Sula, Sethe, and Dorcas enjoy only transient moments of feeling beautiful and loved. Since these women are dependent on others to invest them with self-worth, they are doomed to the inconsistency of others' perceptions. Pauline's foot is made beautiful by a sensitive Cholly but becomes ugly in the eyes of hardened northerners. Sula's birthmark, at one point a powerful aphrodisiac, later signifies evil. Sula does little to disassociate herself from these connotations and dies with the cancer of her bitterness eating her alive. Sethe needs Paul D to turn her scarification into a badge of incredible courage and endurance. But she cannot sustain the illusion of heroics when Paul D deserts her. Finally, Dorcas, who should have been pretty but, like the young Milkman, possessed a face that did not quite seem to fit into a coherent whole, deserts Joe Trace and his unconditional love (even for her pock-marked face) for a younger lover because, as Dorcas says, "I wanted to have a personality and with Acton I'm getting one. I have a look now" (p. 190).

Without a sense of inner beauty or purpose, Morrison's characters cannot sustain love. Some of them achieve it briefly: the young Breedloves and Deads, Sula and Ajax, Nel and Jude, Jadine and Son, and Joe and Violet. But all suffer under the power of a consumer society to commodify beauty and package it as the elixir for happiness. This commodification of beauty jades all relationships as they become a means to gain power and recognition rather than emotional fulfillment. Those who are beautiful (Margaret and Jadine) or wealthy (Ruth Dead) or respectable (Nel) are valuable assets rather than spiritual copartners.

Morrison sees this mentality informing the state of monogamy. Women and men in Morrison's fictional world, naturally desirous to retain control of their human property, view monogamy as a weapon rather than an ideal state of matrimony: Macon Dead's marriage is a power struggle with Dr. Foster; Valerian owns Margaret; Sula, Nel, and Violet fall apart when they can no longer possess their men. What may begin as love in these relationships turns into varying degrees of violence as lovers sense their waning control. Emotional abuse runs rampant in the Dead and Street families, and physical violence is a daily routine for the Breedloves and an act of desperation for a woman whose name becomes Violent. Even the eminently lovable and loving Jadine and Son resort to ugly and violent confrontation.

Resolution is a pipe dream, if not an impossibility, in Morrison's earlier novels. She cannot reconcile westernized beauty since it has been tainted, like the air and water, with an industrialized pollutant. But in her most recent novel, *Jazz*, Morrison, in a rare moment of optimism, allows for a glimmer of hope in the characters of Joe and Violet Trace, who are able to reconstruct themselves and their marriage in spite of their past and their enculturation. Still, their reconciliation must literally and metaphorically occur under the covers and in the dark—they now sleep during the day—suggesting perhaps that their escape from the appropriating gaze is no more free than the life Joe's mother lived in her cave. The beauty that Joe and Violet and most of Morrison's characters seek cannot flourish in a society that desires selfish gain, because the beauty of the human being is dependent upon the interest of the other. If that interest fades, if the woman and the man age, or are physically, intellectually, or emotionally flawed, she and he become worthless and, hence, unlovable. If interest intensifies, then possession translates into an obsession with thingness. Monogamy becomes a desperate attempt to own exclusive rights to beauty. Morrison sneers at this notion of marital bliss through the characters of Hannah, Sula, and her many prostitutes who know that monogamy is not always a guarantee of fidelity.

Finally, Morrison suggests, in her refusal to glorify or romanticize love and beauty, that human beings, disabused of dehumanizing categories of beauty, have the potential to generate an inner purpose, as Kant would say, or an inner beauty whether with a club foot or a high yalla complexion, with wealth or poverty, respectability or infamy. That person then is lovable as a viable and unique individual rather than as a sycophant to another's ego. Allowed the freedom to exfoliate, human beings can enter into relationships free of insecurities, jealousies, or hatred. Monogamy need not be a prison but a spiritual coupling of two individuals. Williams learned in *Paterson* that the Beautiful Thing is the love of a man and a woman in marriage. He finds that in merging with the Beautiful Thing he will find "a song to make death tolerable, a song of a man and woman" (p. 107). While Morrison might agree, she does not settle for this partial epiphany. For her, love is not the exclusive property of, nor most brilliantly expressed in, marriage. Love, for her, flares in the

most unromantic, asexual settings and between the least likely bene-
ficiaries: a little girl and a scarlet woman in a brothel; a dying old
woman and her nephew on a rock overlooking infinity; a black cook
and her lonely teenaged mistress; a young girl scratching at a screen
door for her cherished friend; three women singing in the candle
light or praying in the clearing; a pregnant black slave girl and a
homeless white straggler; a dead girl and her lover's wife's pathetic
attempt to imitate her dance steps. All of these people experience
snatches of profound love and beauty that, though transitory, are the
very moments worth living for. This spiritual love between people is
the essential prerequisite to communal love, a state of affairs perhaps
too beautiful or awesome for Morrison or any of us to yet imagine.

2

Distant Mothers and Incomprehensible Fathers

Perhaps the most complicated and controversial manifestation of Morrison's double-vision is her portrayal of the black family. While Morrison writes primarily about the need for family and community to nurture and sustain the individual, she never valorizes the traditional structure, which for the majority of whites and blacks in America until very recent times consists, major studies have shown, of two parents and their children. Instead, Morrison chooses to consistently, almost systematically, dissect the nuclear structure. In those novels where the typical family is portrayed, it is either impoverished (MacTeers), sterile (Wrights), decadent (Streets), or just plain Dead. In the majority of Morrison's works, the women, whether alone, with other women, or with members of the community in a network of extended relationships, hold the family together in the face of overwhelming odds, from Pecola's prostitutes' defiance of middle-class mores, to legless Eva and her mysteriously acquired wealth, Pilate's loss of her father, and

Sethe's struggle with her ghost. Morrison suggests that unity cannot be maintained in a nuclear family, illustrating this time and again with the absence of the father from the household: Milkman leaps, Ajax takes off, Son lickety splits, and Paul D gets out. Her impetus, then, appears oppositional not only to her own upbringing but also to the recorded history of the black family in America. But what may appear to be Morrison's fictional resistance to sociological and historical reality could more accurately be characterized as a historical revisioning of the black family. Indeed, the current theory among sociologists and historians of the black family is that existing studies that characterize the black family as predominantly nuclear are flawed because they generally end up comparing black families to the norm of the white family, a methodological approach that at least one sociologist characterizes as apples and oranges.[1] According to K. Sue Jewell, "There is a surfeit of evidence suggesting that black families are unique, and while they may approximate those of white families, they are different in composition, structure, and dynamics over the life cycle of the family unit."[2]

Morrison's own unique notion of domestic tranquility harkens back to an agrarian preindustrial, precapitalistic America when most Americans lived in families that were self-contained and self-sustaining economically, emotionally, and intellectually.[3] Morrison's modern-day fictional version, however, splits significantly from its pastoral antecedent; it does not mandate the presence of the husband who, perhaps because he finds it difficult to fulfill domestic or paternal roles within the established cultural norm, very often takes leave of his family. In defense of her men in motion, Morrison feels no need to "write books about stable black men" and does not "find men who leave their families necessarily villainous."[4] Morrison justifies their leaving as a means of transcendence, especially in *Song of Solomon*: "I chose the man to make that journey because I thought he had more to learn than a woman would have."[5] In allowing the father his freedom, Morrison creates families that do not conform nor aspire to the nuclear family dream. So unusual, so compelling, are Morrison's fictional families, they serve to effectively challenge one of America's most cherished institutions.

That Morrison writes more favorably of nontraditional family

structures in her writings is not to suggest that she wishes to obliterate the nuclear family; indeed, she doesn't care how the family
is organized as long as it is motivated by love. Nor does she want
to eliminate men from families, as she indicates with Mr. MacTeer,
Paul D, and Joe Trace. Rather, what she is writing against is a
patriarchal/capitalistic society that, because it prioritizes male domination and materialistic gain, has had a destructive impact on the
traditional nuclear structure, especially as it pertains to the black
family, since black men have often been denied access to jobs that
would allow them to perform the function of primary provider and,
thus, head of the household. While the nuclear family as a structure
does not inherently presuppose a patriarchal arrangement, that certainly has been its predominant configuration in western society, to
the extent that the terms nuclear family and patriarchy have been
conjoined. Morrison conflates the terms herself in a recent interview: "The notion that the head is the one who brings in the most
money is a patriarchal notion. . . . This is not true. And the little
nuclear family is a paradigm that just doesn't work."[6] For Morrison,
it appears the nuclear family, in general, doesn't work in the context
of patriarchy/capitalism; specifically, it fails for black people, who
cannot rely on a racist marketplace to establish the male as provider
and head.

While Morrison does not want to excise men from families, she
recognizes their need to escape an essentially flawed system and ultimately an impossible situation. In turn, she venerates the women—
and the few men (Mr. McTeer, Sydney)—who stay behind to create whatever arrangement will keep the family and, hence, black
people alive. Although Morrison says she does not see men who
leave their families as villianous, she does illustrate in her fiction
how their absence causes chaos and confusion to the women and
children who must then scramble to restructure their families and
lives. These creative alignments are anything but traditional, but
they do reflect the ways in which black families have historically
adapted and changed in reaction to or in isolation from the social,
economic, and political whims of an oppresive society. As Jewell
says, "Restucturing out of economic necessity as well as for maturation has been a salient characteristic of black families. Moreover,

the economically depressed status of black families, linked with the absence of a national social policy designed to promote economic independence, has served to facilitate the establishment of a complex social exchange system."[7] Indeed, the dramatic, often bizarre changes that Morrison's own fictional families undergo from novel to novel—the MacTeers as nuclear family; Eva's extended family as both blood and fictive kin; Pilate's feminine triad; the Streets as a biracial, cultural extended family; the unworldly household at 124; and finally, the ménage à trois on Lenox Avenue in which one member of the threesome is dead—reflect not only her dissatisfaction with the traditional nuclear family, but any familial construct—even her own fictional ones—that has become so static, so institutionalized, so comfortable with itself in theory that it no longer fulfills its purpose in practice.

To understand Morrison's disaffection with the traditional nuclear structure it is necessary to investigate how the myth of the ideal American family has all too often become a source of frustration and disillusionment for many blacks, as well as for whites. This is not to suggest that all black people were somehow psychologically and emotionallly debilitated by the inacessibility of this particular institution. As Jacqueline Jones states, "Any examination of the mechanics of racial prejudice risks reducing its human subjects to victims, helpless before a many-tentacled monster that invades every part of one's body and soul. The cultural distinctiveness of black community life and the attempt by black working women to subordinate the demands of their employers to the needs of their own families . . . reveal the inherent weakness of the 'victimization' perspective."[8] Jones provides anecdotal evidence of how black people "struggled, with varying degrees of success, to define their lives according to their own terms."[9] Any historical/sociological recounting of black family life is at best an approximation of a very complex social phenomenon.

When the cult of domesticity and ideal womanhood emerged in the nineteenth century, the role of men and women in the family changed dramatically as a result of the industrial revolution. Though colonial women enjoyed a relative autonomy as vital copartners in the operations of their homes, their nineteenth-century sisters, who had originally been the first to work in factories, were quickly displaced by an influx of foreign labor and, thus, separated not only from the external work world and their husbands who soon joined the manufacturing labor pool, but also from a productive and meaningful way of life as factories eventually produced the goods that had been made at home.[10] In the face of this newly imposed inferiority, women sought a moral superiority and nominated themselves as the social engineers who would create cultural hegemony from the chaotic industrial revolution that was transforming America.[11] But first, women had to re-create themselves in order to legitimize their self-proclaimed status as arbiters of taste and culture. To be a true woman, one "must possess piety, purity, submissiveness and domesticity,"[12] the most important virtue being submissiveness, since the husband's success in the work world, indeed the future of the industrial America, was predicated on the notion that women stay at home to provide a tranquil refuge for the husband, and for the children who would eventually replace him. Women, once managers of their families' survival, were now hostesses of their leisure time.

While white women grappled with their diminished roles, "the 'cult of true womanhood' that emerged during the nineteenth century had an intensely demoralizing impact on enslaved black females."[13] Slaves "accepted patriarchal definitions of male-female sex roles. They believed, as did their white owners, that woman's role entailed remaining in the domestic household, rearing children and obeying the will of husbands."[14] This acceptance is not surprising considering their immersion in the dominant culture and the fact that African families were also headed by patriarchies; indeed, "White male observers of African culture in the 18th and 19th centuries were astounded and impressed by the African male's subjugation of the female."[15] Unfortunately, this willingness to accept the domestic ideology—while systematically being denied access to it—created the double-consciousness Du Bois speaks of in *Souls of Black Folk*, since the reality for the majority of black women was that they were forced to work in the fields or outside the home.[16] While "originally displaced African women attached no stigma to female labor in the fields," they soon "assimilated white American values . . . [and] accepted the notion that it was debasing and degrading for women to work in the fields."[17] Black women sought to prove their femininity but could do so only if they assumed the "role of home-maker supported, protected, and honored by a loving husband."[18] The cruel irony of this situation was that "a hundred years ago more than 90 per cent of Negro families subsisted in abject poverty, and as late as 1900 the overwhelming majority was still confined to the lower reaches of the lower class."[19] Ideal womanhood was no more an option for black women than blue eyes were for Pecola.

Black men were no less affected by their inability to establish themselves as head of the household. During the late nineteenth century, black men were systematically denied equal access to those jobs in the work force that would provide sufficient income to allow their wives to stay at home. As a result, both black men and black women relied on each other to support the family financially. While Jacqueline Jones sees this as "a more equal relationship . . . in the sense that the two partners were not separated by extremes of economic power or political rights,"[20] she also acknowledges that this situation could, in some instances, lead to domestic violence: "If whites attempted to cut 'the britches off' black fathers and husbands, then these men would try to assert their authority over their households with even greater determination. At times that determination was manifested in violence and brutality."[21]

Instances of domestic violence in black families were not interpreted by nineteenth-century black or white social workers and leaders as a manifestation of economic frustration but as an indication of the general unsuitability of the black male. This critique of the unworthiness of the black male was based on the observation that black women both supported the family and assumed the burden of domestic responsibilites. Thus, white social workers and black writers and educators, in alternately praising the hardworking black woman and condemning the "worthless" black male, were responsible for initiating the "black matriarchy thesis." As Jones says, "The image of the strong, overburdened black mother persisted through the years, and it was usually accompanied by the implicit assumption that women wielded authority over men and children in Afro-American families."[22] Jones sees this as "cruel irony" since black women "lacked the control over their own productive energies and material resources that would have guaranteed them a meaningful form of social power." [23]

Such black feminists as Bell Hooks, Angela Davis, and Michele Wallace have shed light on the continued negative impact on blacks who have struggled to establish a patriarchy. As Hooks states, "Just as 19th century black male leaders felt that it was important that all black men show themselves willing to be protectors and providers of their women as a sign to the white race that they would tolerate no more denial of their masculine privilege, 20th century black male leaders used this same tactic." [24] Hooks sees the civil rights movement not as liberation for black people but as "a move to gain recognition and support for an emerging black patriarchy." [25] Leaders of the movement were "obsessively concerned with asserting their masculinity while black women imitated the behavior of white women in black sex-role patterns." [26] In fighting off the myth of the matriarchy perpetuated by E. Franklin Frazier and later intensified by the now infamous Moynihan report,[27] black women found that "the stereotypical image of the black woman as strong and powerful so dominates the consciousness of most Americans that even if a black woman is clearly to conform to sexist notions of femininity and passivity she may be characterized as tough, lazy, and strong." [28] Even as late as the sixties, seventies, and eighties, black women, inundated by images in advertising and the media, continued to aspire to the Victorian concept of true womanhood.[29]

The extreme psychic frustration of this situation is exacerbated by the current state of black males. While many black women may still be afflicted with the aspiration to ideal womanhood, they cannot wish their men into the role of head-of-the-household providers. Indeed, the entire notion of a black patriarchy is undermined by the economic, political, and social forces that militate against such a structure. In her essay on black male-female relationships, Audrey Chapman paints a very dismal picture for black males. She estimates that "40 percent of the Black male population is functionally illiterate;" that while the number of doctoral and professional degrees for black women increased between 1976 and 1981, they decreased for black men; that unemployment for black men between the ages of eighteen and forty-four increased at a greater rate during 1983 than they did for black women; and that "there is also a high mortality rate among Black men; many are incarcerated, in mental hospitals, drug addicts, in the military (overseas), or simply not interested in Black women."[30] Given the fact that so much emphasis is placed on men as sole provider,[31] it takes no stretch of the imagination to envision the frustration of many black men and women who aspire to an ideal that is increasingly unattainable.

Like the civil rights movement, the women's movement from the turn of the century until recent times did little to liberate the black male and female from the restrictive cultural norms. When it seemed apparent that black males would get the vote before white women, white women activists turned against a political force they should have embraced and adopted a racist and sexist attitude in hopes of turning the tide in their favor. Many suffragettes portrayed black people as "incompetent barbarians" and themselves "as mother-figures, whose fundamental raison d'être was the nurturing of the male species."[32] Their invocation of motherhood thus served to undermine the premise of the movement—"the elimination of male supremacy."[33] When the movement began again in earnest in the 1960s and 1970s, middle-class white women did little to address or integrate the needs and concerns of working-class black women. Having never been allowed the leisure of staying at home, and forced to accept the most backbreaking, demeaning jobs, black women did not understand the white woman's desire to get out of the house and find meaningful jobs.

Thus, while black men and white women have sought to acquire power from a male-dominated society, black women have largely been excluded from major attempts at social revolution and reorganization, even though their actions have been decidedly subversive of the oppressive patriarchy. Expected to be submissive to their men, and historically neglected by their white sisters, black women have struggled along in a no-win contest. Even their attempts to be supportive of black males have often been futile, since they have no control over the vagaries of the marketplace. Complicating their dilemma even further is the class separation within the black community itself, in which black women who have become part of the bourgeoisie and who practice its ideology tend to denigrate those blacks who compose the working-class or underclass majority. As Michele Wallace points out, "Everyone knows that whites have traditionally been prejudiced against blacks, but what people do not know, or do not care to know, is the extent to which blacks are now prejudiced against each other."[34] No wonder, then, that Toni Morrison, in her fictional world, chooses to deny those values that consistently frustrate, demoralize, and divide black society. Instead, she creates individuals or family groups that do not conform to middle-class mores and that, while imperfect, certainly would appear more attractive to blacks long deluded by a fantasy of normalcy that has all too often become an exercise in futility.

Futher exacerbating the state of affairs of the black family is that historians and sociologists, in an effort to square the black family in the eyes of white society, produced elaborate statistics and detailed studies to prove that black families were predominantly patriarchal/ nuclear in structure. In one study, Elizabeth Pleck discovered in her research of the black family in late nineteenth-century Boston that the most typical household in Boston (82 percent) included the "husband, wife, or a husband, wife, and children."[35] This percentage was not peculiar to the East since "overall figures from Southern urban Southern rural, and Northern urban centers in [the] late nineteenth century demonstrate a striking similarity in the percentages of two-parent households."[36] These numbers remain consistent for the first half of the twentieth century, though E. Franklin Frazier warns of an increasingly single-parent, woman-dominated household suggested by the figures from the 1940 census: "In the urban areas of southern states 31.1 per cent of the Negro families were without male heads while the proportion for rural nonfarm areas was 22.5 per cent and for rural farm areas 11.7 per cent."[37] While this census tends to belie Frazier's anxiety, a recent study confirms it: "In 1960, 22.4 per cent of Black households were headed by females . . . in 1970, the figure . . . rose to 28.3 per cent . . . by 1980, more than half of all Black children under eighteen years of age were in homes headed by one parent."[38] And finally, in a report published in 1988, researchers found that just 10 percent of all "households are now made up of a breadwinner husband, homemaker wife and children" and that nine out of ten black children "will live with a single parent at some time before their 16th birthday."[39]

The problem with these studies is that they tend to oversimplify the historical configuration of the black family by characterizing it as either patriarchal or matriarchal—terms that imply an overt power struggle and a successful institutionalization of a familial structure that has never been effected. In addition, they ignore major studies that document other manifestations of the black family that are neither reflective of nor dependent on the scenario of a nuclear or single-parent family.

In her study on the conceptualization of black families, Jualynne Dodson has isolated two schools of thought in the research on the black family: the cultural ethnocentric approach represented by E. Franklin Frazier and Daniel P. Moynihan, which views the black family as dysfunctional because of what they see as its increasingly fatherless, matriarchal structure; and the cultural relativistic view supported by Andrew Billingsley, Wade Noble, J. W. Blassingame and others, which "maintains that the black family is a functional entity."[40] Contrary to the beliefs of the cultural ethnocentrics, the cultural relativists insist that slavery did not "totally destroy the traditional African base of black family functioning"; indeed, it derives its strength not from its American cultural heritage, but from its African one.[41]

The cultural relativists move beyond the simplistic characterization of the black family as either matriarchal or patriarchal and identify, instead, other forms of family organization. In *Black Families in White America*, Andrew Billingsley categorizes the black family into three groups, primary or nuclear families (which he readily acknowledges comprise the majority of black families), extended families, and augmented families. He further subdivides primary and extended families into three more groups, incipient, simple, and attenuated suggesting the multiple and complex manifestations of the black family. Rather than lament the fact that the black family is increasingly moving away from the nuclear structure, Billingsley celebrates it.[42]

While such cultural relativists as Billingsley have taken great strides in debunking the notion of the black family as deviant, they have suffered from flaws in their own methodological approach. According to K. Sue Jewell, the controversy surrounding the issue of whether the black family is deviant, variant, or similar "is related to the inordinate proportion of black families with female heads."[43] The problem with this impetus to "confirm or deny the prevalence of the black matriarchy has led to the systematic comparing of black families to white families."[44] For social scientists to understand the nature of the black family, they must first, Jewell says, forgo the comparison with the "normative paradigm":

> Theoreticians, those in the cultural deviance and relativism schools, continue to examine black families using a middle-class, nuclear model as the barometer. But not all factors that affect white family structures impact similarly upon the structures of black families. The primary difference is that black families, because of social and economic hardships, developed unique family arrangements. Hence, black families became dependent upon external informal support systems to a greater extent than did their white counterparts.[45]

What social scientists must also realize, in order to fully comprehend black families, is that they are not static but inherently dynamic in structure. "Over the black family life cycle, a variety of changes are likely to occur within the family structure. While the frequency of structural change is related to socioeconomic status, black families are characterized by changing structures across all social classes. Hence, a developmental approach is a necessity for analyzing black family structure."[46]

Toni Morrison places these variant and ever-increasing family structures in the forefront of a distant and not so distant past and in so doing, she acts as a historical revisionist who dispels the myth of nuclear familial bliss. Instead, she revoices her own families to adapt to the social/historical context of her novels. She rejects the tendency to naturalize the conditions and ideology that go with the traditional family—male domination or patriarchy, female submissiveness or the cult of domesticity, and true womanhood—concepts that have retained a grip on the American psyche much to the psychological detriment of white women who were pressured into restrictive role playing, and more so, to the mental malaise of black men and women who were encouraged to embrace the myth of the perfect family but denied the means to fulfill it.[47] But more than rewriting history, Morrison, like Houston Baker's jazz musician, chooses to proliferate rather than restrict interpretations of that chameleonic reality into fictive possibilities that neither exclude nor deny personal expression.

Morrison's familial representations undergo a complex and bewildering evolution. She scrambles the structure, locus, ideology, and value system of the family, dramatically illustrating that the home is not necessarily housed in a two-parent nuclear family but where the heart is. Morrison says that the nuclear family "is a paradigm that just doesn't work. It doesn't work for white people or for black people. Why we are hanging onto it, I don't know. It isolates people into little units—people need a larger unit."[48] Morrison, however, does not arrive at this juncture automatically; indeed, each of her novels shows an increasing disaffection with her previous family types and a subsequent revisioning of them. She sets up tenuous dyads and triads in her earlier novels only to abandon them as she creates even more complex and bizarre families in her later novels. Her families themselves constitute genealogical lines of fictional descent, some of which become extinct and others that engender aberrant and even startling configurations.

Morrison's first fictional families are dialectical voicings and re-voicings of traditional nuclear families versus women-constructed, women-headed households. The MacTeers, Breedloves, and Geraldines prefigure the Wrights and the Deads, who are collectively antithetical to the merry gargoyles, Eva and Pilate. But after her early novels, Morrison recognizes that the dichotomy she sets up suffers from an oversimplification of the psychosocial, emotional, and spiritual parameters of the family. As a result, she abandons the woman-constructed household in *Tar Baby*, choosing instead to extend the nuclear family from a household to a Street, a dysfunctional family that becomes a synecdoche for dysfunctional society. In *Beloved* Morrison Signifies against her own female-headed households: the idyllic trinity of women singing in the candlelight is re-visioned in *Beloved* as a trinity of women in the clearing, one of whom—

a ghostly daughter—threatens matricide and, thus, the end of the
myth of feminized bliss. The community of women must step in to
free Sethe's family from the tyrannical forces of history and its attendant guilt. In *Jazz* the Trace family on Lenox Avenue is both a
ménage à trois consisting of Joe, Violet, and the photograph of the
dead Dorcas, and a nuclear family of sorts in which Violet can even
imagine Dorcas as her daughter. The love that Violet must generate
to reconcile with her husband and the object of his desire stretches
to the breaking point even Morrison's own unique notion of family.
By the time *Beloved* and *Jazz* emerge, all that is left of the family is
all that Morrison says it should be: an individual awareness of and
commitment to the idea that families are not spatial and geographical constructs united by blood ties, but a collective consciousness of
caring that engenders the universal family.

In her first three novels, Morrison confronts the notion of ideal
family that the black community aspires to and exposes the surface
respectability and security represented by the husband, wife, and
children. The focal point of her criticism, as Susan Willis skillfully
explains in her essay "Eruptions of Funk," is not necessarily the
nuclear family per se, but the capitalistic patriarchy that reifies the
nuclear family.[49] Alongside the traditional nuclear family, Morrison
introduces an alternative lifestyle that very much resembles Frazier's
matriarchy. The difference, of course, is Morrison's perception that
a female-headed household is neither weak nor deviant, but vibrant
and organic, what psychologist Anne Schaef calls the Living Process System.[50] In sharp contrast are the households of the MacTeers,
Wrights, and Deads, which, as their names suggest, range from pure
drudgery to lifelessness—Schaef's Non-Living or Addictive System
in which human beings are animated zombies. Gone from Morrison's alternative family is the rhetoric of the marketplace that, while
embedded in the psyche of people no matter what the economy,
is certainly intensified in a capitalist society that makes priorities
of wealth and material possession. Members of Morrison's female
households are not rigidified or compartmentalized into functions
like workers in an industrialized society, or more specifically, like
members of a capitalist society who emulate in their homes the con-

cept of private production, accumulation, and ownership. Morrison's families are a three-woman household "which do[es] not permit heterosexuality as it articulates male domination to be the determining principle for the living and working relationship of the group, as it is in a capitalist society."[51] Morrison's social alternative "comes into view when Macon Dead peers into Pilate's window; when the child Nel . . . scratches at Sula's screen door; and when the intimidated and fearful Pecola visits her upstairs neighbors, the three prostitutes."[52] Willis calls this life-style "the utopian aspect of her vision" even though she admits none of the utopias are perfect—a further demonstration of "the way consumer society penetrates and impoverishes human relationships."[53]

In *The Bluest Eye*, *Sula*, and *Song of Solomon*, Morrison reserves her most scathing attacks for those black families who appear to have successfully imitated middle-class respectability—Geraldine, the Wrights, the Deads. While outwardly model citizens, they live a reality that is something quite different, for in their obsession with social acceptance they have succeeded in destroying themselves and their children, and ultimately effecting violence on black culture. These families inevitably include a mother and father, though the father is either absent, invisible, or abusive; and the women, faring no better, are portrayed as distant, frigid, arrogant, perverse, and pathetic, what Morrison calls in *Sula* "distant mothers and incomprehensible fathers" (p. 52). These men and women, representing levels of society and degrees of societal repression, typify those members of the emerging black middle class who measure their success in how far they have come in denying their cultural roots and how thoroughly they have adopted white society's values. At once victims and victimizers, Geraldine, Pauline, Helene Wright, and Macon and Ruth Dead have become social half-breeds, torn between two cultures. Neither strengthened nor fructified by this inbreeding, they represent the very antithesis of what social visionaries had hoped would be the answer to racial discord—literal and symbolic miscegenation. E. Franklin Frazier, for example, praised the mulattoes for their "part in strengthening patriarchal traditions," which established a "long history of industry and thrift and a sturdiness of character that differentiate them from the mass of the Negro population." [54]

Morrison takes violent exception to this back-slapping of blacks who wish to excuse themselves from their own ethnicity, that "mass of the Negro population," and instead condemns them for adopting an oppressive and stultifying system in which power and control in the family and community is determined by maleness and material possession. Morrison's condemnation is clarified by virtue of the fact that for every traditional family in her first three novels there exists a nontraditional one that refreshes the stale air of conformity. If Geraldine and Pauline Breedlove exist, so do the lively prostitutes; if the beautiful Creole Helene Wright commands respect in the neighborhood, so does her prostitute mother; if Macon and Ruth Dead possess the power of money, so Pilate exercises the power of love.

In *The Bluest Eye*, Morrison explodes the hope for assimilation that blacks and whites have seen as a natural and necessary social progression. The very tragedy in *The Bluest Eye* is the inability of a community to sustain the life of one little black girl precisely because she is not white enough or pretty enough to fit in. While white society is culpable for its imposition of decadent values, the black community, Morrison makes clear, is also responsible because of its desire to embrace those same values. Pecola, victimized from within and without, has no family or community to insulate her from or fortify her against the ideology of beauty and wealth that treats plain black girls like disposable diapers. Morrison is especially critical of those black families who possess the financial resources and education to make a difference, but who choose instead to devote their energies to distinguishing themselves from Frazier's "mass of the Negro population." Their isolation from the black community into separate competing units of nuclear families is the death of the extended family as an informal social support system.

Morrison unleashes her anger in her portrayal of Geraldine who, like her "sugar-brown Mobile" sisters, takes pride in the distance she maintains from lower-class blacks. An educated woman, she learns "how to behave, the careful development of thrift, patience, high morals, and good manners" (p. 68). She makes the maxim "Cleanliness is next to godliness" her golden rule: "Colored people were neat and quiet; niggers were dirty and loud" (p. 71). Cleanliness becomes an obsession that infects every area of her life including sex, which is a filthy necessity not to be enjoyed, and mother love, which keeps a child clean but not cuddled. In her aspiration for acceptance, Geraldine has relinquished the pleasures and very essence of life, "the dreadful funkiness of passion, the funkiness of nature, the funkiness of the wide range of human emotions" (p. 68).

What Geraldine is fighting in fact is her blackness, the very conditions of her birth that identify who she is. Rather than nourish the seed of her being, she attempts to obliterate it. Consequently, Geraldine forfeits all the joys of life: sex, motherhood, companionship, and ultimately self-expression. Sex is a messy business that could have been simplified by putting "the necessary but private parts of the body in some more convenient place—like the armpit for example, or the palm of the hand" (p. 69). Having never experienced an orgasm, Geraldine finds no pleasure in the sex act and settles for the rather perverse sensations she derives from her cat. Symbolic of her fetishization of cleanliness, she places the cat at the center of her affection and attention, to the exclusion of her husband and son, Junior. If a husband is a necessary condition of domestic respectability, she prefers him absent; if she must be a mother she will unfailingly keep her son clean but will not "talk to him, coo to him, or indulge him in kissing bouts" (p. 71). Geraldine's life has dwindled and diminished to such an extent that she becomes little more than an innocuous feline at the feet of an exacting social code.

Though she poses no threat to the existing order, she adversely affects the lives of Junior, her flesh and blood, and Pecola, a total stranger. Junior, forced to live by his mother's standards, is clipped as neat as a hedge because the "line between colored and nigger was not always clear" (p. 71) and is only allowed to play with white children. Junior suffocates in this rarefied atmosphere and "more than anything in the world he want[s] to play King of the mountain and have them push him down the mound of dirt and roll over him" (p. 71). Frustration turns into cruelty, and Junior, denied access to the pleasures of his own ethnicity, resorts to tormenting cats and little black girls. Pecola bears the brunt of the rage that has seeped into the tidy lives of Geraldine and Junior. In an echo chamber effect, Pecola becomes the victim of Junior who is the victim of Geraldine who is the victim of centuries of oppression. Pecola ceases to exist in Geraldine's eyes except as a type of social disease:

> She had seen this little girl all of her life. Hanging out of windows over saloons in Mobile, crawling over the porches of shotgun houses on the edge of town, sitting in bus stations holding paper bags and crying to mothers who kept saying "Shet up!" Hair uncombed, dresses falling apart, shoes untied and caked with dirt. They had stared at her with great uncomprehending eyes. Eyes that questioned nothing and asked everything. Unblinking and unabashed, they stared up at her. The end of the world lay in their eyes, and the beginning, and all the waste in between. (p. 75)

Pecola becomes the enemy—the dirt, the ignorance, the silence, the needfulness, the history—that which must be stamped out in Geraldine's life. Representing all that Geraldine is ashamed of and which she fights so desperately not to be, Pecola's presence in the house is the ultimate transgression. When she orders Pecola out, Geraldine also dismisses her history, culture, passions, and love. There is no love for Pecola in Geraldine's house because the woman has no love for herself.

Geraldine's rejection of Pecola is a total denial of the way of life she comes from and is in eternal fear of returning to. That life is represented by Pauline Breedlove, who once possessed such joy that it welled up in her in a fountain of colors and bubbled into laughter. Certainly Pecola could retreat into the bosom of that joy and retain a sense of dignity. Yet somewhere along the line, her mother's happiness evaporated with an idyllic childhood that she spent in a mythic South. Like Geraldine, Pauline is also a type—one of many black families in the 1940s to migrate to the industrial Midwest in search of a better way of life. Her problem, a common one to southern blacks, was "how to maintain an Afro-American cultural heritage once the relationship to the black rural South has been stretched thin over distance and generations."[55] While Geraldine has never experienced the funkiness of nature, passions, and uninhibited joy, Pauline has, and carries it with her up north. Her dilemma is how to adapt or exchange one set of cultural values for another, especially when what she must relinquish is all that is dear to her—a spacious home and a loving family unit located in a quaint and supportive rural black community. "As in the ancestral African tradition," Barbara Christian says, "place is as important as the human actors. For the land is a participant in the maintenance of folk tradition. It is one of the necessary constraints through which the folk dramatize the meaning of life, as it is passed from one generation to the next. Setting then is organic to the characters' view of themselves. And a change in place drastically alters the traditional values that give life coherence." [56]

In Lorain, Pauline adjusts to an alien, hostile land, where whites are more numerous than blacks and where she is judged, not by the superior quality of her work but by the relative attributes of her external appearance—even by blacks influenced by the values of an ever-present white society. Her days no longer adequately filled with domestic tranquility, Pauline looks outside her home for a sense of purpose and identity. A devout Christian and a model servant, she earns the respect of the black women who had scorned her unsophisticated southern ways and high praise from the white people whose house she cleans. Her own home becomes "the early-morning and late-evening edges of her day, the dark edges that made the daily life with the Fishers lighter, more delicate, more lovely" (p. 101). She no longer belongs to the home in Kentucky where she "cultivated private pleasures"; the Fisher house is now the sanctuary where she "could arrange things, clean things, line things up in neat rows" (p. 101).

Pauline's existence is schizophrenic, torn between the darkness and chaos of the Breedlove storefront and the hospital-white sterility of the Fisher home. Always on the verge of leaving drunken Cholly, she will stop, struck by the memory of happier times. Her earlier love of him mixes with the blissful moments of her childhood in a rainbow of her psyche:

> When I first seed Cholly, I want you to know it was like all the bits of color from that time down home when all us chil'ren went berry picking after a funeral and I put some in the pocket of my Sunday dress, and they mashed up and stained my hips. My whole dress was messed with

purple and it never did wash out. Not the dress nor me. I could feel that purple deep inside me. And that lemonade Mamma used to make when Pap came in out the fields. It be cool and yellowish, with seeds floating near the bottom. And that streak of green them june bugs made on the trees the night we left from down home. All them colors was in me. Just sitting there. (p. 92)

The colors occur infrequently now, but leave Pauline with sufficient disquiet. As she says, "Only thing I miss sometimes is that rainbow. But like I say, I don't recollect it anymore" (p. 104). All of the colors that swirled inside of her—the reds of her sexual passion, the yellows of her boundless joy, and the greens of her quiet moments—have bleached white. With the rainbow goes her interpretation of life through sensual perceptions. Reduced to judging herself in terms of external measurements—work, church, movies—she is no longer able to trust her subjective reaction to the world and consequently is alienated from it. She bears the burden of her drunken husband as penance for her imagined sins and prays for the salvation of her poor and ugly, thus sinful, family. Her motives are simply to seek some affirmation of her worth even if it is at the expense of her family.

In the midst of Pauline's aspiration to martyrdom is Pecola who, instead of flourishing under the nurturing love of her mother, becomes a victim of Pauline's compulsion to punish her own blackness. In one of the most harrowing scenes in the novel, Pauline strikes out at what should be the pride of her life and instead embraces the little white girl, a symbol of all that has diminished her. The blueberries that had once colored Pauline's own dress in the blush of her youth become Pecola's stain of dishonor as she is burned by the blueberry cobbler, and then slips and falls in the mess by the force of her mother's blow. The irony of the name Breedlove intensifies as "Polly"—another misnomer that is a further diminution of Pauline—hushes the cries of the little girl in pink as her own daughter shuffles away in abject humility.

But Pecola suffers worse humiliation and degradation at the hands of her father, whose crime is not that he rejects her but that his love for her is misplaced and the ultimate cause of her destruction. Cholly, however, is no monster and is at least deserving of our sympathy and understanding—emotions that Morrison purposely evokes to make sense of an otherwise incomprehensible act. Abused and neglected himself as a child, Cholly is not obliged to justify his actions to the very system of justice and morality that failed to protect him. With no mother or father to socialize and nurture him into a normal human being, with no protection from the whimsical intrusion of violent racist elements, and with no access to a decent job, Cholly is released from human responsibility. He becomes "dangerously free. Free to feel whatever he felt—fear, guilt, shame, love, grief, pity. Free to be tender or violent, to whistle or weep. . . . He was alone with his own perceptions and appetites, and they alone interested him" (p. 126). When Cholly rapes Pecola he does so without any sense of right or wrong—a distinction he has never been taught or experienced.

Even though Cholly, Pauline, and Geraldine are victims of a repressive system, they are all in part responsible for Pecola's rape and subsequent loss of sanity. Turning their rage against one of their own, a child no less, they have transgressed the limits of sympathy in spite of the conditions of their lives. Sparing no feelings, Morrison drives this point home when she characterizes the black community as stingy and reluctant to provide succor for Pecola: "They were disgusted, amused, shocked, outraged, or even excited by the story. But we listened for one who would say, 'Poor little girl,' or, 'Poor baby,' but there was only head-wagging where those words should have been. We looked for eyes creased with concern, but saw only veils" (p. 148).

While Morrison implicates the entire community in Pecola's unspeakable tragedy, she does offer the MacTeers as an example of a black family that has not been totally divested of its obligation to the black community. Though the MacTeers endure poverty and hardship, they are sustained by a love for each other that transcends their earthly reality. Rather than seal themselves off into their own private family unit, the MacTeers retain a committment to the idea of the black community as their extended family. Resisting the temptation to retreat into the opium den of movie theaters, like Pauline, or the bottle, like Cholly, the MacTeers have survived with a sense of self and culture that stands in striking opposition to the Lorain community. Mr. MacTeer, though nearly as invisible as Geraldine's husband, is nevertheless a hard worker whose rewards are apparently reaped in terms of keeping his family together rather than climbing a social ladder wrought with broken rungs. In Mrs. MacTeer is a "misery colored by the greens and blues in her voice" (p. 24). Her children, Claudia and Frieda, live on the boundary of a prolonged scolding or a burst of sweet-sad music. The harsh conditions of her life, marked by poverty and a bitter climate, shape her sometimes rough and cruel treatment of her children. Claudia and Frieda are chastised for catching a cold or suffering a bruised knee. Any illness "is treated with contempt, foul Black Draught, and castor oil" (p. 13). Her frustration takes the form of agonizing monologues that leave Frieda and Claudia demoralized and ashamed, for their very existence appears to be a tremendous strain on their mother.

In spite of her often painful rebuffs and unjust punishment of her children, Mrs. MacTeer is, as Claudia recalls it, capable of soft music, warm laughter, and an abiding love:

> Love, thick and dark as Alaga Syrup, eased up into that cracked window. I could smell it—taste it—sweet, misty, with an edge of wintergreen in its base—everywhere in that house. It stuck, along with my tongue, to the frosted panes. It coated my chest, along with the salve, and when the flannel came undone in my sleep, the clear, sharp curves of air outlined its presence on my throat. And in the night, when my coughing was dry and tough, feet padded into the room, hands repinned the flannel, readjusted the quilt, and rested a moment on my forehead. So when I think of autumn, I think of somebody with hands who does not want me to die. (p. 14)

Unlike Pauline and Geraldine, Mrs. MacTeer rises above the conditions of her life and the self-pity that could have consumed her, in order to fulfill her duty as a loving mother.

Because the MacTeers are not obsessed with the need to be beautiful, wealthy, or white, they concentrate their efforts on family and community. When they take in Pecola, they voluntarily increase the weight of the burden that could eventually break them. In one of Mrs. MacTeer's frequent harangues, it appears this additional mouth to feed has become too much for her; yet her anger is not directed at Pecola as much as the family that appears to have abandoned her.

"Folks," she says, "just dump they children off on you and go on
'bout they business. Ain't nobody even peeped in here to see whether
that child has a loaf of bread" (p. 23). She has no sympathy for the
Breedloves, only disgust for their lack of responsibility. "What kind
of something is that?" she asks (p. 23). Mrs. MacTeer's condemnation of the Breedloves articulates a recurring theme in Morrison's
works. "All the time that I write," Morrison states, "I'm writing about
love or its absence. . . . I still write about the same thing, which is
how people relate to one another and miss it or hang on to it . . . or
are tenacious about love."[57] The MacTeers have held on, and they
represent just a few in the world of *The Bluest Eye* who have not
been divested of their humanity. Yet the depressing reality is that the
MacTeers simply do not have the time, energy, or money to adopt
all the Pecolas of the world. The circumstances of their lives leave
little room for the leisure of love. Poverty has blunted their joy and
muted their affection for their children. That they are capable of love
at all is something of a miracle; that they are unable to find room for
Pecola in their hearts is an understandable tragedy.

Though the MacTeer household is very much a traditional family,
it is not intended as an affirmation of patriarchy—Mr. and Mrs.
MacTeer play equal parts in keeping the family together—as much
as it is a testimonial to the ability of unique individuals to sustain
each other no matter what the circumstances. In this respect, Morrison implies—though she does not explicitly make the distinction—
that it is not the nuclear family that is inherently flawed, but the commodifying influences of patriarchy. Unfortunately, the MacTeers
cannot extricate themselves from the social, political and economic
forces that militate against families like the MacTeers who cling to
values of family and community as they teeter on the edge of an
economic abyss. Though the MacTeers are apparently blessed with
a hardworking father and dutiful mother, they must struggle daily
for their own survival, which leaves very little left over for the less
fortunate members of their community.

Their domestic blues, and the general gloominess that persists in
the novel, are displaced momentarily by the world of the prostitutes,
which collectively invokes a subversive response to patriarchy and
Victorian ideas of decency and womanhood.[58] With the merry pros-

titutes, Morrison introduces the female-constructed household that will eventually reappear in the Eva household and reach its highest degree of development in the Pilate home. Though traditionally labeled victims themselves, China, Poland, and Miss Marie do not fit the stereotype of the fallen woman. Morrison avoids the Madonna/whore dichotomy and releases women from a long-standing no-win situation. Still, the household of the whores, while it is certainly a cheerful domicile, falls well short of the ideal concept of family.

Their household is distinctly feminine and uninhibited; absent is the prolonged presence and intrusion of males, and the artificial and stultifying strictures of society and religion. Free to conduct their lives according to their own code, they scorn the hypocritical religious zealots who condemn them, and the macho frauds who, while enlisting their services, become babies in their hands: "In a playful manner, the way grandmothers do with babies, [Mr. Henry] was sucking the fingers of one of the women [China] whose laughter filled a tiny place over his head" (p. 63). Their rejection of men—aggravated no doubt by their dependence on their patronage—is total. To them, men are the most vile of creatures, who claim intellectual and moral superiority over women in one breath, while they beg for perverse pleasure in another. They hate "all men, without shame, apology, or discrimination. They abused their visitors with a scorn grown mechanical from use. Black men, white men, Puerto Ricans, Mexicans, Jews, Poles, whatever—all were inadequate and weak, all came under their jaundiced eyes and were the recipients of their disinterested wrath" (p. 48).

Though they exist on the periphery of society, despised and reviled by so-called good Christians, the prostitutes create an atmosphere of jocularity and freshness that brightens the otherwise moribund mood of the novel. Pecola takes refuge in this world because the prostitutes, unlike Geraldine and Pauline, remain unaffected by the standards of an alien culture; they are, therefore, oblivious to Pecola's ugliness and dirt. Indeed, the Maginot Line pays Pecola the greatest compliment by comparing her to her beloved food: "Marie seldom called Pecola the same thing twice, but invariably her epithets were fond ones chosen from menus and dishes that were forever uppermost in her mind" (p. 44). Pecola listens with rapt attention to the

bawdy stories and lewd jokes that make up the demimonde's conversation. In a room where laughter resembles "the sound of many
rivers, freely, deeply, muddily, heading for the room of an open sea"
(p. 45), Pecola finds the balm to soothe her psychic wounds. Her
contentment is such that she wonders, "were they real?" (p. 49).

While the whores are Pecola's sole retreat from the battlefield of
her life, they cannot provide the manna that will keep her sane. Their
affection for her is real, but it is no substitute for her mother's love.
The social alternative Morrison hints at, and which Susan Willis
sees as utopian, simply does not emerge in the framework of this
novel. The seeds are there in the three-woman household, but do
not develop in the novel any further than the one scene in which
the prostitutes are introduced with Pecola. Morrison's denunciation
of the society that Pecola lives in becomes even more pronounced
by virtue of the fact that the only place Pecola feels a sense of
warmth and humanity is in an establishment that sells love for profit.
Pecola's life is neither enriched nor transformed by the existence of
the whores. Indeed, her longing to be part of their lives is another
in a long list of unfulfilled dreams. She tells Frieda, "China gone
take me to Cleveland to see the square, and Poland gone take me
to Chicago to see the Loop. We going everywhere together" (p. 85).
Frieda tells her to stop lying, knowing, as the reader does, that the
women, though sincere in their intentions, cannot accommodate a
child because of the nature of their business. Pecola perhaps senses
this when, asking Miss Marie if she had any children, the Maginot
Line answers abruptly and the subject is dropped. Though the prostitutes may represent an alternative to the established social order,
it is a world that does not as yet include responsibility for their own
children, let alone Pecola.

In *Sula*, Morrison continues her attack on the capitalistic/patriar-
chal family, but this time eliminates altogether even a minimally
healthy nuclear family, thus allowing the MacTeer lineage to die out.
Instead, she introduces more clearly the dichotomy between nuclear
family and female-constructed household that she had set up between the three prostitutes and the Breedloves. In *Sula* Morrison
places in direct opposition to the Wrights, Eva's household. She also

revoices the merry gargoyles in the form of Rochelle who, like her literary antecedents, tricks patriarchal power by commodifying her own sexuality outside of marriage. As a result, Morrison's despair in *The Bluest Eye*, her tendency toward a naturalistic and fatalistic interpretation of life, is mitigated in *Sula* by the Creole whore and the legless Eva. The evanescent quality of Helene Wright's mother and the almost illusory nature of Eva's home are a far remove from the gritty reality of the MacTeer family and the pleasant, but isolated, realm of the three prostitutes. Even Morrison's critique of middle-class propriety loses some of its sting so that Helene Wright is not nearly the unattractive and pathetic creature that Geraldine is. Nevertheless, despair finally wins the day in the person of Sula, who cannot accept or understand her grandmother's way of life and who destroys her best friend's illusion of domestic happiness. Though Sula and Nel are products of two distinctly different family structures, both fail to sustain and nurture their members into adulthood. Thus the dialectic that Morrison sets up in the households of Nel Wright and Sula Peace is never dissolved, a painful reminder to the reader that happy endings in Morrison's complicated world rarely materialize.

Helene Wright's house, like Geraldine's and Ruth Dead's, is a Dickensian Stonelodge with lace curtains. Clean, respectable and utilitarian in function, it is a twentieth-century remnant of the materialistic rationalism that was the organizing principle in Victorian life. The father, a seaman (a double entendre) who is never home, serves exclusively as a wage earner, while the mother acts as custodian of his property and progeny so that economic security, rather than love, acts as the center and circumference of the home. Helene instills in Nel those qualities that will make her a productive member of society—politeness, neatness, cleanliness, obedience, and hard work—and that will assure an accumulation of wealth and respectability. Aesthetic pleasures, since they produce no material gain, are worthless and, thus, undesirable. Helene does the right thing but not necessarily the good thing in teaching Nel to be "obedient and polite. Any enthusiasms that little Nel showed were calmed by the mother until she drove her daughter's imagination underground" (p. 18). Nel longs for the relative freedom of a world she can only visit. She hates "the oppressive neatness of her home," and prefers "Sula's woolly house, where a pot of something was always cooking on the stove; where the mother, Hannah, never scolded or gave directions; where all sorts of people dropped in; where newspapers were stacked in the hallway and dirty dishes left for hours at a time in the sink, and where a one-legged grandmother named Eva handed you goobers from deep inside her pockets or read you a dream" (p. 29).

Such a scenario would horrify Helene, who is the epitome of ideal womanhood. Dignified, graceful, beautiful, religious, and well-heeled, she has successfully assimilated white values, but only after being whisked from her mother, a Creole whore, and counseled "to be constantly on guard for any sign of her mother's wild blood" (p. 17). Her success is illusory, and despite her trappings as a lady, she finds that in going south to her grandmother's funeral she is subhuman in the eyes of white society. When the train conductor humiliates her she does not rebel but "smile[s] dazzlingly and coquettishly at the salmon-colored face of the conductor" (p. 21). By this action, Helene insures her own oppression and degradation, for even in a society in which capital gain is a badge of honor, Helene's skin color alone attests to her inferiority.

Helene's mother, on the other hand, is clearly subversive to the bourgeoisie in general and all good women in particular. Her oppositional stance is manifested in the semiotics of her being—her job, her marital status, her clothes, and her language. A French-speaking prostitute, she challenges all conventions and approaches near sacrilege. She invades her mother's funeral in a splash of color: "In that somber house that held four Virgin Marys, where death sighed in every corner and candles sputtered, the gardenia and canary-yellow dress emphasized the funeral atmosphere surrounding them" (p. 25). She refuses to see death in anything but natural terms despite all efforts of civilization to make it strange and, thus, control the behavior of individual lives in the here and now by mystifying the afterlife. Rochelle conducts her life according to an inner code; consequently, she is both the Madonna and the whore in her representation of life and her indulgence in earthly pleasures.

Rochelle's appearance in the novel, as fleeting as the bird imagery Morrison invokes, leaves a remarkably strong impression on the reader—and on Nel. Nel is distanced from her own grandmother and her way of life by the French Creole she cannot understand and her mother's unwillingness to acquaint her. Nel is vitalized by the strangeness of the woman's bright and gaudy clothes, her un-restrained laughter, her financial independence, her apparent lack of concern for material possessions, and her compulsive and un-conditional affection. Helene reacts by soaping Nel "head to toe" (p. 27) in an effort to scrub off the woman's filmy embrace and thus the influence of her ideology. Morrison's proclivities, however, cannot be washed away and in the few short pages that Rochelle appears, she, with her halolike hair, is truly virginal. She may sell her body, but she will not prostitute her soul for the sake of social acceptance. By using Rochelle and her other prostitutes, Morrison hopes to shock the reader into acknowledging that preoccupation with sexual morality—especially if becoming immoral is forced upon black women who have very few alternatives to support themselves—is often a beam in the eye of spiritual awakening.

While Morrison offers us only a fleeting glance of Rochelle, she places Eva's household at the center of the novel, moving closer to the periphery the notion of nuclear family represented by the Mac-Teers. Eva's house is a far cry from the drudgery of the MacTeer family, where poverty and disaster rub against the legs of a husband and wife who cannot work harder than they already do to make ends meet. Eva is virtually removed from the influence of the marketplace because she has sacrificed her leg on the altar of economic security. As a result, her household is free to govern itself according to human needs. She does not need a man to support her; she does not need to instruct her children in their proper roles as providers and nurturers; and she does not need to set herself against or above her community since she is no longer a competitor in the work world. Instead, the Peace household is a veritable United Nations in which sex, race, and class are not used to create distinctions but to accommodate a diverse and dynamic community. The house itself is organic and grows according to the needs of the people whose only requirement for entry is a longing for family. Eva's magnaminity extends to any race—Pretty Johnnie, who is mostly white, and the three Deweys, who are black, light-skinned and red-haired, and half-Mexican—

and to both sexes. She welcomes men into her home and despite a dis-
astrous marriage, loves them probably "because there were no men in
the house, no men to run it" (p. 41); and to any class—poor once herself, she never uses her relative comforts as a podium from which to
chastise her neighbors. Indeed, she commands respect from people
who figuratively look up to her while they literally look down at her
in her wagon.

Eva's home articulates the way it should be, but not necessarily
the way it can be, since the vicissitudes of the outside world scar
the inhabitants of her home. Plum returns from war a drug addict;
Johnnie is an alcoholic; the Deweys were neglected children. Even
the remarkable Eva cannot sustain the illusion of a private retreat,
and she initiates the inferno that will eventually consume her son,
her daughter, and her sanity. When Sula returns to institutionalize
Eva, she removes the last hope for the survival of a household that
once held such promise.

Though Nel and Sula adopt life-styles as different from each other
as Helene Wright and Eva Peace, those life-styles clash and meld
into one another so that both come to know the other's joy and
misery. Nel enjoys domestic bliss with Jude until Sula, the Ishmael
of Meridian, returns to destroy it; when Sula learns the pleasures
of companionship, Ajax deserts her. Both women are alone at the
end—Nel in life and Sula in death—contemplating the futility of
their search for wholeness in monogamy and domesticity. And while
they share the commonality of misery, they miss a consensus of happiness that surfaces at times in the Peace household, but withered
and died with Sula. In death Sula takes with her Eva's utopia, thus
heightening the reader's sense of loss. Nel, meanwhile, wanders off,
startled by the realization that she loved Sula more than anything
because that love was unconditional and innocent.

In *Song of Solomon*, Morrison once again pits the nuclear family
against the female-constructed household, the difference being that
Pilate's household, a revision of Eva's, is able to produce an heir
in Milkman. By doing this, Morrison tosses the reader a curve ball:
with one hand she valorizes an ideal female-headed household; with
the other she bequeaths that spirit elan to a male. The women who

should be heirs in Morrison's novels—Hagar, Pecola, and Sula—do not possess the strength of the prostitutes, Eva, or Pilate; they succumb to the corrosive societal climate. Morrison's intention is not to suggest that women cannot sustain their own lineage, but that for families to survive, they must include men who—and this is most important—are feminized. Milkman, Pilate's convert, will appear again in a more symbolic, feminine role in the form of Son who now, an outsider in a dead family, is the only hope for the Street family. Thus, in *Song of Solomon*, Morrison succeeds in both venerating the female response to life and allowing men entrance into a world in which they become both members and prophets.

Morrison takes a protracted look at the masculinized Dead family making it a truly formidable enemy of Pilate's way of life and a major obstacle to Milkman's spiritual rebirth. Morrison launches a vitriolic attack on middle-class respectability and denounces it for the loveless, thing-oriented household that it is. Macon Dead is an entrenched capitalist and lone member of the bourgeoisie in his town. He prides himself on his possessions—his rental property, his car, his wife and children. Indeed, his sole motivation in life is accumulation, as if that act alone will protect him from his father's fate in Lincoln's Heaven. But Macon's properties do not possess the natural beauty and lushness of his father's farm; they are urban excrement that others must inhabit to provide him a living and eventually make him wealthy. Macon's crime is not that he makes money, but that he acquires, then hordes it, at the expense of others. His happiness is derived not from the fruits of his own labor but from ownership of things and people, including his family. His wife, once a valued prize, is disenfranchised initially by marriage to Macon and ultimately by the death of her prominent doctor father. Ruth's desire to retain the esteem her father's prestigious position afforded her, and Macon's realization of the extremes to which she will go to effect that, reflect a break in his ownership of her. If she insists that she is her daddy's daughter, she cannot be appropriated by her husband. If Macon cannot own her, he will not love her. Their marriage becomes a battleground for control and a living hell. Ruth, devoid of the opportunity to expend energy in the work world and denied the expression of love, resorts to secretive acts of subversion—nursing Milkman beyond the normal age, thus, retaining control of the heir apparent, and visiting her father's grave as a symbolic act of rebellion and putative sexual titillation.

Macon intensifies his need for power by exploiting members of his community and by strangling the life out of his children. Incapable of thriving in such an environment, Macon and Ruth's children become reified objects in the Dead household. The girls are highly educated but serve no productive function except to make velvet flowers, an ironic mimesis of nature that reflects their estrangement from it. Approaching middle age without husband, lover, or work, Macon's daughters are dead to social, emotional, and intellectual interaction. Their brother promises to follow in his father's footsteps holding the economic reins of a one-horse town because that is the only goal his father has set for him.

This unpleasant state of domestic affairs is relieved by one of the most powerful scenes in the novel—the three women singing in the candlelight voyeuristically viewed by the pillar of the community, Macon Dead. His desire to return to the simplicity and certitude of his sister's home reflects a subconscious desire in all of us to cast off the ideology of getting ahead, which, whether we like it or not, affects our every waking moment. Macon's nostalgia is fleeting and, like most of us, he returns to the proverbial rat race. Pilate's household represents a retreat from the world of accumulation because it is based on aesthetic and emotional rather than material needs. It is a preindustrial way of life, devoid of capitalistic influence and patriarchal restraints so that the women perform only enough work to satisfy their immediate needs. Because Pilate is a bootlegger (again, an immoral occupation, like prostitution, that supplies the demands of the sinful consumer), she controls the means of production and has no interest in generating excessive profits; her relationship with the consumer is natural, that is, based on mutual needs, not exploitative.[59] The women consume "whatever they had a taste for. No meal was ever planned or balanced or served. Nor was there any gathering at the table. . . . They ate what they had or came across or had a craving for. Profits from their wine-selling evaporated like sea water in a hot wind" (p. 29). Pilate, as manufacturer of a pleasurable product and an adversary to squeezing money out of neighbors—though not necessarily of making it—is the aesthetic antithesis of her utilitarian brother who makes people pay dearly for a basic necessity so that he may live in comfort. Money and power belong to Macon, but it is his sister who reaps the bounty of life by making her family the source of her succor.

Milkman is polarized by these conflicting ways of life, and his confusion is symbolic of the polemical nature—the male and female—in all of us. Won, at first, by his father's command of business and dazzled by the quest for gold, Milkman eventually rejects Macon's materialism and embraces Pilate's aestheticism. How this will translate into his family life remains to be seen, but what is certain is that Milkman understands the importance of family and ancestral ties and the relative wasteland of an existence that commodifies every arena of life. Though Pilate dies, she bequeaths the most valuable of her belongings, a responsibility to value family above profit, thereby insuring the continuance of another generation of Deads. Still, her death is a profound declaration of the near impossibility and fragile nature of any life-style that does not conform to the notion of patriarchy and that is naive to the politics of possession.

In her first three novels, Morrison uses death and insanity as a way to bring the reader back to the reality of the corrupting and destructive forces of an oppressive society. Although hope abounds in her novels, it is usually mowed down. In *The Bluest Eye* Morrison offers only brief glimpses of alternatives to the patriarchal/capitalistic system that imprisons men and women, but her optimism and vision grow in *Sula* and nearly wax poetic in *Song of Solomon*. Still, Morrison exhibits an increasing discomfort with her female-constructed households, and just as the prostitutes are peripheral to and incapable of changing Pecola's life, so too are Eva's and Pilate's homes barely more than mirages in a vast desert soon to disappear in the glaring light of reality. The Peace and Pilate households crumble like the House of Usher, not from internal pressures but from external ones. Eva's son is already dead from the war, and Hannah burns to death. Eva, unable to cope with these losses and her grand-daughter's cruel indifference, lapses into dementia. Sula, the last of the Peace line, is consumed by disease. Pilate is murdered, but not before she witnesses her granddaughter die from lack of love. Only in *Song of Solomon* is there any suggestion that real values will be passed on to the next generation.

After her first three novels, Morrison shifts from polarizing femi-nine households and nuclear families, to exposing the decadence of a white family, and finally to historicizing the emotional and psychological obstacles to familial bliss incurred by blacks. Morrison appears increasingly skeptical about the possibility of even isolated coves of happiness and about her own rendition of functional and dysfunctional families, since the forces of history, culture, and tra-dition spread like an insidious disease into the most private recesses of the mind. She expands her vision of the family beyond the con-straints of time, place, and dimension in an endeavor to reconstruct the origins and significance of family.

In *Tar Baby* Morrison no longer focuses exclusively on the black family and community, using them mainly as a referent for how far blacks have strayed from their "ancient properties" (p. 263). By setting her novel in the Caribbean, Morrison is able to incorporate several different cultures, including the island natives, Philadel-phian Negroes, and western imperialists, all of whom are mutually dependent on one another but who are alienated from any sense of community. Therese, Gideon, and Alme Estee; Ondine, Sydney, and Jadine, rely on the beneficence of the white Streets for their liveli-hood as Valerian and Margaret Street rely on them for their service and devotion. This mutual dependency, based on economic need, is only as durable as the whimsical nature of the paymaster Street. The patriarch of L'Arbre de le Croix, Street dictates the lives of his dependents and is alternately a benign monarch and a tyrant, an icon of the imperialist regime that controls the islands and a symbol of the crumbling—rotting—of western civilization and the manifest destiny that was its impetus for the appropriation of other lands. In addition, the highly dysfunctional Street family, since it controls and incorporates all constituents of the island, becomes a synecdoche for a dysfunctional society in which all members willingly participate in or are affected by a system of repression.

As decadent as their candy is sweet, the Streets' affluence poorly masks the odor of decay that emanates from the hothouse, which is a metaphor for their lives. Valerian Street's impotency and uselessness, apparent in his languid and insipid approach to life, are underscored by the fact that his sole contribution to the world is candy. Still, as head of the family and representative of an established family business, he has effectively appropriated land, house, wife, servants, children, and shaped them to fit his particular life-style. He has acquired the best of everything, island property, the Principal Beauty of Main, and "Philadelphia Negroes—the proudest people in the race" (p. 51).

Sydney, Ondine, Jadine, and Margaret all take pride in the qualities that make them valuable to Valerian but because they define themselves almost exclusively in relationship to him, they become appendages rather than autonomous human beings. As members of a family/society that establishes priorities for human value, they become hopelessly invested in the hierarchy that defines their worth. Margaret was still a teenager when she was swept away by a man who was willing to overlook her lower-class background, her age, and her ignorance simply because she looked "like the candy that had his name. His youth lay in her red whiteness, a snowy Valentine Valerian" (pp. 45–46). Ondine, and especially Sydney, justify their servant status by virtue of being personal attendants to such a rich and important man. Jadine is a beautiful and successful model, accomplished in the arts and highly educated—the epitome of ideal white womanhood. Valerian's dependents exist as manifestations of a culture they have not created and are only as real and significant as the values they imitate and aspire to.

Yet to exist only as a reflection is life-destroying, and the tension that electrifies the house is the unspoken frustration, confusion, and anger that accompanies self-effacement. The occupants of the house become engaged in a subtle warfare in which subterfuge, subversion, and emotional blackmail are employed to gain some measure of control. Ondine lords over the kitchen and purposely prepares exactly what her employers do not want. Mealtime is a battleground that Ondine is sure to retreat from, but not until she has inflicted damage. Margaret remarks to Valerian:

> "They tell us what to eat. Who's working for who?"
> "Whom. If you give Ondine menus for the whole week—that is exactly what she will prepare."
> "Really? You've been doing that for thirty years and you can't even get her to fix you a cup of coffee. She makes you drink Postum."
> "That's different."
> "Sure." (p. 19)

Ondine gets away with this behavior because she knows how valuable she is as a competent cook to a man and a woman who would find it very disagreeable to prepare meals for themselves.

Sydney's oppositional stance is evident in his verbal exchange with Valerian, who regards Sydney as both a confidant and sparring partner without openly acknowledging it. Sydney advises him on his health—he should wear huaraches for his bunions and drink Postum to clear up his ulcer—and on his personal affairs—Margaret needs a boat and no, she doesn't drink. Valerian is conspiratorial and gossipy with Sydney because he is otherwise isolated from his constituency. Sydney is well aware that Valerian probes him for information and knows the extent to which he can exploit that power. At one point Valerian begs, "Don't antagonize an old man reduced to Postum" (p. 17). Sydney is Valerian's only link to his fiefdom, and thus, Valerian must depend on Sydney to allay his own paranoia and guilt: "Mrs. Street, Mr. Street, you, Ondine. Everybody. This is the first time in thirty years I've been able to enjoy this house . . . and everybody is conspiring to ruin it for me" (p. 15). Made privy to Valerian's insecurities, Sydney is allowed the momentary status of equal and granted the perpetual knowledge of superiority over his weak and vulnerable boss.

Ondine manipulates Valerian's health and well-being and Sydney informs his reality—in essence, his body and soul. Jadine completes their control over him by guaranteeing his immortality. She functions as the child who makes the world right in the eyes of the doubting, aging, beleaguered adult. Representing the idealization of womanhood as perceived by western culture, Jadine is the mirror that validates the system and ensures its continued success. Her power over Valerian is emotional; if she repudiates him she disavows his entire way of life. Because of this he needs her to soothe the floorburn of his soul and make him palatable in the eyes of human decency. In addition, Jadine is the child placed between the embittered couple and compelled to arbitrate irreconcilable differences.

The final respondent in the Street dynasty is the most angry and consequently the most subversive and destructive. Margaret, while still a child, is torn from a relatively secure and happy life to be thrown into a world in which her beauty, previously a bonus to the gift of life that kept her in the limelight, is rigidified into her sole raison d'être. Reduced to an objet d'art, Margaret is expected to perform as the perfect lady, a role forced upon her by an exacting and impatient husband. Aware that her every move is scrutinized by him, Margaret crumbles under the burden of perfection to such an extent that even mealtime turns into psychological torture. Since Margaret is uninitiated in the rites of fine dining, she views cutlery, cuisine, and china as the enemy:

> She was usually safe with soup, anything soft or liquid that required a
> spoon but she was never sure when the confusion would return: when
> she would scrape her fork tines along the china trying to pick up the
> painted blossoms at its center, or forget to unwrap the Amaretti cookie
> at the side of her plate and pop the whole thing into her mouth. Valerian
> would squint at her, but say nothing, convinced that she was stewed.
> Lobster, corn on the cob—all problematic. It came. It went. And when
> it left sometimes for a year, she couldn't believe how stupid it was. Still
> she was careful at table, watching other people handle their food—just
> to make sure that never again would she pick up the knife instead of the
> celery stalk or pour water from her glass over the prime ribs instead of
> the meat's own juices. (p. 53)

Margaret's reaction to this intimidation is the most extreme of any of Morrison's other characters. The angel in the household falls to satanic depths. Her peevishness, neuroses, and temper tantrums aside, Margaret alone is responsible for the dissolution of her husband's power when it is discovered that in an attempt to punish her husband she has defiled the symbol of his manhood and immortality, his son. Says Ondine, "She didn't stick pins in her baby. She stuck em in his baby. Her baby she loved" (p. 240). When Jadine can't understand, Ondine supplies the answer: "He kept her stupid; kept her idle. That always spells danger" (p. 240). Though Margaret's action leaves Valerian a near-invalid and broken man, Margaret has not won her independence from him: "Now she's the master, not him?" Jadine asks. "Master, patient, baby—it don't matter. He's still the center of everything" (p. 240).

In the Street household, the dependents gain power and control within the system but do not free themselves from it. All are essentially codependents of the addictive system that has minimalized their lives; yet they cannot live without it, for to do so would require total self-reliance, a concept too frightening to consider. Even after the violent confrontation on Christmas Day, the family remains the same, locked together in a lifeless, static existence. What had kept them together before—fear of losing their jobs, of losing a husband, of losing access to the world of fashion—keeps them together now.

Only Son continues to be a human being capable of spiritual, emotional, and intellectual growth. And as a male, he signals a departure from Morrison's earlier conceptions of woman as spiritual healer and separate from society at large. Representing an integration of (culturally produced) gender roles, Son is both passive/aggressive, intuitive/logical, carnal/spiritual. His arrival at the Street household signals a confrontation: Son does not live by money alone and is, therefore, free from the dependency that afflicts the members of L'Arbre de le Croix. But he is welcomed initially only by the person who serves to lose the most—Valerian. Indeed, Son's presence is considered an insult to Ondine and Sydney, a sexual threat to Margaret, and a cultural reminder to Jadine. They wish him gone because he upsets the balance in their lives by reminding them of what they are not or do not have. A living force, he thumps plants back to life, brings love to Jadine, and renews Margaret's and Valerian's hope of regaining their estranged son. Though Valerian feeds and clothes him, Son feels no obligation since he does not depend on Valerian for survival. Son's disgust with Valerian is equally distributed to those who blind the old man to the truth and who are, thus,

implicated in Valerian's crime against humanity. Since Son has no
motive for lying, he argues with Valerian about his decision to dis-
miss his friends Therese and Gideon. This confrontation marks the
turning point in the novel, the moment Valerian is disenfranchised
of his illusion of superiority. "The evening eyes met those of the man
with savannas in his face. The man who respected industry looked
over a gulf at the man who prized fraternity" (p. 176).

Son attacks his reason and challenges the authority of a man used
to civil obedience. Valerian is incredulous. "I am being questioned
by these people, as if, as if I could be called into question" (p. 177).
Son's bravery opens the floodgates to the pent up anger and frustration in the other family members. Ondine, stripped of the seminal
authority of hiring and firing help, lets go of the ace in the hole she
had kept in fear of losing her job. But her motives are not designed to
improve the quality of life, and although the opportunity for a community of honesty, forgiveness, and love hangs momentarily in the
air, it is blown away by the winds of self-interest. What happens after
the dinner explosion is not a restructuring of familial organization
but a shifting of power away from Valerian to other members of the
house. Margaret now is parent to the childlike Valerian, and Ondine
describes herself as "the woman in this house. None other. As God
is my witness there is none other. Not in this house" (p. 180). Nothing has changed; the system remains intact. Son and Jadine leave,
but Jadine's departure is temporary because she cannot divorce herself from the Streets. Son's decision to retrieve her is delayed by a
journey into myth that, like Milkman's leap, leaves the reader with
vague promises of rebirth and in no way resolves the problems that
debilitate the Street family.

Valerian Street, the quintessential capitalist and patriarch, and his
beautiful wife are at once caricatures and icons of a system long
past its prime. Morrison suggests that they, too, are victims of an
ideology they embrace, but her sympathy for them falls short of that
which she generates for Cholly Breedlove, Eva Peace, and Sethe, all
of whom commit violence on their children. For all except her white
Streets, Morrison provides a harrowing context for their acts so that
their motives, if not always justifiable, are at least understandable.
In defense of Morrison's treatment of the Streets, Demetrakopoulos

states that Morrison "depicts the lives of rich people with compassion. Indeed, except for F. Scott Fitzgerald's stories and novels, I can think of no American literary works that can rival her story of how vacuous and empty wealthy white people can be."[60] In particular, she characterizes Morrison's treatment of Margaret as "a full-blown portrait" to which we have to "pay close attention."[61] How Morrison can be called compassionate for depicting shallowness is an interesting twist, as is the statement that the characterization of Margaret is full-blown. Hardly presenting an in-depth analysis, Morrison offers very little to relieve the reader's disgust toward Margaret. The most she can muster is that because Valerian oppressed her with luxury she was incapable of handling the "needfulness" of her son, and she stuck pins in her son because it was "delicious." To make sure the reader doesn't overlook Valerian's part in all this, Morrison reminds us that "no man should live without absorbing the sins of his kind, the foul air of his innocence, even if it did wilt rows of angel trumpets and cause them to fall from their vines" (p. 209). Morrison offers no detailed analysis of how Margaret and Valerian were themselves victims at one time; thus, the generosity that mitigates Cholly's rape of his daughter and Pauline's blindness to it, stands in sharp contrast to her miserly reluctance to humanize the Streets. Morrison therefore misses an opportunity to expose how pervasive a system is that compels even its most successful members to destroy their own.

Morrison's last two novels, *Beloved* and *Jazz*, represent yet another re-visioning of her fictional families, so extreme in their departure from even Morrison's own prototypes, they almost defy inclusion in the category of family. As if debunking her own myth of a viable female-headed household, Morrison presents families in *Beloved* and *Jazz* that are so completely dysfunctional they literally cease to exist. Once the husbands and fathers have disappeared or been destroyed, the wives and mothers cannot sustain the family and become themselves victims of insanity, murder, and suicide. Even the grandmothers—Baby Suggs and True Belle—eventually give up. Sethe's family is dissolved the moment Beloved is exorcised while in *Jazz* there is not one family that is able to remain intact and unscathed by the forces of oppression that beleaguer it. What is left of the black family in *Jazz* and *Beloved* is a ragtag assembly of friends and relatives, usually held together by sympathetic women relatives or a community of women. Yet Morrison is not suggesting the impossibility of the survival of the black family. Apparently for Morrison, apocalypse is the necessary antecedent to renewal, for it is in apocalypse that oppressive institutions are destroyed, that black people are able to disassociate themselves from the influence of the dominant culture and reclaim their own history. Indeed, after the destruction, Morrison makes another dramatic departure: her men do not disappear this time, but return to their women, emotionally as well as physically, to start a family anew. But before they return, it is the women once again, whether as a community chasing out an evil ghost or a woman too tired to do anything else but love, that initiate both the healing and the rebirth.

Lest readers become inebriated with visions of utopia, Morrison provides her usual sobering note: Paul D's return does not promise permanence or continuity, and Joe and Violet can only survive, actually and metaphorically, under the covers in a self-imposed cave. Though Paul D and Joe Trace do eventually effect a reconciliation with their women, Morrison makes it clear how difficult their decisions were to stay with their families, given the disincentives of racially motivated economic and political discrimination. Paul D and Joe Trace notwithstanding, the majority of families in *Beloved* and *Jazz* are absent a father or husband, either by choice or accident. Halle goes insane, while his two sons desert 124 rather than face the reminder of their mother's incomprehensible act. In *Jazz* Hunters Hunter is separated from his son by the taboo against miscegenation and, even though he functions as Joe's father for a short while, he prefers the woods to human company. Dorcas's father was murdered in the East St. Louis riots, and Violet's father deserted his family in search of economic opportunity. That Paul D and Joe rejoin Sethe and Violet is less a romanticized vision of black life, as one reviewer says of the ending of *Jazz*,[62] and more a reminder of all the men in Morrison's world who do not remain and all the women who suffer accordingly.

Beloved is a retreat into the shadow of the American psyche and acts as a historical precedent to and psychological referent for the acts of child abuse and infanticide that are prevalent in Morrison's books. Parents abusing children becomes Morrison's most effective means of revealing the rage of the oppressed. Sethe's slave status involves total loss of freedom and humanity and serves as the Ur of all subsequent forms of oppression endured by Morrison's other characters, and the motivation for their violent reaction to it. Racial oppression twists Cholly's notion of love into rape; war oppression turns Eva's Plum into a drug addict and forces her to euthanize her son; sexual oppression drives Margaret to burn little holes in her baby. Inevitably, the home becomes the battleground in which the oppressed, denied any sort of expression in the external world, turn their rage against each other or on themselves, much like entrapped animals who will chew off a part of their bodies in order to escape.

Sethe's family is a complicated matrix: power and control, familial roles, sexual relations, and reality continually shift. Family becomes a function of time and place rather than a fixed and static construct of father-role, mother-role, and children-roles. In the historical past, Sethe and Halle serve equally as family sustainers, but with the disappearance of Halle, Sethe alone assumes the responsibility, until she is threatened with death. The miraculous appearance of the white girl signals the creation of a new family, and although Sethe and Amy "never expected to see each other again in this world," they "couldn't care less" because "there on a summer night surrounded by bluefern they did something together appropriately and well. A patroller passing would have sniggered to see two throw-away people, two lawless outlaws—a slave and a barefoot whitewoman with unpinned hair—wrapping a ten-minute-old baby in rags they wore. But no patroller came and no preacher. . . . There was nothing to disturb them at their work. So they did it appropriately and well" (pp. 84–85). The new family is outside of the law, the patroller, and outside of order, the preacher, but within the realm of human decency and morality. Alone in nature and free from the artificial constraints of the patriarchy, Amy and Sethe are allowed to form a family based on need and love; consequently, the family is able to sustain itself and its new member. When Sethe names her baby after Amy, she acknowledges her as kin responsible for Denver's birth. Soon after, Amy leaves the natural world and her new family to re-enter the world of law and order, which would punish her for her humanity: "She wouldn't be caught dead in daylight on a busy river with a runaway" (p. 85). Though Amy chooses to return to society, she does not disavow her experience in the field, insisting that the baby remember its parentage.

Sethe once again is solely responsible for her family and at Baby Suggs's place must decide for her children between slavery and death. Her decision to kill her baby saves the family from dissolution, and at that moment she has served the function of protector/provider. However, in the face of universal condemnation, she relinquishes that role to Baby Suggs whose moral and spiritual strength are necessary, in general, to hold the family together and, specifically, to shield Sethe from the corrosive effects of guilt and shame externalized by the ghostly but invisible presence of the dead baby. But Baby Suggs's resolve eventually gives out and she dies of disillusionment and bitterness.

The family then becomes a bizarre variation of Morrison's three-woman household—the two boys having hightailed it from the ghost-infested house—in which Sethe and Denver recognize the spiritual presence as a family member. Morrison revoices her earlier trinities, adjusting Sethe's household to accomodate history, memory, and the collective unconscious, all of which conjoin in the form of Beloved. No idyllic trinity exists this time; Beloved would rather strangle her mother in the clearing than soothe her. In addition, Paul D, unlike Macon Dead, joins the women in an effort to restore stability and emotional security, a virtual impossibility he is soon to find out, since he is impotent to alter the horrific history and memory that Beloved embodies. When Paul D deserts 124, he predates all Morrison's black males in motion who cannot reconcile the status quo given their historical treatment by it.

To Denver, Beloved is a comfort and staves off the family's self-imposed loneliness, and to Sethe she is a hair shirt that serves as a constant, though not intolerable, reminder of her violent act. When Paul D moves in, he disrupts the tenuous emotional balance and the political dynamics of the family by exorcizing the ghost and assuming the head of the household position. The ghost, however, is only temporarily in absentia and returns in full force to snatch away her mother's imminent happiness and challenge the newly arrived man of the house.

From this point on in the novel, the family at 124 Place engages in manipulation, with Beloved gaining control over Paul D sexually, and over Sethe and Denver emotionally. Beloved's powerful position is solidified when Paul D reveals Halle's fate to Sethe. This knowledge threatens the sense of security Sethe has placed in Paul D since he is as potentially susceptible to mental illness as was Halle: "Why now with Paul D instead of the ghost, was she breaking up? getting scared? needing Baby? The worst thing was over, wasn't it? She had already got through, hadn't she? With the ghost in 124 she could bear, do, solve anything. Now a hint of what had happened to Halle and she cuts out like a rabbit looking for its mother" (p. 97).

Having invested half of herself in her husband, and then discovering that he was not strong enough to endure the humiliation that was hers, she cannot afford the same emotional investment in Paul D who could possibly succumb to the same weakness. Sethe retreats from a normal and happy relationship with Paul D into a highly charged and potentially explosive trinity of mother, daughter, and (holy) ghost—"the three women in the middle of the clearing, at the base of the rock where Baby Suggs, 'holy,' had loved. One seated, yielding up her throat to the kind hands of the other two" (p. 97).

But the intentions of Beloved are anything but kindly, and the family, failing to love and nurture each other, no longer operates as a family. Paul D moves away from Sethe emotionally, sexually, and physically while indulging in sexual relations with Beloved. Sethe and Denver devote their energies to Beloved. When Paul D finds out about Sethe, he finally leaves because he does not have the courage to share in the enormous burden of Sethe's guilt and because he realizes how relatively insignificant he has become to her.

With Paul D gone, the family no longer possesses its stabilizing force and is destined for destruction. Sethe relinquishes all responsibility for earning a living and spends her time attending to Beloved. To keep the family from ruin, Denver seeks employment and essentially assumes the head of the household position. Beloved becomes fat and greedy under her mother's devotion and watches with indifference as her mother wastes away. She acts as a daughter intent

upon making her mother pay for her brutal act and lacks the forgiveness and compassion necessary to make the family whole. But
at this point, her presence, no matter how negative, is crucial to
the guilt-ridden Sethe in need of punishment as the precursor to
redemption. Beloved's divisiveness is intentional and complete: the
family becomes a pit of psychological torture rather than a haven of
love. Sethe's collapse is anticipated by the townswomen who must
intervene to save the family from the diabolical and unrelenting Beloved. Their action is an expression of familial love and concern;
the exorcism cleanses the family that was dissolving under the force
of guilt and shame. When Paul D returns at the end, his arrival
promises the start of a family now free to develop naturally.

In *Jazz*, Morrison continues her investigation of the debilitating impact of history on black families. In this novel, however, Morrison
does not focus on slavery, but its legacy to a generation removed in
time but not place from its grasp. The unrelenting and destructive influence of racism and oppression on the black family is manifested in
Jazz by the almost total absence of the black family. Even Morrison's
mothers, previously incomparable in their strength and endurance,
succumb to the social/economic/political forces of history. Joe, Violet, and Dorcas lose their mothers to insanity (Wild woman), suicide
(Rose Dear), and murder (Dorcas's mother). Their deaths are directly attributable to institutionalized racism. Considered little more
than chattel to the dominant culture, wild woman probably endured
unspeakable abuse. Rose Dear, abandoned by a husband denied the
economic opportunity to support his family, jumped to her death in
a well rather than face homelessness and starvation. Dorcas's parents were innocent victims of the East St. Louis riots. With no father
or mother to speak of, to form their identity, to succor them, Joe,
Violet, and Dorcas are left to be raised by kindly friends or relatives, all of whom themselves are disconnected in various ways from
family and community. Henry LeStory, or Hunters Hunter, is most
at home in the woods; by mythologizing Golden Gray, True Belle
unintentionally taught Violet how to despise her own skin color;
and Alice Manred, in order to protect Dorcas from white men who
would desire her and white women who would hate her because she

was desirable, tried to drive Dorcas's sexuality out of her. By totally excising even the semblance of family in this novel, Morrison exposes the extent to which external conditions have conspired against not just the nuclear/patriarchal structure as an option for the black family but any recognizable familial configuration at all.

Nevertheless, Morrison's characters find a way to survive, and in *Jazz* survival is ironically tied to that which has been most assaulted—their humanity, their capacity for love. And in the tradition of Morrison, it is once again the woman—Violet—whose decision to love rather than hate the victim of her husband's passion begins the process of healing in her family. Violet collects what is left of her humanity and turns it into a remarkable display of love. Barely three pages into the novel, after having attempted every form of revenge she could enact on Dorcas and Joe, Violet "decided to love—well, find out about—the eighteen-year-old whose creamy little face she tried to cut open even though nothing would have come out but straw" (p. 5).

The result of Violet's efforts is one of the strangest (second only to *Beloved*) family gatherings in Morrison's canon: a whimpering, middle-aged, two-bit cosmetics salesman; a scrawny, jet-black, unlicensed hairdresser; and the object of their intense passion, the photograph of a pockmarked, high yaller teenage girl. But it is not, ultimately, the oddity of this configuration that captures the reader's attention, but the fact that it exists at all, that Violet and then Joe do learn to forgive and love in spite of everything. As the narrator says, having incorrectly predicted a repeat of violence in the Joe, Violet, and Felice threesome, "I was so sure it would happen. That the past was an abused record with no choice but to repeat itself at the crack and no power on earth could lift the arm that held the needle" (p. 221). The greatest power on earth, Morrison makes clear, is love and it is—and must be—from that motivation, and not socially mandated programs of action that are more often than not inaccessible to blacks, that families originate. The re-visioning of family in *Jazz* is finally apocalyptic; the family rises from the rubble, if not as a phoenix, at least as a vibrant tuft of grass.

In all of her novels Morrison defamiliarizes the notion of family that still dominates the consciousness of the typical reader so innun-

dated by history, religion, the media, advertising, and even political
rhetoric, that she has been forced to see patriarchy as a natural
and desirable form of familial organization, and made to feel isolated or excluded if she does not embrace it, though it is now very
much the exception rather than the rule. Morrison wishes to free her
readers from such psychological handcuffs so that they may enter
into or create a family whose existence is not a reflection or append-
age of a larger economic or social construct. She illustrates time
and again that those families influenced by patriarchy/capitalism
are destined to relate to each other in a highly politicized way because they see themselves as commodities rather than human beings.
What she is further suggesting is that alternative formations—even
those in her own novels—are not often possible because millions
of people still cling to the Dick-Jane-Spot utopia, and because they
cannot completely separate themselves from their social/historical/
economic context.

Her denunciation, while liberating, is also disturbing, for she appears to disavow a way of life that is not always a henchman of
oppression simply because the mother and father happen to reside
in the same place. Morrison is taciturn in regard to her own marriage, but is less so about her own upbringing, a seemingly delicate
balance of economic and emotional security that sustained her into
adulthood and nurtured a genius. Her father did not light out for the
territory but devoted himself to his wife and children; one can only
speculate what might have been lost had he chosen to go it alone.
Morrison's willingness to accept men in motion and her understanding of their sporadic bouts of inconstancy and infidelity in relationship to their families appears to be an ironic dismissal not only of her
own father's lifestyle but of other men's desire—and their success in
being able to stay home, even when external forces make it almost
impossible to do so. In addition, Morrison does not acknowledge a
similar need in women to cast off domesticity; rather, those who wan-
der are often seen as aberrant and self-serving. Sula and Jadine are
unattractive characters because their search for fulfillment—unlike
Pilate's and Eva's—is not used to enrich the community.

What seems to be left of family in Morrison's world is a gathering of women who apparently either have no desire for anything but

the most tangential relationship with men or stay with them out of
default, and men who are flailing about in search of identity. But
this is not to say that these circumstances are what she prefers. A
better interpretation is that she perceives them as the way life is—
because society has been so convincing in its advocacy of family
conformity and so thorough in its ability to keep black people from
that ideal through economic, political, and social means. Morrison's
disaffection is not so much with the traditional nuclear family (even
Morrison's nontraditional families cannot effectively sustain themselves given the forces of societal intrusion) as much as it is with
the patriarchal/capitalistic mindset that perverts the family's—especially the father's—basic function of love, caring, and nurturing.
If Morrison's men leave the responsibility of family-rearing to the
women, they do so because so much of their identity is tied up in
the notion that they provide financial rather than emotional support
for their families. Divested of that seminal authority, they may very
well perceive themselves and be perceived as useless to the family.[63]
And while this instability is destructive to the women who are left
behind, Morrison does not so much place blame as she does stretch
her imagination beyond the limits of the real, redefining, even in
the course of her own novel-writing, the concept of family as not just
men and women under one roof, but a force—regardless of gender,
politics, memory, time, and place—of love and caring, empathy and
compassion that continually strives to ameliorate the difficulty of
being human. Therese, Pilate, Amy, the Maginot Line, Ella, Violet—
these are some of the women in Morrison's fictional worlds whose
households are of the spirit and not the flesh. But Morrison suggests—especially in her later novels—that for the black family not
just to survive but to thrive, men, too, can and must join the family
regardless of whether they reside under one roof or one sky or even
one blanket. Morrison's men are on the run in search of answers
that may eventually bring them back changed; but first, it will take
a journey in an airplane, a leap off a rock, a disappearance into the
jungles of the past, a bout with the supernatural, or the touch of a
cave-dwelling wild woman before Morrison's men come in from the
cold to join the community of women singing in the candlelight.

Finally, and perhaps most importantly, Morrison makes her readership part of both the problem and the solution, regardless of race, gender, or class. While Morrison makes it clear that black women and men must find answers, she also suggests they cannot do it alone. Morrison's most celebratory moments, those instances in which her nontraditional families enjoy happiness, love, and security, are fleeting, nearly illusory. Indeed, the most disconcerting aspect of Morrison's fictional families is that they are so delightful, so invigorating, so spiritually refreshing, but so virtually impossible. Just as we begin to love them, just as they become an important new addition to our psychic and spiritual concept of household, they are destroyed. When Pecola, Hannah, Plum, Eva, Sula, Hagar, Pilate, and Beloved are cast off, die, or go insane, the reader experiences a personal loss and is diminished because these characters have become the reader's family, a part of the reader. How, Morrison seems to ask, can we allow this to happen to ourselves and our own family members? In *Jazz*, the narrator devolves on the reader the power and the obligation to effect change: "Say make me, remake me. You are free to do it and I am free to let you because look, look. Look where your hands are now" (p. 229).

3

Up in the Bottom:

Morrison's Social

Dialectic

Morrison's alienation from traditional family organization and standardized beauty in contemporary society taps into a pervasive anxiety about normality and acceptance. While society proclaims loudly the necessity of adherence to traditional values, it privately allows variance and diversity in the self and family. The majority of Americans may pay lip service to certain standards of beauty and family, but they know the futility of establishing a fixed construct since many of those people may, themselves, at any given time, be unable to meet the social contract. Proclaiming loudly for stability and coherence begins to sound suspiciously like a defense mechanism or denial of the possibility that they, too, could be divested of the status quo and cast into the despised minority, either by choice or chance.

The paranoia inherent in the shrill profession of tradition is symptomatic of the realization that one's status is neither fixed nor static, but subject to the vagaries of fortune. A divorcée, an aging beauty, a business failure, a liberated closet homosexual may all have led the band in the praising of the amorphous American Dream only to have it turn on them profoundly. And while many of these people eventually reintegrate into the inner ring, they cannot return unchanged; their initial shock at being excluded must also act as an awakening to the fragile nature of the human condition and, thus, the absurdity and cruelty of dogma. Those who fall from grace— one might call it a fortunate fall—and even those who have not but secretly fear it, can find succor, if not from the larger majority, at least in the fictionalized world of Toni Morrison in which marginalization is showplaced not as the Achilles heel of the community but its Atlas.

While Morrison's readership may be willing and even eager to embrace Morrison's more liberal definition of self and family, it appears to be less enthusiastic of a similar treatment of the social order. Not so liberating to some of Morrison's readers is her reproach of capitalism and hard work, Christianity and morality, education and performance, and government, law, and order. Morrison's attack, some critics suggest, constitutes a valueless society bordering on anarchy. Cynthia Edelberg wonders what values Morrison would substitute to sustain the black community. She says, "Morrison posits a kind of primitivism as an answer, as something that counters education and work, but this primitivism is rhetorical rather than convincing. . . . Morrison's values are reduced to wishful thinking. To put it another way, she implies that 'ancient properties' are better than education and the work ethic, but dramatically shows us they are not." [1]

In a similar vein of disapproval, Carol Iannone faults Morrison for her refusal "to transcend black and white as categories of good and evil. The icy scorn she levels at the black middle class, especially exemplified in a certain type of black woman who destroys her natural 'funkiness' in the interest of 'thrift, patience, high morals, and good manners,' is itself but a variant of her scorn for the white world, whence such falsely 'good' values supposedly derive." [2]

While Iannone and Edelberg are correct in their assessment of Morrison's disdain for the state of contemporary values, they fail to see that it is not the values Morrison opposes but their misapplication: the work ethic that becomes synonymous with greed, a Christian religion that instills fear and demands conformity, education that breeds mediocrity, a government that serves itself first. Morrison does not disavow values; indeed, her works are replete with the essentiality of home, work, and religion, but as organisms capable of adaptation and evaluation, not entities that stagnate and are eventually subject to decay. If, as Iannone says, Morrison's ideas about middle-class respectability are "somewhat complicated, if not downright contradictory,"[3] then this confusion is a function of the conflict between values as theory and values as praxis.

In practice, values can become institutions, ideology resistant to change. As sociologist Roy Wallis states, while institutions can ensure permanence and stability, they also

> come to possess a life of their own; they impose themselves upon social actors and may constrain their choices. . . . As they become institutionalized, ideas, actions and relationships may lose their excitement, their vitality, their idealism, and come to be valued simply because they are familiar. This may be no bad thing in some cases. . . . But it may sometimes act as a mechanism of control over innovation, repressing the human spirit beneath powerful institutional structures which have long outlived their usefulness.[4]

Morrison resists the institutionalization of once vital elements of society and revivifies them by taking them out of the institution and giving them back to neighborhoods and communities. According to Susan Blake, " 'The community' in Morrison's work is defined by personal rather than political relationships; it is made up of family and neighbors. If one is black, one's community is likely to be black, but blackness does not define it. 'My tendency is to focus on neighborhoods and communities,' she told Robert Stepto. 'And the community, the black community . . . was always there, only we called it the 'neighborhood.' "[5] Her impetus to deinstitutionalize could be characterized as primitive, not in the sense that it is crude or uncivilized, but because it is natural. If it was once considered primitive to live in nature without carefully orchestrated townships and municipalities, Morrison suggests it is now primitive, unnatural, to seal off hermetically in various shades of brick the major components of social interaction.

Her communities are very similar to Victor Turner's *communitas*, "which tends to characterize relationships between those jointly undergoing ritual transition. The bonds of communitas are antistructural in the sense that they are undifferentiated, egalitarian, direct, extant, nonrational, existential . . . It is not shaped by norms, it is not institutionalized, it is not abstract."[6] *Communitas* is the opposite of structure, which Turner defines as "all that holds people apart, defines their difference, and constrains their actions." *Communitas* is "sentiment for humanity," liberating individuals "from conformity to general norms."[7] Morrison's fictional communities do not always effect *communitas*, but even in her failed communities—Lorain, Southside—there is evidence of an antistructural component that challenges social stasis.

What Morrison specifically reacts against is the Protestant work ethic, which, though a noble concept, becomes the catalyst of greed. Her interpretation, hardly shocking or radical, is generally supported by historians and sociologists. The Protestant ethic was promoted by the Calvinists who believed that hard work glorified God. Eventually, with the arrival of the industrial revolution and the emphasis on material production, the work ethic elided seamlessly into the desire for greater production and consumption.[8] Industrialism invaded the social fabric of nineteenth-century life, instilling in American society the importance and magnitude of production. The materialistic rewards of the industrial age dazzled Americans who soon began to translate mechanized economy into a mechanized way of living and thinking. The work ethic became the vanguard on the pulpit, the lectern, and the stump, not exclusively or even primarily as an avenue to inform the meaning of life, but as a way to secure wealth.

Against the materialistic rationalism that still grips America, Morrison does not condone laziness, as Edelberg and Iannone's criticisms imply, but a neoprimitivism, or more specifically, a neocolonialism that combines the values of the African community and preindustrial America. According to Karla Holloway,

What Western civilization defined as *society*, African networks identified as *family*. The *clan* was the basis of economic, religious and political units. Within the clan all of these units functioned. The only significant difference between this African perspective and what has happened in Black America is that the privilege and responsibility of the male within the clan has been replaced with the crushing responsibilities of the female in America. This divergence from our culture is directly linked to the racist/humanist insecurities of Colonial America. What has been retained—the focus on lineage and responsibility for the line—has been kept under the most subversive conditions.[9]

This description of African life provides further context for Morrison's societal structure:

In traditional African communities, which depended to a large degree on the collective solidarity of the people, ritual incorporation or aggregation generally occurred after the initiand had been carefully tutored in the art of communal living. For in a collective society, the community—one that embraced the living and the dead—takes precedence over the individual who exists only as a representative of the whole. The group's survival supersedes that of the individual. Consequently, initiation rites, which often involved circumcision, not only introduced the novice to adult life, but, more important, they educated him, providing instructions in traditions, institutions, and, above all, in the revered ethical values of the group.[10]

The value of community as opposed to the individual is a predominant one in Morrison's novels. While this African value may appear to clash with the American valorization of rugged individuality, recent studies suggest an early America that shared an affinity with the African emphasis on community, solidarity, and education. Michael Merrill has argued that in the late colonial period of America

most rural output was for family or local consumption, that involvement in the market was usually limited, but that a complex network of exchange relations existed within each rural community. Production was geared not to profit but to needs. This in turn generated a rural culture as much concerned with cooperation as with individual advancement and therefore less ripe for entrepreneurial development than the earlier interpretation had suggested. James Heretta, expanding the critique of the significance of the profit motive, has further argued that the single most important feature of rural culture was the strength of family values—the desire to transmit accumulated property and beliefs from one generation to another and the conservation of family interests. Moreover this set of values remained significant far into the 19th century.[11]

As Merrill's and Samuel's descriptions illustrate, in both cultures, community, family, and tradition take precedence over, though they do not expunge, individual ambition and mercantile interests.

Far from offering no value system, Morrison advocates hard work if it benefits the community; education if it trains people to care about family, tradition, and each other; religion if it encourages spiritual as opposed to material growth; and government if it serves the people, not just the most powerful interests. Hers is not a disavowal of getting ahead; it is simply a shift in emphasis from getting ahead at the expense of others to getting ahead for the sake of everyone. According to Joyce Ladner, black culture is nonmaterial and "can be more clearly observed in the emotive responses of Black people than in their artifacts; more poignantly in their spirituals and jazz than in their craftsmanship; more lucidly in the strong bond between mother and child than in the ability to provide that child with all of the material luxuries life can afford." [12] These values are exactly the ones that retain a residual grip on Morrison's fictional communities but that, because of the advent of industrialism and capitalism, have been either subsumed or twisted in a new guise. Morrison's values are painfully apparent; they struggle almost hopelessly, many would argue naively, against a mechanism of greed and self-interest that infests even the sanctity of home and church. Morrison's novels devalorize self-serving individualism and expose it as the anathema to every thread of the social fabric.

Morrison's fictional communities, simultaneous expressions of structure and *communitas*, provide unique insight into the conflicting value systems of America. Entities devoid of direct contact with the white world, they are nevertheless irrefragably tied to it and exhibit both a unique system of beliefs and the values of a society that constitute the frame of their continuing social-historical narrative. While this does not always create an obstacle to growth and fulfillment, it does impose a context from which black Americans may never be free in their struggle for autonomy and recognition. The effects of such a condition include a dialectic tension, an arm wrestling of values, that can breed frustration and resentment, but that often creates a brilliant articulation of divergent social structures. Perhaps only in America does ethnicity announce itself with both anguish and a flourish, enough of each to keep it thriving and writhing in a perpetual dance of survival.

Morrison's social dialectic is evident within black communities torn between conformity and rebellion. Those that have acquiesced to the prevailing ideology are clustered in the industrial Midwest: Lorain, Ohio; Southside, Michigan; Medallion, Ohio; Cincinnati, Ohio; and the City. Those communities that have more successfully retained ethnicity and a measure of independence are located in the South: Shalimar, Virginia; Pilate's Virginian Island colony; Eloe, Florida; and, one might add, the Isle de Chevaliers. Neither set of communities is totally freed from nor obliterated by oppression, and both grapple daily with survival, but the ways in which these communities create a dialectic is in their difference which becomes greater in those towns that are further south, rural, and thus distanced from western values. Morrison's northern communities suffer the greatest hardship and are nearer collapse and ruin because of their proximity to the white world and their susceptibility to its influence.

By setting her northern and southern communities off as antipodes, Morrison makes a connection between geography and ideology: the further south blacks travel, the closer they are likely to come to cultural and spiritual fulfillment, to *communitas*. In this respect, Morrison revoices the cultural immersion ritual that, as Robert Stepto outlines in his study of selected black writers, is prevalent in African-American literature. Stepto explains that both the "ritual ascension and immersion journeys" have been the narrative strategy of a number of African-American texts.[13] Most fascinating, probably because it is most pertinent to this discussion, is Stepto's essay on Du Bois's *Souls of Black Folk*, which Stepto characterizes as a cultural immersion ritual. Du Bois's desire to return south is an attempt to resolve "double-consciousness": "The creation of the illusion that a journey of immersion into the 'deeper recesses' of the

Black Belt conducted by a group of blacks and whites alike will indeed be a moment in and out of time, an occasion of communitas, a 'ritual transition' to a true America." [14]

By choosing the South as the location for effecting this unified consciousness, Du Bois creates what Stepto calls symbolic geography, the notion that "a landscape becomes symbolic in literature when it is a region in time and space offering spatial expressions of social structures and ritual grounds on the one hand, and of *communitas* and genius loci [spirit of place] on the other." [15] Stepto explains that social structures, such as slavery, and ritual grounds, such as slave quarters, the Black Belt, or Harlem "exist in time, while spatial expression of *communitas* and genius loci are, as Turner says of *communitas* alone, 'moments in and out of time.'" [16] Stepto defines *communitas* in distinction to Turner's use of the term, as "not so much a reaction to social structure within a structural topography (that is, ritual ground) as it is an autonomous, fresh space *in* time in that it is anti-structure (or, in the context of this discussion, antislavery and its residuals), and *outside* time in that it is a space and in some sense a vehicle for extra-structural relationships." [17] The impetus toward symbolic geography, Stepto concludes, is "a remarkable expression of how Afro-Americans have persistently constructed real and imagined dominions, responding to spatial expressions of oppressing social structures which are always configurations and manifestations of the color line." [18]

Morrison's works are rife with symbolic geography, but her significant landscapes cannot so easily be restricted to a specific location. Indeed, in four of her novels, *Jazz, Beloved, Sula,* and *The Bluest Eye,* her characters go north; only two novels, *Song of Solomon* and *Tar Baby,* contain immersion rituals. Even though Pilate, Milkman, Therese, and Son, as products of or converts to southern life, come the closest to articulating an anti- or extracurricular structure, it is not accurate to say that Morrison's symbolic geography is only manifested in the South. Rather, in the spirit of symbolic geography of which Stepto speaks, *communitas* often emerges in and out of time in response to or because of the historical and social context in which Morrison's communities are submerged. In the course of her novels, the symbolic nature of the landscape is not fixed—cannot be fixed because blacks were continually denied ownership of property—but is often assigned a significance based on the needs of the fictional characters who themselves alternately travel north and south in a desperate search for *communitas*.

While it would be convenient to analyze Morrison's communities in the order in which she created them, *The Bluest Eye*, *Sula*, *Song of Solomon*, *Tar Baby*, *Beloved*, and *Jazz*, it seems more fruitful to arrange her works in historical order since the novels are generally set in time periods of great importance. Beginning with *Beloved*, Morrison re-creates the historical context for the emergence of the free black community in the South and shows how this development affected the already established communities of their northern counterparts. *Sula* and *Jazz* are set during the great waves of migration. *Jazz* begins seven years after World War I; *Sula* traces a span of about twenty years from 1919 to 1941. Though *Sula* ends in 1965, and offers an interesting coda about integration, the story itself concludes just before World War II, in 1941. *The Bluest Eye* occurs in a single year, 1941, and *Song of Solomon* covers the years from 1931 to the early sixties and the advent of the civil rights movement. Finally, *Tar Baby* takes place in the early eighties, a time of relative black complacency and racial harmony. Certainly Morrison's narratives are never confined to a specific time frame; she mixes past and present as Dwight Gooden does pitches. However, her novels present an almost uninterrupted chronology of social development. In that arrangement can be discovered the major historical influences on the black communities and their social responses to them. This history is testimony to the tremendous struggles of the black community to retain those values that have become buried under rhetoric. The black community as an organism articulates a social dialectic in which traditional values do not mean a return to an earlier social construct, but a reacquaintance with what it means to be human.

In *Beloved* community undergoes a radical redefinition for emancipated blacks. Once dependent for their entire existence on whites, blacks were thrown into social chaos without any material or emotional means to cope. Paul D describes the malaise that followed emancipation:

During, before and after the War he had seen Negroes so stunned, or hungry, or tired or bereft it was a wonder they recalled or said anything. Who, like him, had hidden in caves and fought owls for food; who, like him, slept in trees in the day and walked by night; who, like him, had buried themselves in slop and jumped in wells to avoid regulators, raiders, patrollers, veterans, hill men, posses and merrymakers. Once he met a Negro about fourteen years old who lived by himself in the woods and said he couldn't remember living anywhere else. He saw a witless coloredwoman jailed and hanged for stealing ducks she believed were her own babies. (p. 66)

Paul D's description is that of apocalypse and a return to nature. Emancipated blacks faced a total loss of the civilized society of which they were adjunct. Contending with animals for food, hunted like animals, even, to Paul D's horror, identifying themselves as animals, the freed slaves were completely divested of any social structure. Their return into an asocial existence is an ironic reversal of the condition of Adam and Eve in the garden of Eden, the beginning of existence before memory and history; the man in the woods "couldn't remember living anywhere else." But the freed people, despite their divestiture of the world, were not afforded the innocence of Adam and Eve. They possessed knowledge of a world and then were cast into an Edenic existence. For them, knowledge precedes innocence, an impossibility that turns Eden into Hades.

Their knowledge of the world involves a highly confused and conflicting notion of community. Both prized possessions and despised objects, slaves endured the best and worst of southern life. Paul D's and Sethe's memories of Sweet Home suggest their own transition from innocence to experience, from the bliss of Sweet Home under Garner who regarded his slaves as people to the horror of Schoolteacher whose education destroys their innocent state. Sethe remembers "Sweet Home rolling, rolling, rolling out before her eyes, and although there was not a leaf on that farm that did not make her want to scream, it rolled itself out before her in shameless beauty. It never looked as terrible as it was and it made her wonder if hell was a pretty place too. Fire and brimstone all right, but hidden in lacy groves" (p. 6).

For Paul D, Sweet Home became the battleground for his own manhood. Under Garner, who treats him like a man, Paul D lives outside history and social reality. But Garner's death shatters the illusion: "Nobody counted on Garner dying. Nobody thought he could. How 'bout that? Everything rested on Garner being alive. Without his life each of theirs fell to pieces" (p. 220). With School-teacher's arrival comes a redefinition of Paul's existence and a pain-ful question: "Was [Garner] naming what he saw or creating what he did not?" (p. 220). So thoroughly destructive is Schoolteacher—and one could say Garner for assuming sole responsibility for naming and, thus, for creation—of Paul's identity that Paul D even dis-avows the intentionality of his own acts. He ponders, "Oh, he did manly things, but was that Garner's gift or his own free will? What would he have been anyway—before Sweet Home—without Gar-ner?" (p. 220). Dispossessed of self and family, Paul D wanders for years, a man invisible not only to others but to himself.

Trapped in purgatory between heaven and hell, Sethe, Paul D and, by extension, all emancipated blacks, attempt to create some semblance of order and continuity, however, any effort to establish community is thwarted at every turn by whites: "Eighteen seventy-four and whitefolks were still on the loose. Whole towns wiped clean of Negroes; eighty-seven lynchings in one year in Kentucky; four colored schools burned to the ground; grown men whipped like chil-dren; children whipped like adults; black women raped by the crew; property taken, necks broken" (p. 180).

In spite of suffering every indignity, the black community slowly coalesces or moves north to more favorable climes. Sethe speaks with relish of the twenty-eight days after slavery with Baby Suggs: "Days of healing, ease and real-talk. Days of company: knowing the names of forty, fifty other Negroes, their views, habits; where they had been and what done; of feeling their fun and sorrow along with their own, which made it better. . . . Bit by bit, at 124 and in the Clearing, along with the others, she had claimed herself. Freeing yourself was one thing; claiming ownership of that freed self was another" (p. 95).

But moving north does not dissolve the past or the ever-present threat of white oppression, and the existential freedom that presents itself to Sethe and Paul D in the guise of the traditional ascension

ritual and its promise of a haven, is a lie. Paul D cannot establish manliness when society desires his castration; Sethe can claim
ownership of herself and children but only by executing the very
proof of her existence. When Sethe and Paul D cross paths, they
represent the total alienation and near impossibility of black community: a man who is not sure he is a man and a woman who has
destroyed her greatest biological feat. It is this beginning that shapes
the subsequent social history of the black community.

Because the North does not pan out as symbolic geography in *Beloved*, its characters are forced to create their own ritual ground in
a hostile environment. When Paul D seeks out Sethe, he attempts a
return to community even though he had been "resigned to life without aunts, cousins, children. Even a woman, until Sethe" (p. 221).
His feelings for her give him new meaning and purpose, a sense of
rootedness. He takes Sethe and Denver out of isolation, into society
represented by the carnival: "Paul D made a few acquaintances;
spoke to them about what work he might find. Sethe returned the
smiles she got. Denver was swaying with delight. And on the way
home, although leading them now, the shadows of three people still
held hands" (p. 49). The carnival itself is a subtext of the momentary
desire of the white world to suspend structure and thus becomes a
perfect occasion for *communitas*: it serves to unify the three with
each other and the community. No longer the freaks themselves,
they set aside the acutely painful otherness of their condition and
blend into the diverse and chaotic circus of humanity.

While Paul D's arrival signals a return to normalcy, it also fore-
shadows the inevitable uncovering of Sethe's secret, which lingers
ominously like the shadows leading the happy threesome. Since
Paul D is ignorant of Sethe's act, he cannot fully enact a healing
and reconciliation of community. When the secret is revealed, his
fledgling sense of hope and renewal is quashed.

So inimical is Sethe's murder that it signifies, as the ever-present
past, a concrete barrier to any sense of future with family or community. Even Baby Suggs's iron will and faith in God are annihilated,
not so much by the murder or by the white people "who don't know
when to stop" (p. 104), but by the community's lack of compassion and understanding: "To belong to a community of other free

Negroes—to love and be loved by them, to counsel and be counseled, protect and be protected, feed and be fed—and then to have that community step back and hold itself at a distance—well, it could wear out even a Baby Suggs, holy" (p. 177).

Baby Suggs retreats to the bedroom and the color blue—a regression into an almost preexistent state outside of time and eventually in death. In a similar fashion, Paul D obliterates thinking about Sethe's act by drinking, and Sethe becomes embroiled in a guilt struggle with Beloved. Chaos and collapse threaten the very framework of their existence.

While the history of their lives clouds the future for Sethe and Paul D, Denver is not constrained by the same concerns. Indeed, she is impatient with any discussion of the past unless it deals exclusively with her birth. A past in which she was not included is exclusion and isolation, just as the ghost is "rebuked. Lonely and rebuked" (p. 13) because it is not part of the present. Thus, Denver does not drag her mother's guilt or Paul D's and Baby Suggs's acquiescence into the community when she asks for help. "So it was she who had to step off the edge of the world and die because if she didn't, they all would" (p. 239). Denver "would have to leave the yard; step off the edge of the world, leave the two behind and go ask somebody for help" (p. 243). She turns to Lady Jones, somewhat ostracized herself by her mulatto skin, whose kindness to Denver "inaugurated her life in the world as a woman" (p. 248). Lady Jones immediately sets community in action by contacting the church's committee on hunger. Denver is suddenly the recipient of communal love and kindness. She "paid a second visit to the world outside the porch, although all she said when she returned the basket was 'Thank you.'" Her neighbor's response is a telling "welcome" (p. 249). The simple act of giving allows Denver to reclaim her past and her community, which had been shut out by Baby Suggs, whose own disgust and guilt were intensified by the condemnation of the neighbors.

Denver's move is a healing for the community as well: "Maybe they were sorry for the years of their own disdain. Maybe they were simply nice people who could hold meanness toward each other for just so long and when trouble rode bareback among them, quickly, easily they did what they could to trip him up" (p. 249). The community leader, Ella, takes action because "whatever Sethe had done, Ella didn't like the idea of past errors taking possession of the present. . . . Daily life took as much as she had. The future was sunset; the past something to leave behind. And if it didn't stay behind, well, you might have to stomp it out. Slave life; freed life—every day was a test and a trial. Nothing could be counted on in a world where even when you were a solution you were a problem" (p. 256).

This rationalization and the subsequent exorcism by the women of the town provide the context for the development of the black community and *communitas*. No matter how vile or horrendous the act of an individual member, the community must remain intact. Therefore, the business of getting ahead at another's expense or setting oneself above others is inimical to the survival of the black community. The work ethic, Protestantism, law and order, and education work only if the individual brings something back. Perhaps whites who do not confront the enormity of the struggle with identity and their place in history cannot appreciate that community and social organization for blacks is not a convenience but a dire necessity, economically, historically, and spiritually. According to Andrew Billingsley, "In a stream of historical development reaching back to centuries in Africa—broken partly by the slave system—Negro families have placed heavy emphasis and reliance on interactions with both relative and nonrelative outside the immediate nuclear family. . . . Many a Negro man or woman can point to a member of the community who made the difference in his success or failure in life." [19] The symbolic geography in *Beloved* is most certainly not the North, but the land on which, at any given time and place, blacks immerse themselves in a loving consortium called community.

In *Sula* and *Jazz* Morrison moves forward in time from Reconstruction to the Great Migration just after World War I. While hopes for change in the black condition ran high during Reconstruction, they soon were to dissolve in an ever-increasing racist America. According to David Nielson,

> The last decade of the nineteenth century and the first three decades of this century were, literally, the Negro American's modern "time of troubles." In spite of gains over former conditions in many spheres,

their status in the society as a whole had deteriorated markedly. Black America realized by the 1890s that the hopes and promises of emancipation were empty ones. As a result, Negro America became institutionalized; it became a society within a society, coming into existence and growing to early maturity during this period, while white society played the dual role of parents and midwife.[20]

A major cause of increased racial tension, especially in the North, was the Great Migration. As southern blacks by the thousands migrated to the industrialized North in search of a more secure economic future, black and white communities in the North, which had maintained a relative atmosphere of calm, gave way to increased tension. A Cleveland native, Langston Hughes, described it as a "great dark tide from the South" turning "sheds and garages and store fronts . . . into living quarters. As always, the white neighborhoods resented Negroes moving closer and closer."[21] Black neighborhoods spilled over into white ones across the "de facto 'fall lines' that existed in all communities."[22]

Soon realizing that the dominant society, struggling with its own unique urban problems, would do little to ameliorate conditions of crowding and hardship, blacks turned their energies to the development of their communities, which were imitative of white society but which in turn "allowed more and more blacks to avoid contact with the white world."[23] Forced into isolation from the mainstream, blacks responded with racial pride: "In this sense the rise of black racial consciousness was an entirely rational response to the reordering of the white social community underway at the time."[24] By 1920 the black community had become a distinct entity, even though they "had been molded into a distorted facsimile of white society."[25] Left almost entirely to his own devices, the black American became "inherently nationalistic while at the same time he retained American identity. He was not trying to preserve a cultural heritage in his nationalism; he was building one."[26] In the context of these historical movements, Morrison presents three communities set in the time period between the two World Wars. In *Jazz* Morrison analyzes the psychological lure of the City, which offers blacks a retreat from the capriciousness of white southern rule, but which also effects isolation and loneliness. Bottom, in *Sula*, represents a northern community geographically and socially isolated from the dominant community, while Lorain in *The Bluest Eye* is typical of northern communities reeling under the influx of black southerners. While it would be an exaggeration to characterize these or any other black community real or imagined as white distortions, they nevertheless juggle the values and traditions that have come to identify them as a distinct ethnic culture with those often contradictory values and beliefs that are uniquely American.

In *Jazz* Morrison attempts to reconstruct the complex set of factors that motivated black people to migrate to the city in the first place and those factors that compelled them to stay. Morrison cites economic opportunity and social equality as primary reasons for flight, but while initially "running from want and violence" (p. 33), black people, Morrison shows, sought more than a safe job and a secure environment, amenities even the city could not guarantee. Perhaps most importantly for black people, the city represented indifference. A community of steel and concrete more so than people, the city protects black people from constant scrutiny, from the ever-present, appropriating glare of a racist society that defines and shapes their identity. Thus separated by the enormity of the city from the look, black people can reclaim the freedom of self-definition that is tied to their anonymity: "There, in a city, they are not so much new as themselves: their stronger, riskier selves" (p. 33).

But as is always the case in Morrison's worlds, what is apparent and what is real are never so neatly in sync. Black people may experience a newfound sense of individuation and autonomy in the city, but they relinquish a sense of responsibility to community and the selfless love that communities require to survive: "And in the beginning when they first arrive, and twenty years later when they and the City have grown up, they love that [stronger, riskier] part of themselves so much they forget what loving other people was like— if they ever knew, that is" (p. 33). The inhabitants of city life become so enamored with the city as a monument to self-indulgence that they cease to see people as necessary to their survival. Indeed, people in the city value each other only to the extent that they defer to or facilitate the very agent of their dehumanization. "What they start to love is the way a person is in the City; the way a schoolgirl never pauses at a stoplight but looks up and down the street before stepping off the curb; how men accommodate themselves to tall buildings and wee porches, what a woman looks like moving in a crowd, or how shocking her profile is against the backdrop of the East River" (p. 34). The schoolgirl, the men, the woman in the crowd or by the river are little more to each other than tableau vivants, aesthetically pleasing snapshots that adorn the cherished city of opportunity, of pleasure, and of self-interest.

As a mecca of opportunity the city represents double jeopardy: it allows for personal freedom, which necessitates separation from community and is wrought with all the dangers that freedom of choice implies. The narrator warns early on, "Do what you please in the City, it is there to back and frame you no matter what you do. . . . All you have to do is heed the design—the way it's laid out for you, considerate, mindful of where you want to go and what you might need tomorrow" (pp. 8–9). As long as "you pay attention to the street plans, all laid out, the City can't hurt you" (p. 8). But to be mindful of the dangers inherent in the city—to be aware that it is essentially a trap—is to avoid the allure that drew black people to it in the first place—a license to indulge in any pleasure, sin, or temptation that would allow them to forget the very limited choices available to them in the external world. For black people the city invites hedonism as an act of self-affirmation. As a result, it "pumps desire" but does not promote love: "That kind of fascination, permanent and out of control, seizes children, young girls, men of every description, mothers, brides, and barfly women, and if they have their way and get to the City, they feel more like themselves, more like the people they always believed they were. Nothing can pry them away from that; the City is what they want it to be: thriftless, warm, scary and full of amiable strangers." The city, like "laughing gas" (p. 34), anesthetizes its inhabitants to the pain of being black, but it also renders them incapable of any form of communication and connection.

The degree to which the city is paradoxically both an escape from oppression and an entrapment into private hells is manifested in the lives of Joe and Violet Trace. Their decision to move north reflects the complex impulses behind the great migration. Joe, less willing than

Violet to move north, is initially indifferent to but finally intrigued
by the promise of economic opportunity: "The money to be earned
for doing light work—standing in front of a door, carrying food on a
tray, even cleaning strangers' shoes—got you in a day more money
than any of them had earned in one whole harvest" (p. 107). The
lure of financial security, however, is perhaps less significant than
the vision of the North as a way out of a South that thwarts every
effort to establish a community. Driven out of Vienna, Virginia, "encouraged by guns and hemp" (p. 173), Joe wanders from job to job
relying almost exclusively on the whimsy of white people to make
decisions about his future. Though Joe resists the North for fourteen
years, he "abruptly . . . changed his mind" (p. 106). Joe's impulsive
decision to move, never fully explained, is motivated, perhaps, less
by greed than by a desire to escape the insanity in the woods that
is his mother and the memory of her abandonment and rejection.
Violet, consumed with her own desire to distance herself from the
memories of her absent father and suicidal mother, will not realize
Joe's reason to move north until after the tragedy with Dorcas: "No
one, not even Violet, knew what it was that permitted him to leave
his fields and woods and secret lonely valleys" (p. 107).

But Joe discovers a different kind of haunting loneliness in the city
from that which tormented him in the woods. Because Violet and,
perhaps, Joe are blind to the true motives of their flight—a desire
to escape their own personal tragedies—and because the city diverts
them from self-analysis and contemplation, they eventually become
estranged in separate worlds. Violet's regret at not having children,
a decision she made after having experienced the neediness of her
own childhood, drives her to shut out Joe and create the same wall
of silence that triggers Joe's memories of his mother. Joe laments,
"They said the City makes you lonely, but since I'd been trained by
the best woodsman ever, loneliness was a thing couldn't get near
me. Shoot. Country boy; country man. How did I know what an
eighteen-year-old girl might instigate in a grown man whose wife is
sleeping with a doll? Make me know a loneliness I never could imagine in a forest empty of people for fifteen miles, or on a riverband
with nothing but live bait for company" (p. 129).

Since Joe's decision to remain a faithful husband "is unappreciated," indeed lands him in the loveless position he had thought he escaped, he feels duped for "being faithful [to Violet] in the first place" (p. 120) and consequently absolves himself of any moral or ethical responsibility to his wife or his community. Frustrated by his inability to break the cycle of silence that has been his lifelong onus, Joe succumbs to the temptations of the city, the only arena that provides him a measure of autonomy and self-worth. But the choices Joe is left with are destructive to him, his family, and community and thus are really no choices at all. Joe may be "free to do something wild" but "not free to break loaves or feed the world on a fish. Nor to raise the war dead" (p. 120). When Joe commits adultery with Dorcas he does so because he thinks he is "hungry for the one thing everybody loses—young loving" (p. 120). But his love for Dorcas is really possession—a desperate act of a spiritually defunct man in an indifferent universe. As the narrator predicted, Joe falls victim to the fallacy of his own freedom: "That's the way the City spins you. Makes you do what it wants, go where the laid-out roads say to. All the while letting you think you're free" (p. 120).

What the narrator does not predict so accurately, however, is Violet's response to the tragedy that first jars her out of her own misery and into that of her husband, and then into a state of forgiveness and love. Having grossly miscalculated the omnipotence of the City, the narrator incorrectly assumes that Joe and Violet, like hapless rats in a maze, are doomed to repeat their mistakes. But Violet, in an act perhaps as close to existential freedom as any character will come in Morrison's novels, learns to love Dorcas. Violet alone, without the support of community—and *Jazz* is notable for its very lack of a viable and established community—and against the quicksand consistency of an amoral city, effects *communitas* by pulling herself—and eventually Joe, Alice Manred, Felice, and, by example, all members of her community—out of despair into hope, out of hate into love, and out of spiritual death into life. The narrator must finally admit, "It was loving the City that distracted me and gave me ideas. Made me think I could speak its loud voice and make that sound sound human. I missed the people altogether" (p. 221).

The narrator realizes that *communitas* cannot be suppressed even under the most spiritually arid conditions, for in spite of the illusion of power that a city emanates, its meaning is essentially indeterminate; it is neither good nor evil. Morrison, perhaps like William Carlos Williams's *Paterson* in which the poet suggests the man is the city, finds that the city is neither more nor less than the sum of its people. They are the music that makes the city hum, and it is their music-making, whether with a brass instrument or the ongoing rhythm of their lives, that constitutes the vitality of the city; indeed, it re-visions the very notion of inner city. The narrator, reconstructing the essence of city life as possessing the potential as symbolic geography, characterizes its black inhabitants as the elan vital that pulsates subconsciously in the psyche of all of its inhabitants: "For me they are real. Sharply in focus and clicking. I wonder, do they know they are the sound of snapping fingers under the sycamores lining the streets? When the loud trains pull into their stops and the engines pause, attentive listeners can hear it. Even when they are not there, when whole city blocks downtown and acres of lawned neighborhoods in Sag Harbor cannot see them, the clicking is there" (p. 226). It is the "click of dark and snapping fingers" (p. 227) that provides the rhythm for life in the city. Whether it "lurk[s]" or "hover[s] kindly," whether a benign shadow or "an increase to be beaten back with a stick" (p. 227), the beat of pain and suffering, of joy and redemption, goes on.

In *Sula*, which begins fifty years after emancipation, Morrison shows in her community of Bottom that time progression does not equal social progression. Indeed, toward the end of the novel, just before the outbreak of World War II, Bottom, once a living viable entity, collapses under the weight of economic need and the encroachment of an ever-greedy white world. The novel does not end in 1941, but 1965, historically considered a period of great change and social upheaval. But what historians see as progress, Morrison recognizes only as an exchange of one set of values for another. Black Bottomites, having moved into the white community, relinquish family, community, and tradition for the almighty dollar. Young people had "growed up . . . with the cash-register keys around their necks" (p. 163). The material poverty of Bottom residents becomes the spiritual dearth of integrated blacks. Reflecting the unending nature of black oppression and confusion, Nel's "fine cry" at the end of *Sula* "had no bottom and it had no top, just circles and circles of sorrow" (p. 174).

Nel's cyclical notion of time is dialectically opposed to the linear notion of time. For Nel, and most African-Americans, Morrison would say, time moves in rounds, never beginning or ending, a mind-set in contradistinction to the way most Americans view time, as starting at one point and ending in significant segments only to continue in a straight line into infinity. These conflicting ideas constitute the major difference in how blacks and whites of Medallion perceive themselves and reality. For whites, all aspects of life become linear—there is a bottom and by implication, a top—but for blacks, lineality is an illusion, the straight edge of one time period eventually bending into the circle of the ages. How the two cultures view time dictates their respective sets of values. Lineality drives the dominant society to industry, to become work-centered almost at any price; for blacks, the idea of time as cyclical instills a sense of calm and inevitability. Having no effect on the movement of time, blacks feel no need to fight against it; thus, they can concentrate their efforts in human relationships. This dichotomy, as clearly drawn as it may seem, is necessarily spiced, Morrison tossing in her usual pinch of ambiguity, because both cultures profoundly affect each other. What eventually happens in *Sula* is a mixing and melding of values, a swapping of one structure for another, which creates, in Morrison's eyes, ideological miscegenation of the worst sort.

Morrison's notion of time as cyclical is based on the rhythms of nature: one season ends and another begins; the cycle repeats itself over and over in an almost invariable pattern. According to Barbara Christian, "As the beginning is in the end, the end is in the beginning. Time becomes important only as it marks an event, for the people of the Bottom do not see its reckoning as an autonomous terminology." [27] Bottomites and, as Morrison suggests, all black people, accept nature as being as inevitable as white oppression. There exists little faith in the maxim Things Will Get Better in Time, because time for them is not a ladder but a revolving door. Chronological structure, Christian continues, is always transforming itself, for in fact we do not move forward in a straight line. Rather a particular point in time is but the focus of intertwining circles of other times and events. It is as if we were hearing an old African folktale—mythological in tone—in which context revitalizes an empty terminological system. The then is in the now; the now in the then; and the teller spins ever-intricate webs of connectiveness, until the web is completed or broken.[28]

Such a concept of time is hardly new. Christ's death and resurrection is a metaphor for cyclical time, as is the beauty and mystery of nature and the endurance of the human spirit. In a more recent era, modernist experiments with the notion of time as a psychological construct gave us the profuse and discontinuous thoughts of Bloom and Mrs. Dalloway.

For blacks time does not necessarily ensure resurrection, nor is it the exclusive construction of the psychology of the interior. What is more significant to them is the external time that is the indifferent agent of continued physical, emotional, and psychological suffering. A rather bleak notion for sure, and one that jars with the prevailing optimism of Christianity, but it is one also that strikes a chord deep in the psyche, a pessimistic belief that society never really improves, just repeats itself.

The linear versus cyclical dialectic of time that informs the narrative structure of *Sula* is an attempt by Morrison to, as Michael Awkward says about double-voiced narration in *The Bluest Eye*, "explore *structural* means of merging two almost antithetical 'selves.' "[29] While Awkward contends that "*The Bluest Eye* can present merged Afro-American consciousness only in its strategies of narration,"[30] in *Sula* Morrison resists any type of structural closure that would suggest a resolution of double-consciousness. Though the story proper begins in 1919 and ends in 1965, Morrison subverts the linear/ chronological narration of the novel by reinforcing the concept of cyclical time. Nel's "fine cry" at the end of the novel intensifies rather than mitigates the permanency of irresolution: "It had no bottom and it had no top, just circles and circles of sorrow" (p. 174).

The story unfolds in a linear, chronological fashion from 1919 to 1965. In addition, representing the linear concept of up and down,

Medallion and Bottom constitute the binary opposition, or *actants*, that generate the story. Eventually the two communities become *roles* because they are assigned "social or cultural qualities."[31] The "semantic opposition" of Bottom and Top (Medallion) "leads to situations and actions which are characterized by this same opposition. The basic number of actants in a narrative sequence is two, and the basic actions are disjunction and conjunction: separation and union, struggle and reconciliation."[32]

Although Morrison structures her narrative in an overtly linear fashion, she also subverts those traditional expectations in a number of nonlinear ways. She marks off each chapter by a year, but she inevitably invokes nature and setting for contextualization, thus undermining the apparent chronological progression of the years. Time is marked by natural phenomena that tap into a paradigm of other natural events. For example the year 1937 is irrelevant to the fact that Sula was "accompanied by a plague of robins" (p. 90), since Bottomites do not identify evil omens with a year. Instead they "remembered the time when the sky was black for two hours with clouds and clouds of pigeons, and although they were accustomed to excesses in nature—too much heat, too much cold, too little rain, rain to flooding—they still dreaded the way a relatively trivial phenomenon could become sovereign in their lives and bend their minds to its will" (p. 89). The inevitable return of nature, even in its most malignant form, belies the attempt to improve human nature, itself as incontrovertible and predictable as the arrival of the four seasons.

Another way in which Morrison undercuts the apparent narrative structure is by purposely misnaming the very actants of her narrative, thus violating lineality and invoking circuity—the Bottom is really the top, the residents of each community eventually moving from one to another, not in a straight line but in a circle. In addition she begins the novel with the end of Bottom and ends it with an uneasy social stasis. Thus, while the actants engage in a separation and struggle, there exists a union without any real reconciliation. Social calm exists in appearance only—it only seemed better—while the reality of the situation is just another round in a circle of sorrow.

Morrison provides a subtext to her narrative to emphasize the parallel contending ideologies in Bottom and Medallion. A dominant

structure, highly flawed, imposes itself on Bottom residents and ultimately violates their social fabric. As Norris Clark says, "Her novels
question counterfeit white ideals, social standards that warp the
black family and neighborhood, and moral chaos in black America
as a consequence of and reflective of the disorder in white American
and international conflicts."[33]

The opening paragraphs of the novel establish the setting as a way
of delineating the differences between the two communities. The
Bottom is really the top of a hill; the real bottom contains the rich valley land of Medallion that a white farmer did not want to relinquish
to a former slave. The Bottom begins as "just a nigger joke" (p. 4),
a way for the white farmer to cheat the black man. This transaction
establishes the relationship of the two communities and their respective states of experience and innocence. The white farmer will cheat,
lie, and deceive in order to retain a valued possession; the black man
trusts him to fulfill the promise he has been given. In many ways
the neighborhood becomes the bottom of heaven: "It wasn't a town
anyway, just a neighborhood where on quiet days people in valley
houses could hear singing sometimes, banjos sometimes, and, if a
valley man happened to have business up in those hills—collecting
rent or insurance payments—he might see a dark woman in a flowered dress doing a bit of cakewalk. . . . The black people watching
her would laugh and rub their knees, and it would be easy for the
valley man to hear the laughter and not notice the adult pain" (p. 4).

The Bottom is a community of people, not an aggregation of
houses surrounding a business district. In the Bottom, a *communitas*
of extrastructural relationships, there is music, laughter, and fun;
the valley represents business, commerce, and industry. The valley
people voyeuristically indulge in the simple but profound pleasures
of the hill people—spontaneous laughter, artistic expression (singing, playing the banjo, donning a flowered dress), and freedom of
movement (high stepping). The hill people release the joy of life for
the man bent on the linear track of accumulating money.

The valley man's pleasure in the Bottom is echoed throughout the
valley: "Those heavy trees that sheltered the shacks up in the Bottom
were wonderful to see. And the hunters who went there sometimes
wondered in private if maybe the white farmer was right after all.

Maybe it was the bottom heaven" (p. 6). The desire of the valley people to appropriate a once undesirable place represents an escape from the constructs of their social reality, and a creation of their own myth of ascension. The whites long for a return to community, where people take time out for each other, and a return to the primitive—shacks barely discernible from the trees—where heat, dust, and progress are distant memories.

But the longing of the valley people blinds them to the pain of the Bottomites. Having destroyed the Edenic setting of the valley, the town now looks toward the hills, oblivious to the fact that the land itself does not guarantee happiness, only those who occupy it can do that. While the valley people long for a lost paradise, the Bottom residents, at no leisure to fantasize, must deal exclusively with the struggle to survive and understand "what they themselves were all about, tucked up there in the Bottom" (p. 6). Having had no choice in their setting, and divorced from the mainstream, Bottom people, like their slave ancestors Sethe and Paul D, must create an identity and a purpose that must necessarily include an identification with both a culture that shuns them and a heritage that threatens to escape them. Their separation is a geographical antonym and a misnomer. The confusion inherent in this eschewed condition filters into the lives of all the residents. In the midst of this confusion a community is influenced by the same value system that generated Medallion. The residents long for meaningful and life-sustaining work. The tunnel represents their last hope, "the same hope that kept them picking beans for other farmers; . . . kept them knee-deep in other people's dirt; kept them excited about other people's wars; . . . kept them convinced that some magic 'government' was going to lift them up, out and away from that dirt, those beans, those wars" (p. 160). Hardly disparaging the work ethic, Bottom people crave it as a sign of their existence, even though they are not allowed to directly enjoy the fruits of their labor. They see the tunnel as economic security and freedom from the white valley. When it mocks their aspirations, they attempt to destroy it but end up destroying themselves. The collapse of the tunnel on National Suicide Day constitutes a direct disavowal of the myth of resurrection. Lulled into a false sense of spring on an unusually warm January day, Bottom residents rush headlong on a wave of hope into a metaphoric still-birth: "They found themselves in a chamber of water, deprived of the sun that had brought them there. . . . Pressed up against steel ribs and timber blocks. Young boys strangled when the oxygen left them to join the water" (p. 162).

The death of the tunnel victims initiates the death of a community and its distinctive quality of life. Morrison laments the dissolution of Bottom and its apparent assimilation into the valley: "It was sad, because the Bottom had been a real place. These young ones kept talking about community, but they left the hills to the poor, the old, the stubborn—and the rich white folks. Maybe it hadn't been a community, but it had been a place. Now there weren't any places left, just separate houses with separate televisions and separate telephones and less and less dropping by" (p. 166).

In the valley in 1965 the blacks have moved in, apparently in reconciliation. Nel notes, "Things were so much better in 1965," but immediately qualifies herself, "or so it seemed" (p. 163). The "things" Nel refers to are blacks living and working together with whites. But Nel's qualification indicates that what blacks have traded in is not worth what they lost. Though the young people are "working stores with a measure of responsibility," they no longer "plowed, hoisted, lounged" (p. 163). The youth have exchanged physical labor for commerce, community for property, neighbors for a town. The quality of life has improved in the material sense but diminished in the spiritual.

In *Sula* Bottom and Valley rather than melding into a congeniality, simply switch places. "Just like that, [whites] had changed their minds and instead of keeping the valley floor to themselves, now they wanted a hilltop house with a river view and a ring of elms. The black people, for all their new look, seemed awfully anxious to get to the valley, or leave town, and abandon the hills to whoever was interested" (p. 166). In an endless quest for happiness, fulfillment, and order, like dogs chasing their tails, the whites move geographically and intellectually in a whimsical, cyclical fashion, while the blacks react in a desperate attempt to define themselves in a topsy-turvy, fickle world. Chronological time means very little when history, though certainly in a different guise, repeats itself. The years may change, but the plea, like the headstones in Sula's family plot, remains the same: "PEACE 1895–1921, PEACE 1890–1923, PEACE 1910–1940, PEACE 1892–1959" (p. 171).

In *The Bluest Eye* Lorain represents one of the northern urban communities reeling under the influx of southern migrants. Supposedly promising a better economic environment, Lorain attracts the likes of Cholly and Pauline Breedlove who do not suspect the prejudice and resistance they will face from their northern brethren beleaguered by a mass of largely uneducated poor blacks. The Breedloves give up the relative stability of their lives in exchange for a way of life that is not only foreign but hostile. While Bottom was a spatial configuration of *communitas*, separated as it was from the valley, Lorain is a mix of cultures in which blacks are under constant pressure to conform. As a result Pauline and Cholly are met with ridicule and scorn by northerners who see their ignorant and unsophisticated ways as a threat to the tenuous racial stability: "To the old settlers [northern blacks] especially, these new arrivals seemed to epitomize all that was the worst in the race. The tension produced within the community was striking and evidently consistent across the North."[34] In an attempt to counter the inevitable racist attacks from the white community, blacks attempted immediate and widespread socialization. Says David Nielson, "Certainly as northward migration continued to swell the Negro districts of the urban industrial centers, censure of public conduct became more frequent and immediate. . . . Negro organizations issued broadsides on public manners as the Great Migration came into full flood during World War I."[35] While some of the migrants assimilated easily, "most of the new arrivals ended up merging with the largely undifferentiated mass at the bottom of the black social heap."[36]

Both the old settlers and the new appear in *The Bluest Eye*, the Breedloves representing the bottom of the black social heap at one end and Soaphead Church the remnants of the black elite. Though Cholly initially enters the mainstream through work and male friends, he eventually succumbs to drinking, carousing, and unemployment. Pauline, meanwhile, learns early on that life will be decidedly different from her old Kentucky home: "Everything

changed. It was hard to get to know folks up here, and I missed my
people. I weren't used to so much white folks. The ones I seed before
was something hateful, but they didn't come around too much. . . .
Up north they was everywhere—next door, downstairs, all over the
streets—and colored folks few and far between" (p. 93). This infiltra-
tion of whites into the social fabric of black community introduces
white values that have become cheapened by consumerism and in-
dustrialization. Pauline learns that her worth as a person is tied first
to her appearance:

> Pauline felt uncomfortable with the few black women she met. They
> were amused by her because she did not straighten her hair. When she
> tried to make up her face as they did, it came off rather badly. Their
> goading glances and private snickers at her way of talking . . . and dress-
> ing developed in her a desire for new clothes. . . . Money became the
> focus of all their discussions, hers for clothes, his for drink. The sad
> thing was that Pauline did not really care for clothes and makeup. She
> merely wanted other women to cast favorable glances her way. (p. 94)

Eventually Pauline becomes a respectable member of the community but at the cost of her marriage, since Cholly initially loved her
unsophisticated ways, and her children. Because they were black
and, to her, ugly she had no enthusiasm for bringing them up. Overcome by the new value system, Pauline's own values become diluted
or dissolve altogether. Consequently, the greatest value Pauline can
pass on to her children is fear: "Fear of being clumsy, fear of being
like their father, fear of not being loved by God, fear of madness like
Cholly's mother's" (p. 102).

Pauline's education and assimilation are an ironic echo of the enculturation of Soaphead Church, who represents the dying vestige
of the black elite. A mixed—West Indian and descendent of British
nobility, Soaphead learns from his ancestors "to separate [himself] in
body, mind and spirit from all that suggested Africa; to cultivate the
habits, tastes, preferences that [they] would have approved" (p. 132).
He performs in the best Victorian tradition: "With the confidence
born of a conviction of superiority, they performed well at schools.
They were industrious, orderly, and energetic" (p. 133). But all his
education brings him is a twisted and perverted sense of worth and

value. His high principles and reason translate into a love of things rather than people with whom "the slightest contact . . . produced in him a faint but persistent nausea" (p. 130). His only normal relationship with a woman is destroyed by his melancholy and "academic gloom," and he resorts to fondling little girls because they "smacked of innocence and [were] associated in his mind with cleanliness" (p. 132).

Possessed of a western education, Soaphead acquires an aversion to humanity because it affords him no material comfort. But Soaphead is not oblivious to his warped value system, recognizing the inhuman revulsion that insures his isolation. This self-reflective ability is best revealed to God in a letter, in which Soaphead provides an incisive analysis of his own corrupt being. He admits that the black bourgeoisie adopted the worst white characteristics:

> We were not moral but snobbish, not aristocratic but class-conscious; we believed authority was cruelty to our inferiors, education was being at school. We mistook violence for passion, indolence for leisure, and thought recklessness was freedom. We raised our children and reared our crops; we let infants grow, and property develop. Our manhood was defined by acquisitions. Our womanhood by acquiescence. And the smell of your fruit and the labor of your days we abhorred. (p. 140)

In this letter, Morrison invokes through Soaphead a constant refrain—that the values of western culture are not inherently bad, just errantly and disastrously misapplied. Nobility, authority, education, and passion become means of oppression, while freedom and leisure typify irresponsibility. Material production elides with human growth and development so that human beings are either the possessors or the possessed. The natural world is abhorred because it exists in spite of man's control.

Soaphead and the Breedloves are the extremes, the parameters of a besieged black community. Those in the middle, the MacTeers, survive each day as a small victory, though painfully aware of what they may have sacrificed. Claudia says, "We were not strong, only aggressive; we were not compassionate, we were polite; not good, but well behaved. We courted death in order to call ourselves brave, and hid like thieves from life. We substituted good grammar for intellect; we switched habits to simulate maturity; we rearranged lies and called it truth, seeing in the new pattern of an old idea the Revelation and the Word" (p. 159). All decent human qualities become twisted to the point that even truth is seduced by lies.

The alternative to a life of lies and chaos is perhaps even more frightening, one that Morrison compares to being evicted: "Outdoors was the end of something, an irrevocable, physical fact, defining and complementing our metaphysical condition. Being a minority in both caste and class, we moved about anyway on the hem of life, struggling to consolidate our weaknesses and hang on, or to creep singly up into the major folds of the garment" (p. 18). Values take on secondary importance compared to the primary struggle for survival, to own property as the barrier against homelessness. Absorbed with these daily concerns, people in Lorain have little left over for community and they teeter on the abyss of nonexistence. That despair, repeated in the last line of the novel, is a lament for identity and community: "At least on the edge of my town, among the garbage and the sunflowers of my town, it's much, much, much too late (p. 160).

In *Beloved, Jazz, Sula,* and *The Bluest Eye,* Morrison follows the black community from emancipation and being put outdoors to the slow and haphazard establishment of towns and neighborhoods. By the time period of *Song of Solomon,* the early sixties, land and communities have already become part of black American heritage. "That is why," Barbara Christian says,

> we are first introduced in the novels to the place that the characters inhabit, the land of the community. As in the ancestral African tradition, place is as important as the human actors. For the land is a participant in the maintenance of folk tradition. It is one of the necessary constants through which the folk dramatize the meaning of life, as it is passed on from one generation to the next. Setting then is organic to the characters' view of themselves. And a change in place drastically alters the traditional values that give their life coherence.[37]

This happens repeatedly to Morrison's characters who possess an instinctive affinity for the land but who are always dispossessed of it physically or spiritually by the whites who ultimately own it. For

Sethe and Paul D, Sweet Home is a paradise but only until School-teacher arrives. Cholly and Pauline could not have imagined how their trek north would destroy their sense of self that was nurtured in the southern countryside. Bottom residents become confused about the meaning of their land since whites have misnamed it, as is the case with *Tar Baby*'s Isle de Chevaliers, an island that presents conflicting myths and, thus, confusion as to native history. In *Song of Solomon* Lincoln's Heaven is snatched away and cannot be passed on. The characters in Morrison's world are continually frustrated in their endeavor to establish a tradition and a history that would validate and be evidence of the very existence of the American black.

Perhaps because of these thwarted attempts, many of Morrison's characters adopt the appropriative, rather than custodial, view of land. Claudia observes in *The Bluest Eye*:

> Knowing that there was such a thing as outdoors bred in us a hunger for property, for ownership. The firm possession of a yard, a porch, a grape arbor. Propertied black people spent all their energies, all their love, on their nests. . . . Renting blacks cast furtive glances at these owned yards and porches, and made firmer commitments to buy themselves "some nice little old place." In the meantime, they saved, and scratched, and piled away what they could in the rented hovels, looking forward to the day of property. (p. 18)

This frenzy for ownership manifests itself in its worst forms in *Song of Solomon*, but is countered throughout by the nonappropriative view of life most often represented by the women. In *Song of Solomon* blacks are affected by a double-consciousness of racial values and gender.

While appropriation characterizes the motives of Macon Dead and Guitar Baines, it can be seen earlier in Macon's grandfather, a separatist who attempts to create a private paradise and, hence, a measure of autonomy. Macon's father's philosophy is a mix of the African view of his role as custodian of the land and the American view of ownership and exploitation. The farm, representing an opportunity to an oppressed people, might say, if it could talk to blacks, to "Stop sniveling" and "Take advantage, and if you can't take advantage, take disadvantage" (p. 237). It exhorts them to "grab this land! Take it, hold it, my brothers, make it, my brothers, shake it, squeeze it, turn it, twist it, beat it, kick it, kiss it, whip it, stomp it, dig it, plow it, seed it, reap it, rent it, buy it, sell it, own it, build it, multiply it, and pass it on—can you hear me? Pass it on!" (pp. 237–38). In this passage, the mixing of ideologies represents the confusion inherent in a people torn between two cultures. On the one hand, land is something to be taken forcibly, abused and raped, kicked, beaten, kissed, and plowed—but for the purpose of acquiring more land to enfranchise the black population—"Pass it on!" Thus the means of one culture are used to justify the ends of another. Morrison suggests that this will only lead to ultimate disaster because immediately after this rousing passage she mutes its enthusiasm by reminding the reader of Macon Dead's fate: "They shot the top of his head off and ate his fine Georgia peaches. And even as boys these men began to die and were dying still" (p. 238).

That living death is epitomized by the second Macon Dead who saw in Lincoln's Heaven the necessity for owning land, but not the necessity for community and tradition. He teaches his son not to own land to pass it on but to "own things. And let the things you own own other things. Then you'll own yourself and other people too" (p. 55). Macon Dead, the leader of the community, exploits his neighbors by taking what should be communal land, the most essential element of life. His snatching back land constitutes an egregious break with community. Guitar's Grandmother puts it succinctly: "A nigger in business is a terrible thing to see. A terrible, terrible thing to see" (p. 22). Macon justifies his greed and lack of compassion for delinquent renters by taking note that if he became personally involved with and sympathetic to their plight in particular, and less fortunate blacks in general, "he wouldn't have had any keys at all" (p. 22). To prevent his own disenfranchisement, then, he transfers his values from love of people to love of property. Macon's violation of community is its death, and Southside is a spiritually defunct town.

While Macon Dead embraces the economic mandate of the dominant culture, Guitar Baines's response to the system is to return its most violent manifestation in kind. Like Macon, Guitar recognizes the inevitability of the white world, but rather than work with it, he attempts to subvert it. To justify his killing whites to retain numerical balance of the races, Guitar explains that "the earth is soggy with black people's blood. And before us Indian blood. Nothing can cure them, and if it keeps on there won't be any of us left and there won't be any land for those who are left. So the numbers have to remain static" (p. 159). Guitar recognizes the primacy of the land but his actions, too, constitute a desperate and destructive attempt at ownership that could eventually spill over into the black community. Guitar's philosophy evokes this query from Milkman: "If you do it enough, you can do it to anybody. You know what I mean . . . ? You can off anybody you don't like. You can off me" (p. 162). While Guitar perceives his actions as beneficial to the black community, he is blind to the inevitable consequences of violence. "By Milkman's generation," Susan Blake says, "the concept of political community has become not only irrelevant but perverse, because it violates the concept of personal community, the relationship of kin, friends, neighbors."[38]

Both Macon Dead and Guitar Baines are fighting for the earth, the land, recognizing, even in their twisted ways, that land is the key to their ethnic and personal identity. But in their endeavor to wrest land from the grip of the white world, they eventually resort to the same devices of acquiring ownership, and that technique, no matter for what imagined end, destroys the very sense of identity and community it longs to establish.

This ideology of the land informs and infects all areas of Guitar's and Macon's lives. As Blake suggests, they cannot establish relationships because their values are obscured by the passion for ownership—the very passion that drove whites to murder Macon Dead I and blow up children in a Sunday school. Possessed of value-less vision, they are inept at developing personal and community relationships. Guitar is alone by necessity, Macon lonely by choice. Recognized leaders, they represent isolation and self-interest, an anathema to the very sense of community. Their influence threatens like the Pied Piper to lead the faithful to their own demise.

The exception in *Song of Solomon* to the destructive policies of the two male members of the community is Pilate. In her value system land is not the arena for political or economic empowerment, or an entity that can be owned. For Pilate land simply *is;* it does not belong to anyone. While there may be temporary custodians of the land, the land itself is eternal and thus independent of the generations of people that will lay claim to it. Freed from the obsession of appropriation, Pilate can channel her energies into human relationships and eventually into the community.

While *Song of Solomon* is generally seen as a myth of the male maturation, it also contains the subtext of Pilate's rite de passage and the ritual of cultural immersion. In her history is the process by which she acquires the values that will sustain Milkman and by extension, the black community. Pilate's initiation occurs much earlier than Milkman's. Having been raised in relative isolation in the edenic Lincoln's Heaven, Pilate is abruptly and cruelly cast out as an orphan into the greater reality. Her quest for acceptance, however, turns into rejection, her navel-less belly a semé of exclusion. Thus, in a reversal of the male myth, her initiation does not result in integration into community but isolation from it. She must reach an individual, though parallel, level of maturity: "When she realized what her situation in the world was and would probably always be she threw away every assumption she had learned and began at zero. First, she cut off her hair. . . . Then she tackled the problem of trying to decide how she wanted to live and what was valuable to her" (p. 149). Pilate must first deconstruct herself—symbolized by cutting off her hair—before she can reconstruct truth, which in addition to her two maxims—that she does not fear death and she has "compassion for troubled people" (p. 150)—include traditional values. In her wanderings, Pilate has engaged in the hard work ethic: "Hoeing, fishing, plowing, planting, and helping out at stills" (p. 147). Formal education was not a waste. "I didn't mind it too much," she says, "matter of fact, I liked a lot of it. I loved the geography part. Learning about that made me want to read. And the teacher was tickled at how much I like geography. She let me have the book and I took it home with me to look at" (p. 142). Had it not been for the child-molesting preacher, Pilate would have stayed in school. Instead, she takes her education on the road, learning geography and life through experience.

In addition, and more important than acquiring traditional values, Pilate, isolated from an uncomprehending society, develops compassion, a respect for people's privacy, generosity, and unrestrained laughter. "She gave up . . . all interest in table manners or hygiene, but acquired a deep concern for and about human relationships" (p. 150). That concern leads her back to community, the natural and inevitable completion of her maturation process. Ironically, then, isolation from community inadvertently provides the means for Pilate to develop antistructure.

When Pilate returns to Southside she again endures rejection even though she eventually becomes the answer to Macon Dead's example of a good life. Though she lives at the metaphorical edge of Southside, she becomes its center as evidenced by Macon, at one point the excluded one, longing for inclusion into the home where three women are singing in the candlelight. She represents the antithesis of her brother's way of life, though they essentially share the same values: hard work, education, and family. The difference, however, is again the motive behind those values. Pilate becomes a winemaker because "that still allowed her more freedom hour by hour and day by day than any other work [for] a woman of no means whatsoever" (p. 151). Macon also has an abundance of free time but he uses it to bully people not nurture them, or to acquire more property. Education for Pilate enriches one's humanity; Macon uses it for gain, or points to it as a status symbol. Pilate relies on family to sustain her spiritually and emotionally; Macon views family as a way to continue or enrich his bloodline.

Pilate's otherness is not initially welcomed by Southside residents who see Macon, though begrudgingly, as the natural leader. However, her presence redefines for Southsiders first the meaning of woman and second that of community responsibility. Pilate revivifies black American womanhood because she is so tied to her African heritage, unlike the impure Mrs. Dead who epitomizes the extent of western influence: "They were so different, these two women. One black, the other lemony. One corseted, the other buck naked under her dress. One well read but ill traveled. The other had read only a geography book, but had been from one end of the country to another. One wholly dependent on money for life, the other indifferent to it" (p. 139). Mrs. Dead is light-complected, her African blood polluted by white rapists; she is controlled and frustrated by that

society signified by the corset (body/sexuality) and her unused education (mind) but also addicted to its monetary value system. She,
like the land, has been raped, harnessed, exploited and finally enslaved by the system that oppresses her. Pilate, perhaps like Africa, is
black, unfettered, expansive, and free. If these two women invoke the
metaphor of Mother Earth, then one is a commodity and the other an
aesthetic given. Still, they are both women who share a commonality
that transcends their social-economic differences: "Their similari-
ties were profound. Both were vitally interested in Macon Dead's
son, and both had close and supportive posthumous communication
with their fathers" (p. 139). Their common concerns bridge the syn-
aptic gap of difference that still exists, but which shows promise in
Southside.

That transformation will occur through the character of Milkman,
whose education in value begins with his aunt's arrival. Because
Pilate is indifferent to most of the social mores, she is initially perceived by Milkman and the community as demented: "She was the
one who was ugly, dirty, poor, and drunk. The queer aunt whom
[Milkman's] sixth-grade schoolmates teased him about and whom
he hated because he felt personally responsible for her ugliness, her
poverty, her dirt, and her wine" (p. 37). But Milkman's perspective
changes dramatically as he is drawn to the spiritual force that suffuses her being. "Instead she was making fun of his school, of his
teachers, of him. And while she looked as poor as everyone said she
was, something was missing from her eyes that should have con-
firmed it. Nor was she dirty. . . . And unless he knew absolutely
nothing, this woman was definitely not drunk. Of course she was
anything but pretty, yet he knew he could have watched her all day"
(p. 37). Once Milkman disabuses himself of these artificial considerations—cleanliness and physical beauty—he is able eventually to
comprehend the most valuable lesson of all—loving thy neighbor.

Some critics do not see Pilate in a heroic mode, criticizing Morrison for reproducing the myth of the male hero and relegating the role
of woman, in this case Pilate, to that of the helper who never fully
shares in the knowledge and epiphany of the male hero. According
to Cynthia Davis, Pilate "lacks [Milkman's] recognition of meaning. By contrast to his final state, she seems intuitive, personal, and

rather passive." This bothers Davis because she feels it reinforces male/female stereotypes, the universal myth as a male story, and "the difficulty of the heroic mode for a woman." Davis concludes by challenging Morrison to create a uniquely female hero.[39] Pilate may certainly appear passive at the end (a bullet in her head no doubt having something to do with that condition) but her life has been marked by action—traveling, learning, working, fighting. Indeed her last words are testimony to her willfulness—the verb "love" being the most active word in the English language.

But to defend Pilate against typically female traits is to fall into the old trap of valorizing traditionally masculine ones. As Virginia Woolf says, "The values of women differ very often from the values . . . [of men]; naturally this is so. Yet it is the masculine values that prevail. . . . And these values are inevitably transferred from life to fiction. This is an important book, the critic assumes, because it deals with war. This is an insignificant book because it deals with the feelings of women in a drawing room." [40] Davis demands, on the one hand, a unique female hero, but ignores on the other the very feminine qualities that create one.

In addition Morrison does not neatly divide male and female characteristics. For the first thirty years of his life, Milkman is the epitome of passivity, doing little but drinking, womanizing, and collecting rents. By contrast, his aunt has spent the majority of her life making a living in the most dire circumstances. When she returns to Southside, she is approaching old age; thus, her relative lack of energy at the end of the novel is more likely a function of age than gender. More the wise elder than the simpering female, Pilate is content to pass on her knowledge to the younger Milkman. While it is true that Pilate finally needs Milkman to see the whole truth, the reverse is also true: Milkman cannot experience transcendence without Pilate. Her final words crystallize for him the essence of meaning. Both Milkman and Pilate, then, play the role of helper and hero. Pilate, who has had to act like a man to survive, helps feminize Milkman. As Craig Werner suggests about myth in *Tar Baby*, they need a double-consciousness, not so much of race as gender, in order for any transformation to take place.[41]

Milkman's change, however, cannot be effected solely by Pilate;

thus, he embarks on a traditionally male mythic journey that Morrison implies is a bull-in-a-china-shop arrival at the obvious. Pilate possesses intuitively the knowledge that Milkman will partially arrive at conceptually. His education takes him south through Danville and then Shalimar. These two communities retain a history and permanence that stun Milkman out of his self-absorption. Danville, though a community crippled by white oppression, possesses a past. That history is transmitted to Milkman by the elders. Milkman finds kinship: "It was a good feeling to come into a strange town and find a stranger who knew your people. . . . he hadn't known what it meant: links" (p. 231). He also learns the meaning of valuable work: "The more he heard about the only farm in the county that grew peaches, real peaches . . . the more he missed something in his life. They talked about digging a well, fashioning traps, felling trees, warming orchards . . . breaking young horses, training dogs" (p. 236). Finally, he is passed on the tradition that is his by birthright, the nearly larger-than-life men who were his father and grandfather.

But the tradition has been interrupted by the absence of the second Macon Dead and the brutal slaying of the first. The elders of Danville, whittled down by years of injustices and cruelty, look to Milkman for some affirmation of their existence which had been so tied to the success of Macon Dead: "The good times, the hard times, things that changed, things that stayed the same—and head and shoulders above all of it was the tall, magnificent Macon Dead, whose death . . . was the beginning of their own dying even though they were young boys at the time" (p. 237). They are buoyed by Macon Dead's material successes, feeling some vindication. But their joy is only a reflection of how dependent they are upon the dominant culture for validation. Macon Dead's conquests are also a form of capitulation, unlike his father's farm, a utopian sore thumb to the white community. The black community of Danville limps along clinging to tradition, but without the vitality to generate any. This inertia motivates Milkman, but to the wrong action. Their enthusiasm for his father's material wealth ignites in Milkman a need to be as valued as Macon Sr., which he sees as attainable through gold: "He wanted to get up right then and there and go get it. Run to where it was and snatch every grain of it from under the noses of the Butlers, who were dumb enough to believe that if they killed one man his whole line died. He glittered in the light of their adoration and grew fierce with pride" (p. 238). At this moment, Milkman's maturation and education are arrested. He has learned all he can from Danville, itself only a satellite of Shalimar, the community furthest removed geographically and ideologically from white society, which provides the cathartic moment for Milkman's transformation from disconnection to connection.

In Shalimar is a social vision and dialectic that can only be described as neoprimitive, spiritual, and highly feminine and perhaps the closest Morrison comes to symbolic geography: a ritual ground in and out of time that is "a space and in some sense a vehicle for extrastructural relationships."[42] The myth of flying that distinguishes Shalimar served as the antistructure to slavery, but for Milkman, it becomes the vehicle for escape from the distorted values that have corrupted his own home and community.

When Milkman arrives in Shalimar, he is struck by its atypicality—no commerce, no transportation, no government. It even defies the myopic eye of the map. For all intents and purposes, Shalimar does not exist in civilization. Milkman's first lesson in Shalimar is offered not by the male elders, but by the women, who, like Pilate, and most unlike the men of the Dead line, have no need for material possession: "The women's hands were empty. No pocketbook, no change purse, no wallet, no keys, no small paper bag, no comb, no handkerchief" (p. 262). Milkman immediately recognized Pilate as their kin. "That's the way Pilate must have looked as a girl, looked even now, but out of place in the big northern city she had come to" (p. 266).

The women in the community are indifferent to Milkman, unlike their male counterparts who apparently are not as content with their lot as the women. The men react violently to the well-dressed Milkman. "His manner, his clothes were reminders that they had no crops of their own and no land to speak of either. Just vegetable gardens, which the women took care of, and chickens and pigs that the children took care of. He was telling them that they weren't men, that they relied on women and children for their food" (p. 269).

Milkman's presence in the community represents the intrusion of western influence, but interestingly enough, the men do not react against what he stands for but what he has that they do not. Even in Shalimar, in the male population, possession is a link to the very values of a culture that Morrison rejects. And though Shalimar is united by the religious myth of the flight of Shalimar, it is not that myth alone that Morrison suggests will revivify the black community. The spiritual force that sends Milkman airborne to face yet another confrontation with a male brother over material possession, is the vision that emanates from a woman. Pilate needs Milkman to uncover a truth for her, but not *the* truth, the one that is of the utmost concern to her: "I wish I'd a knowed more people. I would of loved 'em all. If I'd a knowed more, I would a loved more" (p. 340).

Some critics argue that Milkman's discovery is not liberation. According to James Coleman, "While folk myth and primeval response keep Shalimar alive and active in a way that Danville is not, there is no indication that the people can use the myth, which they largely think of as superstition, to reach beyond their provinciality or to progress and make their lives better. There is no indication that Shalimar can move beyond the 'Neanderthal' level where Milkman finds it."[43] Coleman feels that Milkman's act is isolated, unrealistic, and futile. More pertinent and useful to the black community is Guitar's philosophy in which the "creative, imaginative, and practical Black survival responses to oppression inevitably merge into strange and destructive behavior that is a consistent, unbreakable cycle in the Black community."[44] Milkman's flight, on the other hand, while it may be liberating for him, is useless to the community because "he is now outside the community and his act is incomprehensible to them."[45] Coleman contends that Milkman's act is individual and thus the "situation for the black community is just as dismal as it was before Milkman left Michigan."[46] The novel would have been more effective in Coleman's eyes had Morrison focused on the black community as a whole rather than the transcendence of one character.

Coleman's characterization of Morrison's town as Neanderthal and provincial suggests a valorization of civilization, culture, and sophistication that is exactly Morrison's onus. In addition, Coleman's penchant for tragedy is a further validation of western ideas of good literature—it must be tragic to attain what Matthew Arnold calls high seriousness, otherwise it does not ring true to reality. Morrison offers possibilities, avenues of change, escape, and hope that speak to the inviolate self. Indeed it is self, the individual, who must first undergo realization, who must originate; otherwise, change becomes the possession of fate and accident rather than intentionality. What Milkman brings back to the community is the very essence of its meaning. As Susan Blake says, "Community through community"[47] is the key, and "community . . . is closely related to individuality, for it depends on individual relationships, which in turn both produce and measure decency in individuals."[48]

The social dialectic in *Tar Baby* is multifaceted and highly complex. Consisting of inter- and intraracial conflict, class and gender conflict, the Isle de Chevaliers is a microcosm of modern society. At the heart of these conflicts is the real and imagined ownership of the island, which involves both a physical and spiritual preoccupation with the land. Both cultures lay claim to a symbolic geography: the white imperialists justify occupation by their commercial interests and the belief that a hundred French cavaliers haunt the island; the natives lay claim to the island by virtue of their presence and the myth of the shipwrecked blind slaves.

The respective myths of the white and black inhabitants determine their relationship to the island. For the whites, the French horsemen with their steel sabers poised represent aggressive and brutal action, a necessary evil for development. As a result of their ideology, the Isle de Chevaliers, once a subtropical paradise, is now "the end of the world," an expression suggesting apocalypse and revelations, but also the last victim of exploitation. The French have so defiled the island that even the river, the source of life, has become a "witch's tit . . . a shriveled fogbound oval seeping with a thick black substance that even mosquitoes could not live near" (p. 8). The natives identify with the blind slaves who came to the island totally divested of every material possession and unexpectedly are given their freedom. Blinded, they must be dependent on the land to sustain them since they lack the vision to manipulate or transform it:

> Somewhere in the back of Son's mind one hundred black men on one
> hundred unshod horses rode blind and naked through the hills and had

done so for hundreds of years. They knew the rain forest when it was
a rain forest, they knew where the river began, where the roots twisted
above the ground; they knew all there was to know about the island and
had not even seen it. They had floated in strange waters blind, but they
were still there racing each other for sport in the hills behind this white
man's house. (p. 177)

With that relationship established, they feel a connectedness with
the land that trivializes the apparent white ownership. When Therese
convinces Gideon to return to the island, he feels tricked into be-
lieving that she owned land. But by property "she must have meant
herself because when he got there that's all there was left: no land,
no hills of coffee bush" (p. 92). Gideon soon realizes that Therese's
idea—once again a feminine perspective—is to take care of property, acting not as an owner but a custodian because land, in her
opinion, can never be owned. Gideon soon adopts her right reason,
recognizing that whites had no concept of how to work the land "and
were dependent on the market" while "the poor . . . ate splendidly
from their garden, from the sea and from the avocado trees that grew
by the side of the road" (p. 93).

This difference in the mythic beliefs and land ownership informs
the relationships of all the characters in the novel to each other and
the communities in which they live. According to Craig Werner:

Focusing on the novel's four male-female pairs, who present a con-
tinuum spanning the Afro- and Euro-American worlds, Morrison investigates a variety of ways of understanding myth. At one extreme, Therese
and Gideon are content inhabiting the mythic blackness of the islands;
at the other Valerian and Margaret occupy positions in a later-day version of the plantation myth. Poised uneasily between these extremes,
Sydney and Ondine attempt to maintain their economic security in
Valerian's household while preserving the core Afro-American values of
family loyalty and personal dignity. Morrison's primary focus, however,
is on Son and Jadine, the only characters she presents explicitly in terms
of the tar baby story. Whatever their specific history, whatever racial
myths they accept, Morrison's characters consistently seek to evade the
painful aspects of their experience and retreat to some version of an
encompassing myth of "safety."[49]

For Valerian, his safety net is a self-enclosed community in which he is master and ruler exploiting both land and people in the tradition of western imperialism: "They could defecate over a whole people and come there to live and defecate some more by tearing up the land and that is why they loved property so, because they had killed it soiled it defecated on it and they love more than anything the places where they shit" (pp. 174–75). He imposes on his community the efficacy of education, hard work, industry, order, and beauty but, as Morrison suggests, the standards he sets for them are not necessarily the ones he sets for himself. He perceives land and people as the playthings of his mythic fantasy, and himself as omnipotent ruler.

Most telling is his relationship to work. Valerian is an advocate of the hard work ethic, as long as it is not contingent upon him to do it. His brief brush with work apparently was sufficient to reinforce his convictions and even retain a residual nostalgia for it. He remembers a poignant moment at his father's death when a black washerwoman helped him deal with the grief by scrubbing a pillow case on a washboard until his knuckles were red. As a consequence of that, he finds pleasure watching, if not engaging in, that same work. He builds a separate washhouse, "looking at it through his greenhouse window knowing there was a woman in there doing something difficult but useful in peace. A soothing thought to concentrate on while his own house was prickly with tension and unanswered questions" (p. 122). Valerian, the quintessential utilitarian and capitalist, enjoys the work ethic voyeuristically.

As with the work ethic, Valerian invests in values so that he can enjoy them without practicing them. He's an educated man but now reads only mail, "having given up books because the language in them had changed so much—stained with rivulets of disorder and meaninglessness" (p. 11). He appreciates beauty, but in isolation and under artificial circumstances; thus, he "loved the greenhouse and the island, but not his neighbors" (p. 11). His wife no longer holds the allure for him she once had; her aging beauty is an indication of imperfection rather than endearment. In all respects, Valerian practices the letter of the law but not its spirit, leaving that to his perceived inferiors. In spite of his humanity he assumes godhead, and the intoxicating effect of divination eventually distorts his judgment and destroys his community.

Sydney and Ondine, appendages to Valerian's system, have no connection to the land and only a mixed bag of values, finding identity as ancillary background to Valerian. Their myth resides in their pride as Philadelphia Negroes, blacks who have ingratiated themselves to white society and who are then suitable to serve him. They are the plantation house servants who view with disdain both the master they serve and the black and uneducated field hands, Therese and Gideon. Their near-slave status precludes community because they are neither completely of one world or the other. They arrogantly shut out those of similar ethnic background, thus perpetuating and reinforcing the system that exploits them. Yet in an effort to retain a semblance of their African-American roots, they attempt to instill in Jadine the value of family commitment. Lacking the capability of perceiving themselves in the scheme of things, they sever the tie to their own people and history and almost lose their future, Jadine.

Jadine adopts the world as her community, having been jettisoned off the island blind much in the same way the black slaves were cast on it. But her myth entails a wide open vision of the world as a candy store and she, the beautiful woman, with an unending supply of pennies. Jadine takes very little of her African roots with her into adulthood and is very much a by-product of the Street system. She is successful, beautiful, and educated, but lacks any sense of family and community. Consequently, she possesses almost a sociopathic disinterest in the welfare of her aunt, uncle, Gideon, Therese, and the youths in the ghettos of New York City. Jadine turns a deaf ear to Ondine's explanation that a "daughter is a woman that cares about where she came from and takes care of them that took care of her" (p. 242), perceiving Ondine's lesson as merely a burden on her life-style, an understandable interpretation considering the self-absorption of her patron. For Jadine, like Valerian, the world remains hers for the taking with no strings attached. Her philosophy appears liberating, but it soon becomes a prison of futility and loneliness. So completely westernized is Jadine that she understands only that individualism is the prime consideration. Says Stephanie Demetrokopoulos:

The mobility of American culture is symbolic of how individuals are early and often cut off from their pasts. Self-reliance, autonomy, separation from family as the hallmark of maturation, children weaned like cats from the nest with the explicit message that no more needs will be met, adult children living far away from ailing and aging parents—these patterns of American individualism are all so strong in my life that they are as if written in concrete.[50]

Jadine remains a lost soul searching the world for happiness and fulfillment, not recognizing that the most obvious component of a meaningful life is human commitment.

Son represents an entirely different notion of community than does Jadine. His myth of utopia is firmly embedded in Eloe, a Floridian version of Shalimar outside of time, politics, and progress. Eloe, like Shalimar, cannot be reached by public transportation. Houses are spread out and not "all crunched up together" (p. 211). Eloe represents land and community, something Son sees as crucial to human identity. He says to Jadine, "You're not *from* anywhere" (p. 229), as by implication he is firmly grounded in time and place. That sense of history and permanence is symbolized by Eloe women whose breasts represent family continuity and tradition.

As picturesque as Eloe is, it is not the ultimate answer to community, in spite of Son's efforts to romanticize it. In this respect, Morrison refigures the cultural immersion ritual that transformed Milkman. The trip south to Eloe offers no space for ritual transition. Eloe, according to Jadine, "was rotten and more boring than ever. A burnt-out place. There was no life there. Maybe a past but definitely no future and finally there was no interest. All that Southern small-town country romanticism was a lie, a joke, kept secret by people who could not function elsewhere" (p. 223). While this interpretation is somewhat jaundiced, it reveals Son's own reservations about the continued vitality of Eloe. Eloe appears to lack direction and purpose, being content to exist on the periphery of the dominant culture, even fading into anonymity and nonexistence. Son senses this on the island, watching Therese and Gideon at work. "You would have thought," Son says, "that something was leaving him and all he could see was its back" (p. 120).

That "something" Therese will call his "ancient properties," which have disappeared altogether in New York City and remain only figurally in Eloe. What those properties are is key to the island natives' concept of community. For them, land is primary but not in the same way it is for western imperialists. One must work with the land, not against it; that cooperation and dependency are traced back to the mythic blind slaves who could not even see the land and, thus, had to rely on it exclusively. The natives are convinced that they will remain through a string of occupations, since their values represent harmonic convergence rather than forced possession. This sense of the relationship between the land and people becomes the metaphor for community, the antistructure in contradistinction to the Street occupation.

This is the basic property that Therese wishes to impart to Son. Though partially blind herself, she possesses a vision and an understanding that have been lost on the other characters in the novel. Craig Werner states that Therese's understanding is severely limited because she refuses to recognize the white world and without this operating double-consciousness she is incapable of effecting transformation for Son or the black community. Her "myths of disengagement," he says, "however necessary to the historical development of the Afro-American community, are no longer adequate."[51] Still, Therese is more vital in relationship to the other characters because she retains origin, which she prepares to impart to Son. Therese takes him to the island in an attempt at deconstruction. Emerging from the sea in the dead of night, crawling on all fours, Son undergoes an infantilization process that will enable him to relive his ancient properties—land, family, community, and tradition—not as memories of distant hometown places, but as the modus operandi of his life.

How Son will proceed is not answered; thus, there is no point beyond that of recognition for the black community to proceed. As Craig Werner says, "In the context of Afro-American experience, almost all myths must be apprehended with a full operating double consciousness to be comprehensible. Very few characters, however, have anything approaching an adequate understanding of both Euro- and Afro-American mythic processes."[52] If there is finally no total vision in this novel, historically the most recent, perhaps it is a commentary on the current state of affairs in which community has become an anachronism, an old-fashioned impediment to the hedonistic impulses of the me generation.

From *Beloved* to *Tar Baby* Morrison historicizes the black community, its traditions and evolving value systems, following them north and south in a cyclical search for symbolic geography and its attendant *communitas*. By doing this, she defamiliarizes notions of family and community and revivifies the meaning of community— either placing it in contradistinctive jeopardy of the dominant class or having it unravel in the face of artificial and hollow values. Morrison implies that community is a state of mind, a prelapsarian rediscovery of what it means to be American and African and human. Her women remind us. Pilate says we must love each other; Ondine invokes caring and commitment; Therese retains the ancient properties of mutuality and sharing; Violet rediscovers the divine state of unconditional and all-encompassing love. Collectively they imply a biblical, religious orientation that edifies the primacy of family and community and a spiritual oneness with past, present, and future. Morrison finally suggests that community is not held together by mortar and mercantility or even by land, but by love, exemplifying this by taking the reader through time and history and the timeless cycle of abuse that human beings endure, but also through the timeless ability of individuals, usually women, to create working myths of value and meaning in a world pathetically devoid of both. If her vision offers no practical means to social progress, let it be more than enough that by her passionate commitment to fictionalizing the obstacles to *communitas*, she creates the conditions for its very existence.

The Metaphysical

Argument for

the Supernatural

But they's a

lot of strange

things you don't

know nothin'

about, boy.

—*Song of Solomon*

The previous chapters have emphasized the highly negative impact of double-consciousness on the black community as it is manifested in Morrison's works. This chapter will reveal how Morrison finally, through fantasy, negotiates the divisiveness of double-consciousness by tapping into the animus mundi that unifies all human beings. By using fantasy in her literature, Morrison is able to some extent to mitigate the problem of double-consciousness and articulate a spiritual response to life in which human beings are treated to possibilities for growth and development denied in their real lives.

The double-consciousness or multiconsciousness that compels Morrison to use fantasy is a result of transenculturation, or as Henry Louis Gates Jr. says of the black vernacular tradition and Standard English, her "symbiotic relationship between the black and white." [1] Her affinity for fantastic forms—myth, folk tales, fairy tales, and biblical stories—is derived not only from Africa and black America, but from Euro-America, Europe, and Greece.[2] According to De Weever, "The appearance of European fairy tales in the work of a Black American writer should not be surprising for, as Joseph Campbell has shown, the essential situations, ideas and messages of the greatest tales appear in Asian, African and American Indian tales as well."[3] Morrison draws from, manipulates, and reinvents a superfluidity of fantastic forms, the result of which is a profusion of personas, beliefs, and values that defy categorization and compound signification. At this juncture in her writing, Morrison presents an ontological construct, or genesis, that illustrates the potential for psychic connectedness.[4]

Morrison's generosity in assimilating and transcribing multicultural forms could be evidence of her belonging nowhere and everywhere, for lapsing into contradiction, profound ambivalence, and even incoherence. The implication of this critical angst or hairpulling need to locate Morrison in the paradigmatic scheme of things is perhaps the impossibility of doing so. In her discussion of *Tar Baby*, Lauren Lepow says, "In the convergence of these retold stories, Morrison defines a world where our customary definitions do not stick, where human potential is enhanced precisely to the degree that dualism is transcended."[5] Lepow is referring specifically to Christianity with its dichotomy of good and evil, body and soul, flesh and the spirit. While this affiliation requires voluntary participation, double-consciousness is a culturally imposed mind-set in which race, to invoke Gates again, "has become a trope of ultimate, irreducible difference."[6] Blacks cannot withdraw from it, but they can, as Morrison suggests with her use of fantasy, accommodate, perhaps even manipulate, it. According to Lepow, "Toni Morrison's fiction embodies a powerful critique of dualistic thinking. Dualism—any system of thought that polarizes what we perceive—is a narrowing world view, for it inevitably cuts the individual off from the 'other,' the not-I or the not-good or the not-ordered."[7] Morrison takes on a number of dualisms: materialism and spiritualism, white and black, past and present, good and evil. Though she does not necessarily resolve those dualisms, she does succeed in expanding the limits of human consciousness beyond the either-or mentality that sets people against each other in mutually destructive ways.

While the appearance of the fantastic in Morrison's work is hardly novel, fantasy as a genre has only recently undergone a renaissance of sorts.[8] Kathryn Hume in *Fantasy and Mimesis* defends the use of fantasy in literature against a tradition that has relegated it to a subcategory. According to Hume, fantasy has historically been excluded from consideration as serious literature on the grounds that it provokes excess emotion (Plato), is a "threat to sanity" (David Hume), or a lie (orthodox Christians).[9] Kathryn Hume places the majority of the blame for this wrongheadedness on Plato and Aristotle who "between them tore a large and ragged hole in western consciousness. Ever since this day, our critical perceptions have been marred by this blind spot, and our views of literature curiously distorted. To both philosophers, literature was mimetic, and they analyzed only its mimetic components. Moreover, insofar as their assumptions allowed them to recognize fantasy at all, they distrusted and disparaged it" (pp. 5–6). Even today Hume has found theorists who assume "that the essential impulse behind literature is mimetic, and that fantasy is therefore a separable, peripheral phenomenon" (p. 8).

Citing the postmodern onslaught on the "insufficiencies of mimetic assumptions" (p. 5) and the increasing appearance of fantasy in postmodern literature, Hume attempts to reenfranchise fantasy as a primary rather than secondary component of literature: "Literature is the product of two impulses. These are *mimesis*, felt as the desire to imitate, to describe events, people, situations, and objects with such verisimilitude that others can share your experience; and *fantasy*, the desire to change givens and alter reality" (p. 20). She provides a definition of fantasy that could extend to literature traditionally considered exclusively realistic, or mimetic. Fantasy is "any departure from consensus reality, an impulse native to literature and manifested in innumerable variations from monster to metaphor" (p. 21).

Though a starting point, Hume's definition presents problems of its own, for it fails to define consensus reality other than as the few material givens of the world such as a tree, chair, or wall. She doesn't, for example, clarify those murky areas that cannot be readily reduced to a consensus such as the multiple interpretations of a single event, or the divergent realities in different cultures. Nevertheless,

Hume's revalorization of fantasy can provide needed insight into Morrison's work in several ways. First, Hume's discussion negates the need to view fantasy and mimesis separately. This is crucial to an understanding of Morrison's works since she dissolves the dichotomy between the two. Second, Hume's redefinition of fantasy as a "native impulse" enriches an understanding of the ways in which Morrison believes in fantasy as a means to transcend the oppressive materialism and physical reality that frustrate the potential for human development. Finally, Morrison's work will suffer less the denigration of current and future critics who consider the use of fantasy to resolve complex problems as ineffectual and unsatisfactory.

From her definition Hume goes on to categorize literature, whether mimetic or fantastic, into four groups: (1) the literature of illusion, or escape literature, in which the "author assumes our agreement that everyday reality is boring, unromantic—even depressing"; (2) the literature of vision, which "invites us to experience a new sense of reality"; (3) the literature of revision, which "lays out plans for revising reality, for shaping futures"; and (4) the literature of disillusion, which "insists that reality is unknowable" (pp. 55–56).

Given the overlapping nature of the categories—a reader cannot experience a "new sense of reality" unless the author has already presented a revision of sorts—and the fact that Morrison's works slip easily into any of these categories at various junctures, Hume's categories nevertheless provide a starting point for approaching Morrison's fiction. Though her earlier fiction leans toward literature of disillusionment, her later works most accurately resemble the literature of vision and revision. As a literature of vision and revision, Morrison's fiction is a blend of mimesis and fantasy that incites its readership into awareness and perhaps action. It provides a way to heal the spiritual wounds of double-consciousness or oppression in any guise within the confines of a harsh reality that daily erodes selfhood.

Morrison's first novel, *The Bluest Eye*, is her most mimetic fiction, a harrowing depiction of oppression unrelieved by any liberating use of fantasy. Having hit her own spiritual bottom at this point in her life, Morrison re-creates an autobiographical account suffused with pain. Claudia's narrative bears little resemblance to the optimism of visionist or revisionist literature that will mark Morrison's later works and, with several characters lapsing into dementia and insanity, is more closely aligned to the literature of disillusion, or perspectivist literature: "Where other kinds of literature impose meaning on experience or encourage us to feel that some actions can be meaningful, perspectivist literature simply denies the validity of any such assurance, and implicitly makes any action on our part optional" (p. 124).

For Morrison at the time she wrote *The Bluest Eye*, it appears that the most brutal way to drive home to her readers the reality of life for black people was through mimesis; yet interestingly enough, mimesis becomes a frame for the psychological world of her main characters, Cholly, Pecola, and Soaphead, who resort to internal fantasies in which *they* depart from a consensus reality, creating their own fantastic text of disillusion. With the disintegration of these characters at the end of the novel, the world becomes unknowable not only for them, but for the readers who vicariously witness their demise. Readers can recognize and to a great extent sympathize with the dehumanization of black Americans. However, Morrison pushes her readers one step further by challenging the very construct of a reality that provides guidelines for that decision-making. She suggests, much in the same way Stowe did in *Uncle Tom's Cabin*, that blacks are violated not only by bad whites but by all whites—and blacks—who tacitly or unknowingly support a society that is inherently racist. Her addition of the element of insanity compromises consensus reality, and the reader is never allowed "to integrate the data and make it harmonious" (Hume, p. 139). Indeed, the reader is faced with a compelling ethical argument that as Theresa Enos says, "arises from the union of speaker and listener, writer and reader; the opening up of a world holding within it values that both participants adhere to underlies the whole concept of ethos." It is through ethos, Enos says, that "a discourse achieve[s] identification." [10]

Cholly, Soaphead, and Pecola go insane because reality has turned on them in the most profound way: what they are taught is good—parents, adults, God—becomes evil, an inversion of those values that constitute the foundation of rational thinking. Cholly learns this very early in life through role models: his parents desert him, white folks humiliate him, and his Aunt Jimmy dies after paying tribute to God at a church revival. But, before this point, even in the loving care of his Aunt Jimmy, Cholly is confused. Watching a father break open a watermelon for his family, Cholly is awed by the man's physical power and strength:

> Tall, head forward, eyes fastened on a rock, his arms higher than the pines, his hands holding a melon bigger than the sun, he paused an instant to get his bearing and secure his aim. Watching the figure etched against the bright blue sky, Cholly felt goose pimples popping along his arms and neck. He wondered if God looked like that. No. God was a nice old man, with long white hair, flowing white beard, and little blue eyes that looked sad when people died and mean when they were bad. It must be the devil who looks like that. . . . If the devil did look like that, Cholly preferred him. He never felt anything thinking about God, but the idea of the devil excited him. (pp. 106–7)

Cholly wants to perceive God as black and strong, larger than nature itself; however, he has learned that God is white, somewhat effeminate (a nice old man) and diminutive (little blue eyes.) The embodiment of God in an aged white body distant from human contact restricts the young Cholly's ability to see God everywhere. But instead of denying the powerful black man, Cholly readjusts his ideology to fit him in. He invokes the antithesis of God, the devil, the only other figure of omnipotence he has been exposed to. As Lauren Lepow points out, this also happens with Son in *Tar Baby*: "Son strongly evokes the traditional Satan: like Milton's, he brings out the intrinsic 'evil' in others. But, as Gideon's and Therese's theft demonstrates, traditional 'evil' is actually no more than the challenge to authority and liberation of knowledge."[11] Like Son, the father is a symbol of authority, "his arms higher than the pines" and defiance, ready to dash the melon "bigger than the sun" to the earth as if it were the earth itself. But his actions are essentially benevolent; he's in the act of feeding the multitudes and providing pleasure. Thus, to the devilish nature of the man is added the dimension of Christ. As Lepow says of Son, "The very actions that initially evoked the satanic now require us to see [him] as its opposite."[12] In this novel, however, the father is a fleeting star in the dark sky of Cholly's life and he is left only with an outline of godhead that he eventually creates in his own warped image.

Cholly's confusion becomes complete in a series of rapid events— the death of his aunt, the hunters' humiliation, and his father's rejection. Abandoned at the age of thirteen, Cholly has no sense of good or evil. After a final rejection by his father, Cholly "was alone with his own perceptions and appetites, and they alone interested him" (p. 126). It is at this point that Cholly has essentially gone insane. He is released of a conscience that will dictate right from wrong: "Free to be tender or violent. . . . Free to knock [a woman] in the head, for he had already cradled that head in his arms. . . . He was free to live his fantasies, and free even to die, the how and the when of which held no interest for him" (pp. 125–26).

Immediately after this analysis of Cholly's pitiful life, Morrison describes the rape scene, the result of which is that the reader is left emotionally numb, confused about the role of victim and victimizer. Given the circumstances of Cholly's life, the reader has great difficulty reinforcing his or her own assumptions about reality, about right and wrong, about good and evil. This is compounded by the confluence of emotions that flood Cholly before the rape as he struggles to find a means to love his daughter: "The sequence of his emotions was revulsion, guilt, pity, then love." Confronting the pathetic and loveless condition of his daughter's life, Cholly asks, "What could his heavy arms and befuddled brain accomplish that would earn him his own respect, that would in turn allow him to accept her love?" (p. 127). When he rapes Pecola, he confuses love and lust, tenderness and violence, father and lover and ends up destroying Pecola.

Pecola's insanity is a function of her and her family having ingested western notions of worth and goodness—for a little girl, beauty in the form of blue eyes—to the point of her own disintegration. Learning that her mother's fist against her jaw and her father's rape are somehow tied to her ugliness, she attempts to become beautiful by denying her own physical existence. The result is that "a little black girl yearns for the blue eyes of a little white girl, and the horror at the heart of her yearning is exceeded only by the evil of fulfillment" (p. 158). "Evil" used in this context takes on new meaning. While whiteness, blue eyes, and blond hair may be good in the sense of providing aesthetic pleasure, they become evil when set up as a cultural given, a measure of individual worth, and the sole measure of physical beauty. By institutionalizing and then nearly deifying a definitive set of physical features, society creates a monolithic bully in a pluralistic society. The impossibility for Pecola of attaining these physical features is translated into her own evilness, or unworthiness. The choice becomes whether to be evil— ugly—or beautiful and godlike, no choice at all since goodness in her society is genetically engineered. Pecola chooses goodness and in a remarkable strength of character goes insane to convince herself of her essential humanity and worth. As Claudia says, "She, however, stepped over into madness, a madness which protected her from us simply because it bored us in the end" (p. 159). Pecola's madness is not boring but profoundly unsettling. Few readers could have imagined the effect of standardized beauty on a black person, even though to a lesser degree they are victims themselves. Faced, however, with the endorsement of the same cultural assumptions as Pecola, the reader finds himself or herself forced into alignment with the perspective of a crazed and tormented adolescent.

In his letter to God, Soaphead Church challenges the religious definition of good and the origin of evil. Instead of accepting blame for his own twisted nature, Soaphead accuses God, the very embodiment (or disembodiment) of goodness. Not only does Soaphead refuse responsibility for his own actions, he succeeds in convincing himself that he is equal and finally superior to God. Soaphead sees God as a Dr. Frankenstein and himself as a superior monster because he can recognize the evil in his creation. Soaphead's position is most convincing because he challenges God to answer a question that continues to nag even the most devout believers: Why does evil exist?

As a seemingly successful product of a civilized and rational culture, Soaphead would be the last person to challenge the authority of his parents, culture, and God. Yet so repressive was his Victorian upbringing, with its obsession with cleanliness and fetishization of the flesh, that Soaphead has become a freak unable to enjoy not just healthy adult sex, but almost any human contact—the exception being little girls who represent for him, and the culture, purity. Molesting little girls becomes "A Thing To Do Instead. Instead of papa. Instead of the Cloth. Instead of Velma and I *chose* not to do without them" (p. 141). Soaphead's perversity is both a rebellion against and an affirmation of the system that created him: he rebels against his father and his church by committing a vile act, but one, in Soaphead's mind, that is somewhat in sync with the notion of denying the flesh. To justify his actions and retain an identity, Soaphead reaches a compromise with himself in which he is not an agent of evil, but an inevitable participant in an evil system: "Since decay, vice, filth, and disorder were pervasive, they must be in the Nature of Things. Evil existed because God had created it" (p. 136). God is responsible for evil; therefore, Soaphead is essentially godhead. He equates his miserable life with his creator's: "I have been a bad man too, and unhappy man too" (p. 142). Soaphead completes his own metamorphosis from subordinate of God to equal and finally superior. He says about giving Pecola blue eyes, "I did what You did not, could not, would not do: I looked at that ugly little black girl, and I loved her" (p. 143).

Condemning God for deserting the innocent and the vulnerable, Soaphead asks a question almost rhetorical in nature: "Tell me, Lord, how could you leave a lass so long so lone that she could find her way to me? How could you?" (p. 142). Soaphead's letter tempts the reader to make the same assumptions he does about the nature of God, of good and evil. But more than that, it provokes an inevitable response: it is not God who has deserted this child, but I, the reader, in my complacency and my indifference to the suffering of the world, nation, community, neighbors, and battered little girls. At this juncture, Morrison, having made an ethical appeal to her readers, consequently effects identification: her readership accepts an invitation to join or become the fictive audience that she has both created and herself become a part of.[13] What happens in this literature of disillusion is a self-reflexive moment in which the reader is faced with ambivalence, uncertainty, conflict, and guilt. Hume says, "An author can lay the blame for our warped perspectives on our membership in the human species, with all the culturally imposed assumptions which that brings. The author usually demonstrates these inescapable weaknesses to his protagonists and expects us to apply the message to ourselves and our own blindness" (p. 125). The reality presented in this novel is disturbing: evil proliferates when goodness is in abeyance. While goodness should be eternally vigilant, it is not. And we have only ourselves to blame.

After the disillusionment of *The Bluest Eye*, Morrison increasingly integrates elements of the fantastic into her novels. These works fall under the aegis of the literature of vision and revision. A novel of vision

> invite[s] conscious comparison of our own vision of reality with that which we confront in the stories. They seem designed to call attention to the differences. They make us feel the limitations of our notions of reality, often by presenting one that seems more rich, more intense, more coherent (or incoherent), or somehow more significant. Not only do these visions invite comparison, they encourage strong emotional response. Creating a separate reality and calling attention to it is one characteristic of great, as opposed to merely competent, fiction. (Hume, p. 82)

By creating these categories, Hume provides insight into Morrison's black community as an alternative reality in both the mimetic and fantastic sense. Since the black community has been invisible and unreal in many ways to mainstream society, its reconstruction, in a mimetic sense alone, is a defamiliarization, "especially effective for forcing us to realize that our view of reality is not privileged" (p. 86). Add to that reconstruction the element of the fantastic—myths, signs, prophesies, omens, dreams, witches, superhuman powers, and ghosts—and the communities of Bottom, Shalimar, and Eloe are elevated to the level of myth and profoundly challenge existing notions of reality. While this visionist literature may provoke action to change reality, it even more "encourages emotional response and reflection rather than action, and provides no blueprint for a future program" (p. 83).

What distinguishes the literature of vision from revision is the "presence of a program of action" thus placing revision in the category of didacticism. While visionist literature often provokes self-reflection, a revisionist novel wishes to quell critical opposition and "demand full affirmation of its vision of reality and by implication asks for revisions in the reader's life" (p. 103). In revisionist literature, fantasy sweetens what is often a bitter message thus making palatable what might otherwise be indigestible. As a mix of mimesis and fantasy, it "allows people to escape from their culture's imperfect systems of authority supposedly based on reason, and lets them experience other possibilities for ordering experience, whether religious or utopian" (p. 123).

As visionist novels *Sula*, *Tar Baby*, *Song of Solomon*, and *Beloved* are strong on inciting powerful overflow of emotion and thought, but short on prescribing remedy. Still, they can also be called revisionist because they present realities that necessarily redefine "normal" or "natural" and thus provide a sense of liberation to their readership. Morrison could have achieved this effect, following the lead of Wright's *Native Son*, in a strictly mimetic fashion. However, she chose to include fantasy, not as a literary gimmick, but as an essential component of the real world. For Morrison, to create ghosts and witches is not her attempt at the sensational, but an almost mimetic impulse. In her own upbringing

> she absorbed the black lore, music, language, myths and rituals that give her prose its special flavor and tone. "We were intimate with the supernatural," she recalls. Her parents told thrillingly terrifying ghost stories. Her mother sang constantly. Her grandmother kept a dream book and played the numbers off it, decoding dream symbols to determine what number to bet on. Morrison's world, like the world of her novels, was filled with signs, visitations, ways of knowing that reached beyond the five senses.[14]

When Morrison recreates these elements in her art, she purposely departs from consensus reality, not to foreground the supernatural as a unique expression of the black community, but as a way to Signify the difference between culturally imposed ways of seeing. Morrison's assumption in her writing, her consensus reality, is very different from Kathryn Hume's because the supernatural does exist, outside of literature and, in a revisionist fashion, presumes a truth that is unassailable. The most compelling evidence of Morrison's belief in the supernatural is her conviction that she maintains a relationship with her dead father. In her oft-quoted *Newsweek* interview, she told Jean Strouse about her father's run-in with racist whites. Strouse's recorder did not pick up that segment of the interview, and Morrison explained to Strouse: "I know why. I told you something I wasn't supposed to tell you. So my father took care of it. I'm not surprised. He's done that before." [15] But Morrison's ultimate purpose in using the supernatural in art is not to prove its existence—her novels intentionally represent it ambiguously—but to create this ongoing dialectic between the seen and the unseen, the known and the unknowable, the signified and the Signified—the supernatural as a trope on reality. The effect of this is a redefinition for some and reaffirmation for others of a consensus reality that dilutes the debilitating effects of double-consciousness, racism, and oppression.

In *Sula* Morrison uses the supernatural as a way to explain illness and death. Bearing little resemblance to the causality assigned by modern medicine, death and illness in *Sula* are rarely accidental, chance, or natural. All of the people who die in the book die a horrible death. None of these things are attributed exclusively to fate and an indifferent universe but to agents of evil or self-neglect. The system of belief in *Sula* incorporates conjure women, signs, witches, and dreams. In spite of the infusion of the fantastic, Morrison shies away from an unambiguous representation of the supernatural as the cause of death and illness, choosing instead to emphasize the psychological aspects of oppression that result in the need to rely on an alternative explanation for misfortune.

Morrison's characters' perspectives on illness and death are derivative, in part, of their African heritage. In a study of nonwestern medical systems, George Foster discovered two explanations for causality of death and illness: personalistic and naturalistic. While Foster's definitions help to explain the Afrocentric notions of death and illness, they only provide a backdrop to the complicated fictional world of *Sula* in which supernatural explanations of death and illness are used to encourage subsequent reinterpretations of life and health. Foster defines "a personalistic medical system" as

> one in which disease is explained as due to the *active, purposeful intervention* of an *agent*, who may be human (a witch or sorcerer), nonhuman

(a ghost, an ancestor, an evil spirit), or supernatural (a deity or other very powerful being). . . . Personalistic causality allows little room for accident or chance; in fact, for some peoples the statement is made by anthropologists who have studied them that *all* illness and death are believed to stem from the acts of the agent.[16]

Sula is perceived by the community as the evil agent responsible for much pain and suffering in her community. However, not all disaster is attributed to her. Eva, with a slightly different perspective than the townspeople, also integrates into her causality the naturalistic, "which explains illness in impersonal, cosmic terms. Disease is thought to stem, not from the machinations of any angry being, but from such *natural forces or conditions* as cold, heat, winds, dampness, and above all, an upset in the balance of the basic body elements." [17]

We first see naturalistic causality in *The Bluest Eye* when Aunt Jimmy catches cold at the camp meeting: "She went to a camp meeting that took place after a rainstorm, and the damp wood of the benches was bad for her" (p. 107). The remedies suggested to her are all aimed at realigning her body elements: "Don't eat no white eggs." "Drink new milk." "Chew on this root" (p. 108). Aunt Jimmy gets worse and M'Dear is called in, a midwife and a diagnostician who "knows the appropriate herbs, food restrictions, and other forms of treatment such as cupping, massage, poultices, enemas and the like." [18] Her diagnosis is "You done caught cold in your womb. Drink pot liquor and nothing else" (p. 108). Aunt Jimmy transgresses, however, eats peach cobbler and dies.[19]

In Morrison's world naturalistic and personalistic causality "are rarely if ever mutually exclusive as far as their presence or absence in a particular society is concerned. Peoples who invoke personalistic causes to explain most illness usually recognize some natural, or chance, causes. And people for whom naturalistic causes predominate almost invariably explain some illness as due to witchcraft or the evil eye." [20] For example, presaging Hannah's horrible death by fire were a number of signs and omens, the first being a wind that brought no rain and the second, Hannah's question of Eva if she ever loved her children. The third strange event is Hannah's dream of the wedding in the red dress. Sula's acting up is the fourth, though

Eva's not sure if that should be counted or not: "Because she was thirteen, everybody supposed her nature was coming down, but it was hard to put up with her sulking and irritation" (p. 74). Finally, Eva can't find her comb which was "the fifth (or fourth, if you didn't count Sula's craziness) strange thing. . . . Nobody moved stuff in Eva's room except to clean and then they put everything right back. But Eva couldn't find it anywhere" (p. 75). After Hannah's death, Eva reconstructs the sign of Hannah's dream: "Weddings always meant death. And the red gown, well that was fire." (p. 78) and the unusual wind that may have fanned the flames that consumed Hannah. Having assigned naturalistic causes, she adds the personalistic, or evil agent element: "Sula had watched Hannah burn not because she was paralyzed, but because she was interested" (p. 78). Thus Eva attributes Hannah's death to both naturalistic and personalistic causality by suggesting that the wind somehow contributed to her death and that Sula must be possessed of an evil spirit to watch her mother burn. Eva interprets Sula's reaction and assigns an unnatural label to what may have been simply the stunned reaction of a thirteen-year-old watching her mother burn to death.

In *Sula* Bottomites mix these two systems of belief to give meaning to the often chaotic rhythm of their lives. These beliefs allow them some measure of control over the evil that greets them daily: "They did not believe doctors could heal—for them, none ever had done so. They did not believe death was accidental—life might be, but death was deliberate. They did not believe Nature was ever askew—only inconvenient. Plague and drought were as 'natural' as springtime. If milk could curdle, God knows robins could fall. The purpose of evil was to survive it and they determined . . . to survive floods, white people, tuberculosis, famine and ignorance" (p. 90). They can avoid certain foods or weather or cast out the witch doctor—actions they can take in lieu of any significant political action as an oppressed group. Too painful would be the realization that their lives are locked in an endless and self-perpetuating cycle of pain and suffering. Rosemary Jackson recognizes this indulgence in fantasy as "negative relationality," a subversive response to the reality imposed by the dominant culture (quoted in Hume, p. 17).

In an effort to assign causality to incomprehensible events, Bottomites look to nature and search for an evil agent. Sula becomes the evil scapegoat, and thus the focal point of a community in need of a common enemy. Sula eventually leaves Bottom but her return is immediately identified with evil cosmic forces: "Accompanied by a plague of robins, Sula came back to Medallion" (p. 89). The event takes on exaggerated proportions, having a greater effect on them than even the chaotic extremes of nature. Their reaction is to embrace the odd occurrence: "In spite of their fear, they reacted to an oppressive oddity, or what they called evil days, with an acceptance that bordered on welcome. Such evil must be avoided, they felt, and precautions must naturally be taken to protect themselves from it" (p. 89).

Sula becomes the convenient personification of evil. While she is connected to a multitude of sins—sending Eva to a nursing home, sleeping with Nel's husband—she is ultimately condemned for her sexual relations with white men. They "regarded integration with precisely the same venom that white people did" (p. 113). Sula's crossing the racial barrier is tantamount in their eyes to crossing the line between good and evil. Having identified her as evil, they fulfill their own prophesy by interpreting seemingly insignificant signs—her birthmark, youthful appearance, her disregard sexually for husbands, and her chance appearance at minor accidents—as evil manifestations.

The consensus of Sula's evilness changes the townspeople: "Once the source of their personal misfortune was identified, they had leave to protect and love one another. They began to cherish their husbands and wives, protect their children, repair their homes and in general band together against the devil in their midst" (pp. 117–18). But the bond they form is tenuous, based on a presumption of evil that may or may not exist. Rather than analyze the complex and difficult conditions in their lives, they reduce those complexities to the simplistic moral absolutes of good and evil, then personify evil as a way to contain it.

When Sula dies, "a falling away, a dislocation was taking place. Hard on the heels of general relief that Sula's death brought a restless irritability took hold" (p. 153). They perceive Sula's death as a sign of good things to come, then endure their greatest misfortune with the collapse of the tunnel—another unfulfilled promise by white society. Without Sula, "the tension was gone and so was the reason for the effort they had made. Without her mockery, affection for others sank into flaccid disrepair" (p. 153). The community begins to fall apart, the final effects of which will be the collapse of Bottom and the eventual integration of blacks and whites.

While Morrison implies that the evil assigned to Sula is more psychological than supernatural, in *Song of Solomon* she further blurs the lines between mimesis and fantasy. In this novel Morrison uses myth as a form of transcendence, a device that mitigates double-consciousness by collapsing the dichotomy between black and white. Myths are "the prototypes of all narrative, the ancestors and models of later developments." [21] According to Jack Zipes, myth, placed in the context of history and culture, redefines the existing order while it gives rise to a new one.

> By relocating the historical origins of the folk and fairy tales in politics and class struggle, the essence of its durability and vitality will become more clear, and its magic will be seen as part of humankind's own imaginative *and* rational drive to create new worlds that allow for total development of human qualities. The utopian impulse has its concrete base. "The magic in the tales (if magic is what it is) lies in people and creatures being shown what they really are," and one could add, in being shown what they are really and realistically capable of accomplishing.[22]

Myth, as it is used in *Solomon*, is not only a metaphor but a course of action that, as it muddies the distinction between spiritual and physical flight, provides fuel for the collective imagination.

Solomon is based on several myths of flying. According to De Weever, "In presenting the evolution of a song in the possession of a particular family, the author uses a variety of myth and folk tale: Biblical and Greek myth and European fairy and folk tales." [23] It is also based on the Icarus story:

> In classical myth Icarus is clearly a hero of the phallic type—the youth attempts to break free of the earth; intent on self-gratification and overestimating his own potential, he rejects his father's guidance; his wings

are melted by the fiery, masculine symbol—the sun; and he falls back into the sea, earth's watery element, feminine symbol of change and rebirth. Thus, the Icarian mythic pattern is one of personal quest, sensual and egocentric, to test the individual's potential. It is a flight in the double sense of the word—a flight from authority and repression and a flight towards freedom; it is also a flight which ends in a fall.[24]

Myth often operates on the principle of binary opposition, "a narrative sequence," Greimas says, "which embodies this mode by the employment of two actants whose relationship must be either oppositional or its reverse; and on the surface level this relationship will therefore generate fundamental actions of disjunction and conjunction, separation and union, struggle and reconciliation."[25] Binary opposition constitutes *Song of Solomon*'s mythic structure "following the clear pattern of birth and youth, alienation, quest, confrontation, reintegration common to mythic heroes as disparate as Moses, Achilles, and Beowulf. Such a mythic chronology emphasizes the hero's rejection and eventual assimilation into his society."[26] Morrison emphasizes less this reintegration into society, suggesting that Milkman is taking a more important step by realigning himself with his history.

While this pattern traditionally involves a male, it is appropriated by Morrison for her female characters as well. Pilate, in her youth, is alienated from society because she lacks a navel; the guilt she harbors retards reintegration into society until just before her death when she is confronted with the knowledge that Macon did not kill the white man after all. Morrison also varies the mythic structure by delaying the initiations of Corinthians and Hagar into society until late in life thus depicting "the extreme difficulty of the black woman's search for self-determination, and certainly the results of these initiations underscore that point."[27] Thus even within the mythic structure, binary opposition is at work, contrasting the relative ease of Milkman's transcendence to the near impossibility for most women in the novel of achieving a similar transformation.

By drawing on and manipulating a variety of mythic patterns, Morrison hopes to achieve, in the final analysis, a new world. When Morrison chose a myth to base her story on, she did not do so for its charm or allure, but to present the reader with an alternative to modern society. As she says, "We have to acknowledge that the thing we call 'literature' is pluralistic now, just as society ought to be. The melting pot never worked." [28] In a pluralistic society many different realities exist and truth becomes relative. According to Damian Grant, there are two kinds of truth, correspondence and coherence. Correspondence, where "truth proposed is truth that corresponds," is whatever the majority of people perceive truth to be, based on empirical and scientific observation. Coherence or intuitive perception is "created in the very act of perception." [29] While Morrison exhibits both truths in *Solomon*—Pilate's intuition and Macon's pragmatism—she is obviously wary of the select group that dictates truth to others and attempts to shape their reality with the force of an iron cast. The inhabitants of Southside often rebel against the empiricists with intuitive truth: a hospital of Mercy does not exist in the black community; the supernatural does constitute a reality; letters can be sent to a street that was never mapped; and men and animals do talk to each other. Macon Dead has forfeited his coherent truth for correspondent truth and it is that condition Morrison wishes, by showing its effects on Milkman and Macon, to reverse in the reader.

In *Solomon* Morrison disorients what Grant terms the conscientious realist who looks for scientific, not romantic, truth. By doing so she directs the reader to a conscious realism: "Truth in art: which is therefore a kind of 'knowing,' not an abstract or scientific kind of knowing that expresses itself not in description, repetition, or imitation, but in making, making new." [30] The world of Southside is an old one recognizable to the conscientious realist. However, when reality elides into allegory, the reader must employ conscious realism to share in the epiphanic ending and all of its ramifications for contemporary society. Because *Solomon* refuses to defer to a preconceived reality, the reader is faced with the genre of the fantastic, which "manifests itself in ambiguity, in the hesitation felt by someone who knows only natural laws, when faced with an event which is apparently supernatural." [31] These events are so numerous in *Solomon* that reality and fantasy are indistinguishable and the beleaguered reader has little recourse but to accept the fantastic as an established corollary to the real world. Pilate can talk to her dead father, Ruth's watermark does grow each day, and Shalimar and Milkman can fly. By casually mingling the real and bizarre, Morrison "has achieved a subtler and more satisfying synthesis between those crude abstractions reality and imagination, and those equally crude adjustable spanners of criticism, objective and subjective."[32] Readers cannot approach *Solomon* armed with a reality as if it were a geometric given; they must seek a reality in "a continuous process that never allows the concept to stabilize or the word to offer a convenient mould of meaning."[33]

Once readers can accept this, they, the real audience, can merge with the fictive one, its writer, and with the text to recognize with Milkman at the end of the novel that the impossibility becomes the stunning probability. Milkman learns this sporadically from different characters as part of his maturation process. Pilate tells him, when he is only twelve, of the man whose imagination was responsible for his own death. When Milkman asks how she explained to a jealous wife her life-saving grip on the man, Pilate responds, "The truth. That I was trying to keep him from falling off the cliff" (p. 41). To Pilate it is the truth since the cliff in his mind was just as real and fatal as any ledge that existed outside his imagination. This parable strikes a chord in Milkman whose own imagination creates conflicts in him. When he witnesses his mother and the surreal dance of the tulips, "he called it a dream because he didn't want to tell [Guitar] it had really happened, that he had really seen it" (p. 105). Later, despite his faith in his own altered reality, he laughs at Freddie's tale that a white bull killed his mother. Freddie scolds, "But they's a lot of strange things you don't know nothin' about, boy" (p. 110). With Pilate's help and his own experiences to deal with, Milkman permits the possibility of the fantastic. When he meets Circe, dreams and reality fuse in a spectacular array of color and sound; Milkman has cracked the facade of civilized truth and can tap the intuitive knowledge that says if "out of the toothless mouth came the strong, mellifluent voice of a twenty-year-old girl" (p. 213), then anything is possible: Ryna still bemoans the loss of Shalimar; Macon Dead I lives; Shalimar flies.

Morrison's world is apocalyptic in vision, and ancient in its suggestion of remedy. Love and freedom replace oppression as the only beliefs worth adhering to. Males do not control females or whites blacks for " 'otherness' no longer functions as an extension of domination,"[34] and communities nurture rather than starve their members. If readers can accept the validity of the world in *Solomon*, Morrison asks that they take one more step—the application of literature to life that will transform the dirge of America into a psalm.

In *Tar Baby* Morrison again relies on myth, ghosts, and evil, intensifying their mystical qualities by placing them in an isolated setting, a Caribbean island. Variant in structure from *The Bluest Eye* in which a very realistic community provided the setting, *Tar Baby* is set in a supernatural environment, an overtly visionist and revisionist construction of reality. Because of the conflicting myths of the black and white inhabitants and the almost sentient quality of nature on the island, Morrison provides *omnipotence of thought*:

> What Freud playfully calls "familiar" ground: the old animistic conception of the universe characterized by the idea that the world is peopled with spirits of human beings, and by narcissistic over-evaluation of mental processes, or belief in magic based upon omnipotence of thought, and all the other inventions by which man "strove to fend off the manifest prohibitions of reality." In fiction, of course, this supposed situation *is* in fact the case: the universe of the fiction *is* animated by an omnipotence of thought shared between the author and the reader.[35]

The reality that Morrison attempts to fend off is one in which whites are set against blacks, women against men, culture against primitivism, and civilization against nature. Morrison challenges these dualities by creating an atmosphere of omnipotence in several ways: (1) in the sentience of nature, (2) through the competing myths on the island, and (3) through the psychic experiences of Jadine and Valerian. While her characters are, on one level, conscious of and attentive to the realistic dilemmas of their lives, they are also programmed in a subtle way to that very omnipotence of thought that suggests that other forces are at work that will influence them. Whether it be the presence of nature possessed of an intelligence or an intelligence imposed by its human inhabitants, reality in *Tar Baby* is a smoke and mirrors act that continues to elude the residents of L'Arbre de la Croix.

Morrison opens and closes her novel with a description of the island, a primary character in *Tar Baby*. The Isle de Chevaliers is a thinking community of plants, animals, and weather suddenly confronted with extinction at the hands of a people with whom communication is impossible. Because Morrison establishes consciousness immediately, she underscores the importance of the island to the reader and the lives of the characters who, at this juncture, are not even aware it is in danger of annihilation:

> When laborers imported from Haiti came to clear the land, clouds and fish were convinced that the world was over, that the sea-green green of the sea and sky-blue sky of the sky were no longer permanent. Wild parrots that had escaped the stones of hungry children in Queen of France agreed and raised havoc as they flew away to look for yet another refuge. Only the champion daisy trees were serene. After all, they were part of a rain forest already two thousand years old and scheduled for eternity, so they ignored the men and continued to rock the diamondbacks that slept in their arms. It took the river to persuade them that indeed the world was altered. (p. 7)

Once in a state of pristine majesty, the island, at the hands of the western imperialists, has become defiled and is doomed. But with the ability to articulate its state of affairs the island takes on more than just ecological significance; it is a living organism with a soul that has been turned into a sinkhole of human waste. Facing the destruction of its beauty at the hands of developers, the island prepares for war:

> After thirty years of shame the champion daisy trees were marshaling for war. The wild parrots that had escaped the guns of Dominique could feel menace in the creeping of their roots. During day they tossed their branches; at night they walked the hills. At dawn their new formations challenged the wit of the chevaliers. Their brothers over on Dominique knew nothing of the battle plans for they were in a rain forest tamed for tourists that came by bus from the Old Queen Hotel, gallant and royal since 1927. Now she was dying from behind. Her front on Rue Madelaine was still seacap white and the columns at her entrance showed no signs of wear. Yet at her great round-skirted rear among breadfruit trees and lime, the cells of a motel were growing. (p. 236)

By allowing the island a voice, Morrison assigns intentionality and intelligence in her personification of Nature, which makes all the more tragic its limited capability to act. Nature's reaction to the invasion creates an illusion of movement. The clouds and fish "were convinced," the wild parrots "escaped," and the champion daisies "were marshaling for war." The daisies "tossed their branches," "walked the hills" and "challenged" the chevaliers, but were still "dying from behind." The island demonstrates violence of feeling stymied by an equally impotent ability to act. The result is that the reader at once gains a new sense of reality into a dimension of nature, and experiences the frustration of its vulnerability to exploitation. Nature no longer appears an unfortunate and necessary sacrifice for the advancement of civilization, but an entity that is powerless to communicate its own importance. The omnipotence of thought that suffuses the island becomes an additional burden on the conscience of the reader who can no longer afford the either-or mentality that has been the impetus behind expansion and imperialism.

Omnipotence is also created by the contending racial myths of the island, both of which suggest that there are greater things at work than themselves. But while it appears that both Valerian and Son believe in something other than empirical reality, they attach themselves to myths that, though in some ways very similar, are antagonistic. The irony implicit in such a situation is that both races acknowledge a level of consciousness not empirically retrievable but use it for division rather than union.

Son is naturally attracted to the myth of the islander. He "asked who were the blind race so Gideon told him a story about a race of blind people descended from some slaves who went blind the minute they saw Dominique. . . . What they saw, they saw with the eye of the mind, and that, of course, was not to be trusted" (pp. 130–31). Unlike the white imperialists who saw the trees, river, and birds as building materials for their own contrived paradise, the blind slaves could not see the island to appropriate it. Equipped only with the mind's eye, they had to rationalize that their very existence depended on their ability to work with, not against, the land. Blindness was their window to understanding that eluded the imperialists who did not trust what they could not see empirically, or chose not to see beyond their own selfish needs and desires. The blind horsemen still ride through the jungle though they can't be seen and "can't stand for sighted people to look at them without their permission. No telling what they'll do if they know you saw them" (p. 131). How they can be looked at if they can't be seen is less a curiosity than why they don't want to be viewed by a sighted person. The reason may be that sight is no guarantee of insight: seeing alone is not a reliable means of divining truth especially if it is divorced from perception.

Valerian's myth is similar to the natives': "Somewhere in the back of Valerian's mind one hundred French chevaliers were roaming the hills on horses. Their swords were in their scabbards and their epaulets glittered in the sun. Backs straight, shoulders high—alert but restful in the security of the Napoleonic Code" (p. 177). In Valerian's myth, like that of the blind slaves, men and horses combine to create a striking image of beauty and dignity. Very different from the slaves, they are arrayed in accouterment that is antithetical and threatening to the natural. Rather than rely on the benevolence of the land, they are dependent on a man-made code as their course of action. They view themselves as superior to the land and with their swords are ready to slash or mutilate whatever stands in their way. Though the chevaliers and the blind horsemen in their courage and bravado appear to have derived from one universal fraternal order, they are worlds apart in their relationship to the land. The lines are clearly drawn in the characters of Son and Valerian: "The evening eyes met those of the man with savannas in his face. The man who respected industry looked over a gulf at the man who prized fraternity" (p. 176). This conflict is not resolved in the novel, but because it is analogized in mythic form, it appears less the Gordion knot of race relations and more a cat's cradle.

The mythic struggle between the races is also the struggle between culture and primitivism, civilization and nature that, if irresolvable, will result in the destruction of all inhabitants of the island. Perhaps that is why Therese wishes to return to the island one of its own— provide nature with human beings who can save the island in ways that the slaves and nature cannot. She exhorts Son to find "the men. The men are waiting for you." She was pulling the oars now, moving out. "You can choose now. You can get free of her. They are waiting in the hills for you. They are naked and they are blind too. I have seen them; their eyes have no color in them. But they gallop; they race those horses like angels all over the hills where the rain forest is, where the champion daisy trees still grow. Go there. Choose them." She was far from him now, but her voice was near like skin. (p. 263)

Therese asks that Son, as a product of both cultures, choose the blind men who understand there is infinitely more to reality than what can be perceived with the senses, and to somehow bring this back to a civilization dangerously at odds with itself.

A further indication of the omnipotence of thought that pervades the island and its inhabitants is the fact that the two most encul-turated and sophisticated characters—Jadine and Valerian—experi-ence a number of supernatural visitations. By giving consciousness to the dead and having them visit the male and female icons of a spiritually deprived culture, Morrison provides Jadine and Valerian a way not only to confront their own immediate and distant past, but also a chance to reflect on what they may have missed in their en-deavor to embrace the status quo. In addition, they face a dimension of reality that—though it does not change them significantly in the end—disturbs them enough to question the validity of their values and beliefs.

When Jadine sinks in the swamp, she is observed by an ancient intelligence—women who are in sync with nature in a most intimate way. The jungle women perceive Jadine's efforts to extricate herself as a denial of the natural:

The women looked down from the rafters of the trees and stopped mur-muring. They were delighted when first they saw her, thinking a run-away child had been restored to them. But upon looking closer they saw differently. This girl was fighting to get away from them. The women hanging from the trees were quiet now, but arrogant—mindful as they were of their value, their exceptional femaleness; knowing as they did that the first world of the world had been built with their sacred proper-ties; that they alone could hold together the stones of pyramids and the rushes of Moses's crib; knowing their steady consistency, their pace of glaciers, their permanent embrace, they wondered at the girl's desperate struggle down below to be free, to be something other than they were. (p. 157)

Morrison's invocation of Mother Nature as the feminine metaphor identifies immediately the distinction between Jadine and real women. She appears as "something other than they were," an artificial construct, an adversary. Soon the women take on more concrete shape and meaning, appearing in the guise of any number of women who have made Jadine feel inauthentic: "She just lay there, too frightened to do it herself for then she would have to walk through the crowd of women standing in the pitch-dark room whom she could not see but would have to touch to get through them. And she felt them nudging each other for a better look at her, until finally being frightened was worse than anything they could do to her so she got mad and sat up" (p. 222). Initially intimidated by these women, Jadine repudiates them for "nudging each other for a better look at her," incensed that they would set themselves up as superior in spite of her culture and training. Jadine interprets the women as wanting to grab her and fit her into their mold: "They seemed somehow in agreement with each other about her, and were all out to get her, tie her, bind her. Grab the person she had worked hard to become and choke it off with their soft loose tits" (p. 224). Jadine runs away rather than reconcile the fragmentation she feels as a member of an ethnic group for which she feels no affinity and a product of a culture that finds no value in her ethnicity.

Valerian entertains ghosts, who appear in a carefully revised state, as a way of smoothing the wrinkles of his past. He is visited by the ghost of his first wife, whom he misses even though she was an "unlovable shrew" (p. 123):

> She started visiting him in the greenhouse with the regularity of a passionate mistress. Funny. He couldn't remember her eyes, but when she came, flitting around his chair and gliding over his seed flats, he recognized her at once. In nine years of marriage she had two abortions and all she wanted to talk about during these visits was how relieved she was that she'd had at least that foresight. He wished she felt something else. You'd think in death, in the Beyond, she would have felt something else.

> Or nothing at all. He was not alarmed by her visits; he knew he conjured
> them up himself, just as he conjured up old friends and childhood play-
> mates who were clearer to him now than the last thirty years were, and
> nicer. But he was astonished to see—unconjured—his only living son in
> the dining room last night. (p. 123)

Valerian's wifely ghost feels nothing else in the Beyond about her
abortions because from her perspective, considering the outcome of
Valerian's son, abortion was the less painful alternative to what Valerian is now suffering. After this revelation, the reader, though not
Valerian, is hardly at all astonished to see Valerian's son since he is
the final ghost with whom Valerian must come to grips.

Both Jadine and Valerian are treated to supernatural manifestations that profoundly challenge the data base of their reality. While
they have mastered education, hard work, sophistication and self-
control, they have lost out—in Valerian's case the joys of childhood
and fatherhood, nature and love; for Jadine, her heritage, history,
and selfhood. Though Valerian drifts in the unclarified mist of his
past, Jadine takes off to new parts, perhaps suggesting that she may
still be in search of a way to integrate the night women—her heritage—into her life.

In *Tar Baby* the world is cluttered with spirits and myths that inevitably minimize individual differences. Given a more complete perspective, individuals can release themselves from their own limited
vision and open up to creative solutions. If Jadine and Son, Valerian
and Son, Ondine and Jadine, Margaret and Michael cannot solve
their problems, it is because they do not possess total knowledge.
Morrison provides her characters with that missing information by
way of the supernatural, although they may not always be able to
adequately interpret it. The reader, however, is not often lost to Morrison's purpose, the effect of which is first to liberate the reader from
restrictive or dualistic thinking, and then to bring him or her back
armed with the weapon of imagination to effect change.

Beloved is Morrison's most unambiguous endorsement of the
supernatural; so rife is the novel with the physical and spiritual presence of ghostly energy that a better term than supernatural would
be uncanny, defined by Schelling as "the name for everything that

ought to have remained . . . secret and hidden but has come to light." [36] In this case, that which ought to have remained secret is slavery, what Morrison suggests most Americans would like to bury since it is the historical reminder of a national disgrace. Morrison herself delayed the writing of this novel because she could anticipate the pain of recovery and confrontation. She says, "I had forgotten that when I started the book, I was very frightened. . . . It was an unwillingness and a terror of going into an area for which you have no preparation. It's a commitment of three or four years to living inside—because you do try to enter that life." [37] Despite "this terrible reluctance about dwelling on that era," Morrison says she went ahead with the writing of the book because "I was trying to make it a personal experience." [38]

The metaphor for Morrison's reluctance to recall this episode is the configuration of Beloved, part ghost, zombie, devil, and memory. Morrison reveals Beloved in tantalizing degrees until she is manifested as a full-blooded person. Like a childhood trauma, Beloved comes back in snatches until finally her history is retold, a discovery process shared by Morrison, her characters, and the readers as the primary step to collective spiritual recovery. Lloyd-Smith states that "as texts reveal and conceal the repressed" they "renegotiate the relation between the self and the world through the manipulation of image." [39] What began as purgation for the author becomes cathartic for all engaged in the reading process.

The likely medium for this experience is the genre of the fantastic or the uncanny because, as an unchartered reality, it allows the writer more freedom to manipulate Morrison's fictional world: "Roland Barthes has discussed the withholding of revelation (enigma) and the process of elicitation and suppression (the hermeneutic code) by which it is vouchsafed and disclosed. . . . The writer's cul-de-sac is the reader's labyrinth; a thin line of words is the way in and the only way out, and revelation may come or be denied, to either." [40]

Morrison violates, to a certain extent, this revelation process. The reader is aware early on—whether from advanced publicity of the book or Morrison's pointed clues—that the girl Beloved is the murdered two-year-old daughter of Sethe. Thus, the mystery or enigma in the novel does not reside in the origin of the ghostly presence but in the purpose of its manifestation. Morrison withholds from the reader Beloved's raison d'être—why she finally makes an appearance, why she changes physically and emotionally, and why she ultimately disappears. The answer to this particular mystery lies in the ability of her characters and readers to reintegrate and reconcile past and present. For Sethe, she must confront the guilt of her act and in that self-absolution find a future. For Morrison's readers, reconciliation is intimately linked to their ability to recover the past, to dissolve the lineality of time, and overcome the fragmented and distorted notion of past, present, and future. Supernatural to a world with limited notions of reality, Beloved is nothing more or less than a memory come to life that has too conveniently been forgotten.

For Sethe, Beloved represents more of a psychological than a supernatural phenomenon. In this respect, Beloved can be explained in terms of the double, a theme Lloyd-Smith identifies in the literature of the uncanny:

> Within this category come reflections in mirrors, shadows, beliefs in the soul and fear of death, for the double can be a sort of insurance against the death of the ego, stemming from what Freud calls primary narcissism. When this stage has been surmounted, the double reverses its function, and instead of an assurance of immortality it becomes "the uncanny harbinger of death." All of these interpretations, however, have to do with the doubling of the self: what we have often occasion to remark in fiction is the doubling of the *Other*, and especially the other as woman.[41]

The theme of the double is useful in understanding the unusual relationship that develops between Sethe and Beloved. On one level Sethe and Beloved are reunited as mother and daughter, but as the relationship evolves, then disintegrates, more is at work than the reunion of the two. Beloved becomes a monster of sorts, bent on sucking dry the life of Sethe. Though Beloved has every reason to hate her mother, and to desire retribution for a nearly incomprehensible act, she—her spitefulness in particular—seems more a projection of Sethe's imagination than a reincarnation of her daughter.

Beloved's appearance coincides with the surprising and welcome return of Paul D, the very person who can make Sethe happy for the first time. But Sethe knows that life with Paul D cannot be a reality unless she deals with the guilt of the infanticide. Serving a confrontational function, then, Beloved acts as Sethe's double, reliving in stages the moments of her mother's life from infancy to sexual awakening to attempted murder. Beloved becomes Sethe's hair shirt, a painful attempt to heal herself by rediscovering the steps leading to an unspeakable act. Instead of reconciliation, however, Sethe finds those events so repugnant that her life becomes negligible and her double, Beloved, nearly destroys her.

Days after Paul D's arrival, Beloved appears, developmentally and emotionally a two-year-old; she can barely walk, cannot talk clearly or intelligibly, and lies in bed for days after her arrival staring adoringly at Sethe and sucking on candy. Beloved soon grows up, not as Beloved since her life was snuffed out, but as Sethe's alter ego. In this way Sethe, having conjured guilt in the image of her dead child, can attempt to exorcise it.

In the initial or narcissistic stage, Beloved emerges from the water as an infant who can do little more than ogle her mother in wonderment: "Beloved could not take her eyes off Sethe. Stooping to shake the damper, or snapping sticks for kindlin, Sethe was licked, tasted, eaten by Beloved's eyes" (p. 57). But the relationship is not exclusively child-daughter since Sethe does not relish the same attention from her other daughter, Denver: "Sethe was flattered by Beloved's open, quiet devotion. The same adoration from her daughter . . . would have annoyed her; make her chill at the thought of having raised a ridiculously dependent child. But the company of this sweet, if peculiar guest pleased her the way a zealot pleases his teacher" (p. 57).

The stage of self-love continues as the double regains memory of the past. Beloved feeds off of Sethe's old stories much to the delight of Sethe, who had avoided any mention of it even with Baby Suggs and Paul D, "who had shared some of it and to whom she could talk with at least a measure of calm, the hurt was always there—like a tender place in the corner of her mouth that the bit left" (p. 58). With Beloved there is no such pain: "Perhaps it was Beloved's distance from the events itself, or her thirst for hearing it—in any case it was an unexpected pleasure" (p. 58). Although Beloved's interest is a typically childish proclivity for a parent's distant past, her knowledge of past events that Sethe did not mention—in particular the diamond earrings—suggests a shared memory. Denver wonders about Beloved's recollections: "How did she know?" (p. 63).

Self-love wanes as the double Beloved gets closer to the events of her own death. Gaining strength and conviction from her own martyrdom, Beloved takes it upon herself to be Sethe's judge and jury. But in order to reach this point she must first distance Sethe from Denver and Paul D. She does this systematically, befriending the lonely Denver, seducing Paul D—a transgression less reprehensible if Beloved can be conceptualized as Sethe's double—and finally by demanding exclusive attention and caring from Sethe. Paul D soon walks out and Sethe wonders, not why her life is marked with so much misery, but why "every eighteen or twenty years her unlivable life would be interrupted by a short-lived glory?" (p. 173).

Once the double Beloved has stripped Sethe of any significant other who could provide Sethe with emotional balance, Beloved proceeds to consume her. "Dressed in Sethe's dresses, she stroked her skin with the palm of her hand. She imitated Sethe, talked the way she did, laughed her laugh and used her body the same way down to the walk, the way Sethe moved her hands, sighed through her nose, held her head. Sometimes coming upon them making men and women cookies or tacking scraps of cloth on Baby Suggs' old quilt, it was difficult for Denver to tell who was who" (p. 241). Sethe and Beloved become so exclusive with each other that they allow nothing to interfere with their relationship—not Paul D, not Denver, not the community, not even work.

The narcissistic stage, however, ends abruptly when Sethe discovers the scar on Beloved's neck that marks her crime. The irresolution of Sethe's act becomes a wedge between them. Sethe and Beloved begin to argue, Sethe attempting to impose parental restraints on the spoiled Beloved and Beloved rebelling against a mother she feels abdicated her responsibilities when she slit her throat. When Sethe eventually gives in to the enormity of the guilt, Beloved becomes her executioner, condemning her to a slow death in which redemption, no matter how earnest or feverish the repentance, is denied. Beloved is Sethe's own unforgiving memory, growing obese with Sethe's guilt while Sethe withers to an emaciated condition.

Since Sethe is locked into her self-imposed psychological terror she is incapable of extricating herself from the grip of her double. Denver takes it upon herself to save her mother, an ironic twist since, as Denver says, "the job she started out with, protecting Beloved from Sethe, changed to protecting her mother from Beloved. Now it was obvious that her mother could die and leave them both and what would Beloved do then?" (p. 243). Denver enlists the aid of the community, the women in particular, to intervene in a situation out of control. The ghost-turned-demon Beloved is exorcised by a community that knows too well the corrosive sin of guilt and who, like Ella, "didn't like the idea of past errors taking possession of the present" (p. 256).

While the double can explain Beloved in psychological terms, it cannot explain the fact that Beloved is visible and real to the other characters as well—Denver, Paul D, the women in the community. Her manifestation is a slow and careful process, Morrison purposely offering revelation in degrees. Though initially an invisible force only capable of the typical poltergeist activities—moving chairs, rattling cabinets, frightening dogs and children—Beloved eventually manifests herself as a ghostly apparition, then as a full-blooded human being. Finally, Beloved grows to obese proportions until she explodes under the collective gaze of an indignant gathering of women. Beloved can never be fully conceptualized because she is continually in a state of transition. But the fact that she can be seen at all is testimony to her power as a supernatural force, a semiotic haint.

Beloved represents not only the spirit of Sethe's daughter; she is also the projection of repressed collective memory of a violated people. The ghost of the murdered child, Beloved epitomizes the inconceivability not only of slavery but of the extent to which it dehumanized people. The real Sethe, Margaret Garner, killed her daughter so that she would not become a slave, a more frightening and terrifying prospect than death itself. Such a story plumbs the depths of human depravity, something that most people choose not to contemplate. Morrison says she wrote *Beloved* convinced that "this has got to be the least read of all the books I'd written because it is about something that the characters don't want to remember, I don't want to remember, black people don't want to remember, white people don't want to remember. I mean, it's national amnesia." [42]

The fact that Morrison did write the book and that it is such a success suggests that readers feel the same need as Morrison to purge themselves; once again, writer, audience, and text engage in a dynamic of identification. Beloved, then, functions as supernatural memory relived for the sake of psychic and spiritual rehabilitation. Only through memory can the past be integrated into the present providing meaning to what it means to be human.

Since Morrison's assumption in writing *Beloved* is that everyone wants to forget, she exerts considerable creative energy in making us remember. Her own characters live a daily struggle to ward off the ever-present past. When Sethe suggests to Baby Suggs that they could move from the haunted 124, Baby Suggs responds, "What'd be the point. . . ? Not a house in the country ain't paced to its rafters with some dead Negro's grief" (p. 5). Baby Suggs also suffers memory loss with regard to her eight children, all now gone. She says, "My first born. All I can remember of her is how she loved the burned bottom of Bread. Can you beat that? Eight children and that's all I remember." Sethe remarks, "That's all you let yourself remember" (p. 5). But Sethe, too, only remembers in snatches; her own children are distant memories: "As for the rest she worked hard to remember as close to nothing as was safe" (p. 6). When Stamp Paid approaches 124, he senses the history of incredible pain and suffering that "was the mumbling of the black and angry dead" (p. 198). The atmosphere created by this conglomeration of dead souls Stamp Paid likens to a jungle, but one implanted in blacks by whites: "And it grew. It spread. In, through and after life, it spread, until it invaded the whites who had made it. Touched them every one. Changed and altered them. Made them bloody, silly, worse than even they wanted to be, so scared were they of the jungle they had made" (pp. 198–99). And finally, on Paul D's return to Sethe, he attempts to put the past behind him: "Me and you, we got more yesterday than anybody. We need some kind of tomorrow" (p. 273).

While this chapter in Sethe's and Paul's life ends on a hopeful note—both having come to grips with their yesterdays—the novel does not end with any conciliatory remarks. Lest readers think they can read the book, feel cleansed, and then lay it down, Morrison provides an unsettling coda. "It was not a story to pass on," she says, though indeed that is what she has just done. After acknowledging the unsuitability of retelling this story, she then accuses her characters, and by implication, her readership and herself, of convenient memories: "They forgot her like a bad dream" (p. 274). By drawing attention to the literary production of her novel and to the casual nature in which it is ingested and then forgotten, Morrison has anticipated the inevitable and final reader response.

Despite the pessimism that marks the ending, *Beloved*—as well as her other works—endeavors to transcend the restrictive notion of time, invoking the supernatural as both a figurative and actual means to reunion with the past. The supernatural in Morrison's world may inevitably be historicity—the blind horsemen, the chevaliers, Circe, Ryna, Shalimar, the night women, Macon Dead, Beloved. Only by recovering that past, Morrison suggests, can individuals be provided with a total vision of their world and, hence, a foundation of truth without which there would be no hope for "some kind of tomorrow."

Just as Morrison appears to have stretched the reader's endurance as a participator in the remaking of reality to the extreme, she creates *Jazz*, a metafictional fiction that commits the supreme transgression—it calls into question the very authority of authorship. She effects this with the use of a narrator as enigmatic and ghostly as Beloved and possesed of a similar feminine, African-American consciousness, the difference being that the uncanny, or that which should remain secret, is not a collectively repressed national disgrace, but a collectively dormant national imagination so dependent on the voice of power it never thinks to question the very legitimacy of the narrative itself and, hence, the truth as presented by a single individual. While some critics see this as a failure on Morrison's part, a lapse into the quagmire of indeterminacy, Morrison is not rendering her art impotent, but devolving upon the reader the responsibility for his or her own vision. When the narrator at the end of the novel says that "you are free to [remake me] and I am free

to let you remake me" (p. 229), she exhorts the reader to engage in
creation rather than consumption.

To effect this response from her audience, Morrison pulls out all
the stops in *Jazz*—she creates a literature that is simultaneously one
of disillusion and revision. She suggests that reality is unknowable,
but rather than see this as a condition of disillusionment, she offers
it as an opportunity to alter reality. Morrison relinquishes ultimate
responsibility for prescribing action, thus creating a "universe of
fiction animated by ominipotence of thought shared between author
and reader."[43] Morrison avoids what Robert Roth calls "authorial
dominance." As he says, "Instead of trying to deduce the writer's
intentions, readers are engaged in a productive dialogue in which
their own purposes and practices come into play, often taking the
foreground."[44] If the author abdicates her role as literary Moses this
does not mean she is enslaved to a tyrannical readership. "Rather,"
Roth states, "it leads to a sharing of control, to a breaking down
of the adversarial writer-reader relationship. Instead of designing a
product meant to have a specific effect on another person, the writer
is engaged in a social process." This, in turn, creates "a kind of
audience awareness that has more to do with gift-giving than with
calculating."[45] Morrison herself says, "I don't shut doors at the end
of books. There is always a resolution of a sort but there are always
possiblilities—choices."[46] In *Jazz* Morrison initiates a dialogue with
her readership that may very well create a text of revision in life that
she avoided in fiction.

The relationship between narrative and audience in *Jazz* is medi-
ated by the narrator, a voice that is both speaker and text, the book
itself, and which must be African-American, given the authority,
almost arrogance, with which she portrays black characters and the
uncertainty with which she characterizes whites; and feminine since
her method of narration begs for the distinct feminine desire for
connectedness and shared knowing. Immediately the narrator engages the reader in a conspiritorial process of determining meaning
by whispering to the reader, "Shh, I know that woman" (p. 3).
This form of address suggests that what the narrator is about to
reveal, whispered as it is in secrecy (heard only by the reader), is
gossip or rumor and not necessarily fact. The very nature of gos-

sip—aside from the not infrequent propensity for character assasina-
tion—is dialogic: it invites an exchange between teller and listener
of speculation and interpretation. Indeed, the narrator occasionally
interrupts the narrative to ask the reader/listener questions. Some of
these questions are rhetorical—"What was I thinking of?" (p. 160)—
not wishing to provoke any response; others only seek affirmation
from the reader—"And although the pain is theirs, I share it, don't I?
Of course. Of course" (p. 219). But they presume an awareness of,
and even inadvertently invite, alternative analyses. The narrator con-
sciously arrives at this conclusion at the end of the novel when she
literally and figuratively leaves herself as text in the hands of the
reader: "Look where your hands are. Now" (p. 229).

The narrator treats the reader to not just one but two titillating
stories and sets of fascinating characters—Joe, Violet, and Dorcas;
and Vera Louise, True Belle, Golden Gray, Wild woman, and Hunters Hunter. During the course of both narratives, the narrator expresses an insecurity about her own perceptions. This is especially
true when reconstructing Golden Gray since the African-American
consciousness that informs *Jazz* must find it most difficult and certainly painful to prescribe motives to an essentially racist character.
Morrison's investigation of what she calls the "Africanist presence"
in white American writers' works was primarily a result of her own
concerns about how gender and race influenced her writings. She
says, "I am interested in what prompts and makes possible this process of entering what one is estranged from—and in what disables
the foray, for purposes of fiction, into corners of the consciousness
held off and away from the reach of the writer's imagination. My
work requires me to think about how free I can be as an African-
American woman writer in my genderized, sexualized, wholly racial-
ized worlds." [47]

The narrator wrestles with how to portray Golden Gray, the spoiled
mulatto who denies his black heritage. Possessed only of True Belle's
memory of Golden Gray, she must reconstruct—imagine—Golden
Gray's encounter with his father, Hunters Hunter, and Wild woman:
"I've thought about him a lot, wondered whether he was what True
Belle loved and Violet too. Or the vain and hincty pinch-nose worry-
ing about his coat and the ivory buttons on his waistcoat? Come

all that way to insult not his father but his race" (p. 143). In her rendition, the narrator vacillates between condemnation and praise, hate and love, scorn and pity in an endeavor to arrive judiciously at the truth. Golden Gray's rescue of Wild woman is construed as "his own dark purpose" (p. 146), a way to "impress his father with his willingness, his honor" (p. 154) while his treatment of the bleeding and nearly comatose Wild woman becomes a source of confusion for the narrator: "That is what makes me worry about him. How he thinks first of his clothes, and not the woman. How he checks the fastenings, but not her breath" (p. 151). Eventually, in a fit of rage, the narrator accuses Golden Gray of being the agent of his own dishonest narrative, a "hypocrite . . . shaping a story for himself to tell somebody, to tell his father, naturally" (p. 154). But the narrator's accusation becomes self-reflexive, an acknowledgment of her own inadequacy as a storyteller: "What was I thinking of? How could I have imagined him so poorly? . . . I have been careless and stupid and it infuriates me to discover (again) how unreliable I am" (p. 161).

At this juncture the narrator learns that her emotional reactions to Golden Gray are insufficient and unreliable since they are colored by the narrator's own enculturation: "Not hating him is not enough; liking, loving him is not useful. I have to alter things" (p. 161). To understand Golden Gray, the narrator must deconstruct herself, what Morrison calls the process of *becoming*: "Imagining is not merely looking or looking at; nor is it taking oneself intact into the other. It is, for the purposes of work, *becoming*."[48] By dissolving the subject/object relationship with Golden Gray, the narrator is free to "be a shadow who wishes him well," "dream a nice dream for him, and another of him," or "contemplate his pain and by doing so ease it, diminish it" (p. 161). Once the narrator engages in the imaginative act of merging with the consciousness of Golden Gray, she can "be the language that wishes him well, speaks his name, wakes him when his eyes need to be open" (p. 161), a generosity that constitutes an act of love and an invitation to the readers to engage in their own process of becoming.

While the narrator imposes a most exacting series of checks and balances on her narrative of Golden Gray, she is less scrupulous in her recounting of Violet and Joe, predicting inaccurately that they were bound to repeat the violence that had nearly destroyed their marriage in the first place. Though she blames the city for distracting her, she might more accurately blame her own stubborness in remaining "intact," taking for granted her own racial consciousness as a guarantee of truth: "Busy, they were, busy being original, complicated, changeable—human, I guess you'd say, while I was the predictable one, confused in my solitude into arrogance, thinking my space, my view was the only one that was or that mattered" (p. 220). But while at least one critic calls this indeterminancy a failure on Morrison's part—a "relentless vigilance" that ends up "indicting other writers for failures of vision and apologizing for her own"[49]—it is a remarkable admission of the inadequacy of a single vision, even if that vision enjoys insider status, that is, membership in a particular race. If the voice in *Jazz* calls into question not only her ability to imagine white people, but black people as well, and then offers up her narrative, herself, to the readers to remake, she is telling her readers that they, too, are capable of a vision that incorporates double- or even multiconsciousness. The accuracy of such a vision is less important than the act of imagining itself, especially as it is motivated by love.

Jazz represents the culmination of Morrison's fictional attempts to connect with her readers, to move them beyond sympathy, empathy, and even understanding of what it means to be black in a white America. She wants her readers to tap into an imagination so vivid, so all-encompassing that double-consciousness becomes as much their psychic state of being as it is hers. Indeed, Morrison may very well reject the desire to transcend or resolve double-consciousness in her novels, using, even manipulating, it instead to invoke reader responsibility. Her own canon resists determinancy and absolutism as an anathema to spiritual growth and understanding, implying that the only real meaning in life comes from a healthy respect for and engagement in its capacity for untruth. Like Keats's "living hand fragment" in which he attempts to "touch" the reader—"see, here it is—/I hold it towards you"[50]—Morrison's books, especially *Jazz* in its invocation to the readers to "make me, remake me," attempt to make a connection with the reader. But Morrison finally moves beyond guilt, beyond anger, and beyond fear into the irresistible realm of spiritual love. No longer content with readers misunderstanding her motives, the narrator—and of course Morrison—finally makes public "that I have loved only you, surrendered my whole self reckless to you and nobody else. That I want you to love me back and show it to me. That I love the way you hold me, how close you let me be to you. I like your fingers on and on, lifting, turning. I have watched your face for a long time now, and missed your eyes when you went away from me. Talking to you and hearing you answer—that's the kick" (p. 229). The love affair between books and readers should not remain a clandestine act of secret pleasure but a declaration of love manifest in the process of call and response. In *Jazz*, as in all of her novels, writer, text, and audience converge on the indeterminacy of meaning, and it is in this divine, and perhaps never-ending, process of determination that those afflicted with double-consciousness and those who share their suffering, are made whole.

Notes

Introduction

1. Elizabeth Kastor, review of *Beloved*, by Toni Morrison, in *Washington Post*, rpt. *Raleigh News and Observer*, 23 October 1987, D3.
2. These appear, in order, in the following reviews: Paul Gray, *Time*, 21 September 1987, 75; Walter Clemons, *Newsweek*, 28 September 1987, 74; Michiko Kakutani, *New York Times*, 2 September 1987, C24; Michael Dorris, *Detroit News*, 6 September 1987, L2.
3. Review of *Beloved*, by Toni Morrison, in *Publisher's Weekly*, 17 July 1987, 53.
4. Merle Rubin, review of *Beloved*, by Toni Morrison, in *Christian Science Monitor*, 5 October 1987, 20.
5. Leonard's review appeared in *Los Angeles Times Book Review*, 30 August 1987, 1, and Clemons's review appeared in *Newsweek*, 28 September 1987, 74.
6. Joanne Braxton, *Wild Women in the Whirlwind: Afro-American Culture and the Contemporary Literary Renaissance* (New Brunswick, N.J.: Rutgers Univ. Press, 1990), xxix.
7. Faye Chadwell, review of *Jazz*, by Toni Morrison, in *Library Journal*, 15 April 1992, 122.
8. *Chronicle of Higher Education*, 22 April 1992, A6.
9. Ibid.
10. David Gates, review of *Jazz*, by Toni Morrison, in *Newsweek*, 27 April 1992, 66.
11. W. Lawrence Hogue, "Literary Production: A Silence in Afro-American Critical Practices," in *Belief Versus Theory in Black American Literary Criticism*, ed. Joe Weixlmann and Chester J. Fontenat (Greenwood, Fla.: Penkevill, 1986), 36.
12. Ibid., 34.
13. Ibid., 41.

14. Ibid., 44.
15. Stanley Crouch, review of *Beloved*, by Toni Morrison, in *New Republic*, 19 October 1987, 43.
16. Ibid., 42.
17. Ibid., 40.
18. Patricia Collins, "Learning from the Outsider Within: The Sociological Significance of Black Feminist Thought," *Social Problems* 33 (December 1986): 526.
19. Michael Awkward, *Inspiriting Influences: Tradition, Revision, and Afro-American Women's Novels* (New York: Columbia Univ. Press, 1989), 67.
20. Henry Louis Gates Jr., *The Signifying Monkey: A Theory of Afro-American Literary Criticism* (New York: Oxford Univ. Press, 1988), xxii–xxiii.
21. Ibid., 50.
22. Ibid., 53.
23. Ibid., 51.
24. Ibid., 49.
25. Ibid., 50.
26. Terence Hawkes, *Structuralism and Semiotics* (Berkeley: Univ. of California Press, 1977), 105–6.
27. Ibid., 106.
28. Susan Blake, "Toni Morrison," in *Dictionary of Literary Biography*, vol. 33, *Afro-American Fiction Writers After 1955*, ed. Thadious Davis and Trudier Harris (Detroit: Gale Research, 1984), 188.
29. Hogue, "Literary Production," 43.
30. Houston Baker, "Belief, Theory, and Blues: Notes for a Post-Structuralist Criticism of Afro-American Literature," in *Belief Versus Theory in Black American Literary Criticism*, ed. Joe Weixlmann and Chester J. Fontenat (Greenwood, Fla.: Penkevill, 1986), 18.
31. Harry Reed, "Toni Morrison, *Song of Solomon* and Black Cultural Nationalism," *Centennial Review*, 32 (Winter 1988): 50.
32. Ibid., 63.
33. Ibid., 51.
34. Norris Clark, "Gwendolyn Brooks and a Black Aesthetic," in *A Life Distilled: Gwendolyn Brooks, Her Poetry and Fiction*, ed. Maria K. Mootry and Gary Smith (Urbana: Univ. of Illinois Press, 1987), 82.
35. Ibid.
36. Toni Morrison, "Rootedness: The Ancestor as Foundation," in *Black Women Writers (1950–1980): A Critical Evaluation*, ed. Mari Evans (Garden City, N.Y.: Anchor Press/Doubleday, 1984), 344–45.
37. Awkward, *Inspiriting Influences*, 67.
38. Ibid., 11.
39. Ibid., 12.

40. Ibid., 14.
41. Theresa Enos, " 'An Eternal Golden Braid': Rhetor as Audience, Audience as Rhetor," in *A Sense of Audience in Written Communication*, ed. Gesa Kirsch and Duane H. Roen (London: Sage, 1990), 100.
42. Quoted in Enos, " 'An Eternal Golden Braid,' " 103.
43. Enos, " 'An Eternal Golden Braid,' " 102.
44. Ibid., 106.
45. Robert Roth, "Deconstructing Audience: A Post-Structuralist Rereading," in *A Sense of Audience*, 175.
46. Ibid., 181.
47. Robert Stepto, *From Behind the Veil: A Study of Afro-American Narrative* (Urbana: Univ. of Illinois Press, 1979), xi.
48. See Stepto's discussion of Du Bois's use of the Jim Crow car in *From Behind the Veil*, 52–91.

Chapter 1. Beauty and Love: The Morrison Aesthetic

1. Norris Clark, "Gwendolyn Brooks and a Black Aesthetic," in *A Life Distilled: Gwendolyn Brooks, Her Poetry and Fiction*, ed. Maria K. Mootry and Gary Smith (Urbana: Univ. of Illinois Press, 1987), 82.
2. Ibid.
3. Ibid., 83.
4. Ibid., 92–93.
5. Henry Louis Gates Jr., ed., *"Race," Writing, and Difference* (Chicago: Univ. of Chicago Press, 1986), 5.
6. Interview with Jean Strouse, "Toni Morrison's Black Magic," *Newsweek*, 30 March 1981, 52.
7. See Jane Somerville's discussion in "Idealized Beauty and the Denial of Love in Toni Morrison's *Bluest Eye*," in *Bulletin of the West Virginia Association of College English Teachers* 9 (Spring 1986): 18–23.
8. Toni Morrison, *The Bluest Eye* (New York: Washington Square Press, 1970), 20. Subsequent references to this work will be made in the text.
9. Sander Gilman, "Black Bodies, White Bodies: Toward an Iconography of Female Sexuality in Late Nineteenth-Century Art, Medicine, and Literature," in *"Race," Writing, and Difference*, 231.
10. Ibid., 250.
11. Alice Walker, *In Search of Our Mother's Gardens* (San Diego: Harcourt Brace Jovanovich, 1983), 290.
12. ABC, *Phil Donahue*, 1988.
13. Eugene Bank, "Why Skin Color No Longer Makes a Difference," *Ebony*, May 1980, 182.
14. Walker, *Mother's Gardens*, 299.
15. Ibid., 301.

16. Paraphrased by Missy Dehn Kubitschek in *Claiming the Heritage: African-American Women Novelists and History* (Jackson: Univ. Press of Mississippi, 1991), 96.

17. Ibid., 92.

18. Paula Giddings, *Where and When I Enter* (New York: William Morrow, 1984), 115.

19. Walker, *Mother's Gardens*, 308.

20. Jennet Conant, "A Question of Class and Color: Spike Lee Takes a Hard Look at Black College Life," *Newsweek*, 15 February 1988, 62.

21. Elsie Washington, "The Bluest Eye," *Essence*, January 1988, 114.

22. Harriette Pipes McAdoo, ed., *Black Families* (Beverly Hills, Calif.: Sage, 1988), 153.

23. Michel Marriott, "Light-Skinned Men: Problems and Privileges," *Essence*, November 1988, 133.

24. Ibid., 76.

25. Dahleen Glanton, "Many Shades of Black, and a Caste System, Too?" *Raleigh News and Observer*, 6 September 1989, D3.

26. Norris Clark, "Flying Black: Toni Morrison's *The Bluest Eye*, *Sula* and *Song of Solomon*," *Minority Voices* 4 (Fall 1980): 51.

27. Barbara Christian, *Black Women Novelists: The Development of a Tradition, 1892–1976* (Westport, Conn.: Greenwood Press, 1980), 22.

28. C. A. Davis, "Self, Society and Myth," *Contemporary Literature* 23 (1982): 328.

29. Ibid., 330.

30. Toni Morrison, *Song of Solomon* (New York: New American Library, 1977), 77. Subsequent references to this work will be made in the text.

31. Toni Morrison, *Tar Baby* (New York: New American Library, 1981), 103. Subsequent references to this work will be made in the text.

32. Toni Morrison, *Sula* (New York: New American Library, 1973), 22. Subsequent references to this work will be made in the text.

33. Toni Morrison, *Beloved* (New York: Knopf, 1987), 247. Subsequent references to this work will be made in the text.

34. Toni Morrison, *Jazz* (New York: Knopf, 1992), 29. Subsequent references to this work will be made in the text.

35. E. Ann Kaplan, *Women and Film: Both Sides of the Camera* (New York: Methuen, 1983), 14.

36. Ibid.

37. Ibid., 14–15.

38. Kant is an ironic choice for discussion of Morrison's aesthetic since, according to Gates in *"Race," Writing and Difference*, Kant was an unabashed racist equating "stupidity" and "blackness." Gates says, "One might say that Kant's *Observations on the Feeling of the Beautiful and Sublime* functions to deconstruct, for the black reader, Kant's *Foun-*

dations [of the Metaphysics of Morals], revealing it to be just one more example of the remarkable capacity of European philosophers to conceive of 'humanity' in ideal terms (white, male), yet despise, abhor, colonize, or exploit human beings who are not 'ideal' " (408).

39. Immanuel Kant, "Analytic of the Beautiful," in *Critical Theory Since Plato*, ed. Hazard Adams (New York: Harcourt Brace Jovanovich, 1971), 387.

40. Ibid., 388.

41. Ibid., 393.

42. William Carlos Williams, *Paterson* (New York: New Directions Books, 1963), 116. Subsequent references to this work will be made in the text.

43. Hazard Adams, in the introduction to Kant's "Analytic of the Beautiful," 378.

44. Walter Scott Peterson, *An Approach to Paterson* (New Haven: Yale Univ. Press, 1967), 119.

45. Nellie McKay, "An Interview with Toni Morrison," *Contemporary Literature* 24 (Winter 1983): 422.

46. William Carlos Williams, *The Autobiography of William Carlos Williams* (New York: New Directions Books, 1951), 55.

47. Paul Mariani, *William Carlos Williams: A New World Naked* (New York: McGraw-Hill, 1981), 415.

48. Toni Morrison, *Playing in the Dark: Whiteness and the Literary Imagination* (Cambridge: Harvard Univ. Press, 1992), 17.

49. Kant, "Analytic of the Beautiful," 393.

50. Thom Gunn, "William Carlos Williams," *Encounter* 25 (July 1965): 71–72.

51. Kant, "Analytic of the Beautiful," 393.

52. Morrison, *Playing in the Dark*, 64.

Chapter 2. Distant Mothers and Incomprehensible Fathers

1. K. Sue Jewell, *Survival of the Black Family: The Institutional Impact of U.S. Social Policy* (New York: Praeger, 1988), 13.

2. Ibid., 15.

3. Christopher Clark, "Household Economy," *Journal of Social History* 13 (Winter 1979): 169.

4. Nellie McKay, "An Interview with Toni Morrison," *Contemporary Literature*, 24 (Winter 1983): 420.

5. Ibid., 428.

6. Interview with Bonnie Angelo, "The Pain of Being Black," *Time*, 22 May 1989, 122.

7. Jewell, *Survival of the Black Family*, 19.

8. Jacqueline Jones, *Labor of Love, Labor of Sorrow: Black Women, Work,*

and the Family from Slavery to the Present (New York: Basic Books, 1985), 9.

9. Ibid.

10. Clark in "Household Economy" and Erlene Stetson in "Studying Slavery" investigate the effect of the industrial revolution on the American home.

11. Nancy Armstrong, *Desire and Domestic Fiction* (New York: Oxford Univ. Press, 1987), 201.

12. Barbara Welter, "The Cult of True Womanhood: 1820–1860," in *American Family in Social-Historical Perspective*, ed. Michael Gordon (New York: St. Martin's Press, 1973), 225.

13. Bell Hooks, *Ain't I a Woman?* (Boston: South End Press, 1981), 48.

14. Ibid., 47.

15. Ibid., 16.

16. Deborah White, in *Ar'n't I a Woman?: Female Slaves in the Plantation South* (New York: Norton, 1985), reconstructs the economic contributions of slave women to their households. She finds that they engaged in a variety of hard, physical jobs, especially after their child-bearing years.

17. Hooks, *Ain't I a Woman?*, 48.

18. Ibid., 91.

19. Andrew Billingsley, *Black Families in White America* (Englewood Cliffs, N.J.: Prentice-Hall, 1968), 145.

20. Jones, *Labor of Love*, 99.

21. Ibid., 103.

22. Ibid., 104.

23. Ibid., 7.

24. Hooks, *Ain't I a Woman?*, 94.

25. Ibid., 97.

26. Ibid., 177.

27. Daniel P. Moynihan's *Negro Family: The Case for National Action* (1965) warned, much like Frazier's study, of the deterioration of the black family as a result of the increasing number of female-headed households. His report has been subject to a flurry of attacks by the black community, who see his report as racist in its negative comparison of the black family to the white ideal.

28. Hooks, *Ain't I a Woman?*, 83.

29. Ibid., 182.

30. Audrey Chapman, "Male-Female Relations: How the Past Affects the Present," in *Black Families*, ed. Harriette Pipes McAdoo (Beverly Hills, Calif.: Sage, 1988), 192–95.

31. John L. McAdoo, "The Roles of Black Fathers in the Socialization of Black Children," in *Black Families*, 258.

32. Angela Davis, *Women, Race and Class* (New York: Random House, 1981), 121.

33. Ibid., 122.

34. Michele Wallace, *Black Macho and the Myth of the Superwoman* (New York: Dial Press, 1979), 124.

35. Elizabeth Pleck, "The Two-Parent Household: Black Family Structure in Late Nineteenth-Century Boston," in *American Family in Social-Historical Perspective*, ed. Michael Gordon (New York: St. Martin's Press, 1973), 168.

36. Ibid., 170.

37. E. Franklin Frazier, *The Negro Family in the United States* (1939; rpt., Chicago: Univ. of Chicago Press, 1966), 101.

38. Sidney Willhelm, *Black in a White America* (Cambridge, Mass.: Schenkman, 1983), 32.

39. "U.S. Family Has Eroded Steadily Over Past 8 Years, Researchers Say," in *Los Angeles Times*, rpt. *Raleigh News and Observer*, 21 July 1988, A16.

40. Jualynne Dodson, "Conceptualizations of Black Families," in *Black Families*, 77.

41. Ibid., 82.

42. Andrew Billingsley, *Black Families in White America*, 15–21.

43. Jewell, *Survival of the Black Family*, 12.

44. Ibid.

45. Ibid., 13.

46. Ibid., 15.

47. Much has been written in the last twenty years rejecting Frazier's naturalization of the black patriarchy. Recent research has emphasized that female-headed households are not aberrant, but are a response to culturally imposed economic barriers and as such have served in a highly positive way to sustain the beleaguered black family. See Julianne Malveaux's "The Economic Statuses of Black Families," in *Black Families*, 133–47; Sharon Harley's "For the Good of Family and Race: Gender, Work, and Domestic Roles in the Black Community, 1880–1930," *Signs* 15 (Winter 1990), 346–49; Robert Staples's *Black Woman in America* (Chicago: Nelson-Hall, 1973); and Joyce Ladner's *Tomorrow's Tomorrow: The Black Woman* (Garden City, N.Y.: Doubleday, 1971). Other studies look to African influences on the development of the black family in America. In "Sapphire? The Issue of Dominance in the Slave Family, 1830–1865" in *To Toil the Livelong Day: America's Women at Work, 1780, 1980*, ed. Carol Groneman and Mary Beth Norton (Ithaca, N.Y.: Cornell Univ. Press, 1987), Christie Farnham states that premarital sex was accepted in many African cultures as a natural act and thus, "such a view of sexuality permitted the slave community to be

more accepting of female-headed families than was possible in white society," 82.

48. Interview with Bonnie Angelo, "The Pain of Being Black," *Time*, 22 May 1989, 122.

49. Susan Willis, "Eruptions of Funk," *Black American Literature Forum* 16 (1982): 34–42.

50. Anne Schaef, in *When Society Becomes an Addict* (San Francisco: Harper and Row, 1987), characterizes American society as an addictive system because it forces people to conform to one notion of reality. Individuals tend to measure themselves to a standard they cannot always live up to. Consequently, they retreat into a variety of coping mechanisms such as alcohol, work, or worry. In the Living Process System, individuals are alive because they trust their own perceptions and interpretations of reality.

51. Willis, "Eruptions of Funk," 41.

52. Ibid.

53. Ibid.

54. Frazier, *Negro Family*, 188.

55. Willis, "Eruptions of Funk," 34.

56. Barbara Christian, "Community and Nature: The Novels of Toni Morrison," *Journal of Ethnic Studies* 7 (Winter 1980): 65.

57. Jane Bakerman, "The Seams Can't Show: An Interview with Toni Morrison," *Black American Literature Forum* 12 (Summer 1978), 60.

58. Armstrong, *Desire and Domestic Fiction*, 182.

59. Willis, "Eruptions of Funk," 38.

60. Karla F. C. Holloway and Stephanie A. Demetrakopoulos, *New Dimensions of Spirituality* (New York: Greenwood Press, 1987), 163.

61. Ibid.

62. Ann Hulbert, review of *Jazz*, by Toni Morrison, in *New Republic*, 18 May 1992, 47.

63. As Andrew Billingsley says, in *Black Families in White America*, "Social workers have known for a long time that there is nothing like a good steady job with adequate and dependable income to make a man get married, stay married, remain with his family, and support it, while the absence of such economic viability is highly correlated with the refusal of men to insure the stability of their families" (24).

Chapter 3. Up in the Bottom: Morrison's Social Dialectic

1. Cynthia Edelberg, "Morrison's Voices: Formal Education, the Work Ethic, and the Bible," *American Literature* 58 (May 1986): 236–37.

2. Carol Iannone, "Toni Morrison's Career," *Commentary* 84 (December 1987): 61.

3. Ibid.

4. Roy Wallis, "Institutions," in *The Social Science Encyclopedia*, ed. Adam Kuper and Jessica Kuper (Boston: Routledge Kegan Paul, 1985), 399–400.

5. Susan Blake, "Toni Morrison," in *Dictionary of Literary Biography*, vol. 33, *Afro-American Fiction Writers After 1955*, ed. Thadious Davis and Trudier Harris (Detroit: Gale Research, 1984), 188.

6. Quoted in Robert Stepto, *From Behind the Veil: A Study of Afro-American Narrative* (Urbana: Univ. of Illinois Press, 1979), 69.

7. Ibid.

8. Max Weber's *The Protestant Ethic and the Spirit of Capitalism* (1904) emphasized the correlation between hard work and business growth.

9. Karla F. C. Holloway and Stephanie A. Demetrakopoulos, *New Dimensions of Spirituality* (New York: Greenwood Press, 1987), 71.

10. Wilfrid Samuels, "Liminality and the Search for Self in Toni Morrison's *Song of Solomon*," *Minority Voices* 5 (Spring-Fall 1981): 63.

11. Summarized by Christopher Clark in "Household Economy," *Journal of Social History* 13 (Winter 1979): 171–72.

12. Joyce Ladner, *Tomorrow's Tomorrow: The Black Woman* (Garden City, N.Y.: Doubleday, 1971), 227.

13. Stepto, *From Behind the Veil*, 66–67.

14. Ibid., 74.

15. Ibid., 67.

16. Ibid.

17. Ibid., 69.

18. Ibid., 91.

19. Andrew Billingsley, *Black Families in White America* (Englewood Cliffs, N.J.: Prentice-Hall, 1968), 98.

20. David Nielson, *Black Ethos: Northern Urban Negro Life and Thought, 1890–1930*, 2d ed. (1977; rpt. New York: Dial Press, 1982), 22.

21. Langston Hughes quoted in Nielson, *Black Ethos*, 47.

22. Nielson, *Black Ethos*, 59.

23. Ibid., 97.

24. Ibid.

25. Ibid., 1.

26. Ibid., 216.

27. Barbara Christian, *Black Women Novelists: The Development of a Tradition, 1892–1976* (Westport, Conn.: Greenwood Press, 1980), 155.

28. Ibid., 154.

29. Michael Awkward, *Inspiriting Influences: Tradition, Revision, and Afro-*

American Women's Novels (New York: Columbia Univ. Press, 1989), 12.

30. Ibid., 58.
31. A.J. Greimas paraphrased by Robert Scholes in *Structuralism in Literature* (New Haven: Yale Univ. Press, 1974), 103.
32. Scholes, *Structuralism in Literature*, 103.
33. Norris Clark, "Flying Black: Toni Morrison's *The Bluest Eye, Sula* and *Song of Solomon*," *Minority Voices* 4(2) (Fall 1980): 55.
34. Nielson, *Black Ethos*, 188.
35. Ibid., 187.
36. Ibid., 189.
37. Barbara Christian, "Community and Nature: The Novels of Toni Morrison," *Journal of Ethnic Studies* 7 (Winter 1980): 65.
38. Susan Blake, "Folklore and Community in *Song of Solomon*," *MELUS* 7 (Fall 1980): 82.
39. C.A. Davis, "Self, Society and Myth," *Contemporary Literature* 23 (1982): 339–40.
40. Quoted in Joanna Russ, *How to Suppress Women's Writing* (Austin: Univ. of Texas Press, 1983), 41.
41. Craig Werner, "The Briar Patch as Modernist Myth: Morrison, Barthes and Tar Baby As-Is," in *Critical Essays on Toni Morrison*, ed. Nellie McKay (Boston: G.K. Hall, 1988), 150–67.
42. Stepto, *From Behind the Veil*, 69.
43. James W. Coleman, "Beyond the Reach of Love and Caring: Black Life in Toni Morrison's *Song of Solomon*," *Obsidian* 2 (Winter 1986): 158.
44. Ibid., 151.
45. Ibid., 153.
46. Ibid., 160–61.
47. Blake, "Folklore and Community," 78.
48. Ibid., 80.
49. Werner, "Briar Patch as Modernist Myth," 157.
50. Holloway and Demetrakopoulos, *New Dimensions of Spirituality*, 132.
51. Werner, "Briar Patch as Modernist Myth," 166.
52. Ibid., 163.

Chapter 4. The Metaphysical Argument for the Supernatural

1. Henry Louis Gates Jr., *The Signifying Monkey: A Theory of Afro-American Literary Criticism* (New York: Oxford Univ. Press, 1988), 50.
2. Jacqueline De Weever, "Toni Morrison's Use of Fairy Tale, Folk Tale and Myth in the *Song of Solomon*," *Southern Folklore Quarterly* 44 (1980): 131.
3. Ibid., 132.

4. David Cowart, in "Faulkner and Joyce in Morrison's *Song of Solomon*," traces the presence of Joyce and Faulkner in *Song of Solomon*, in particular Joyce's concern with the myth of flight and Faulkner's emphasis on the importance of personal history. Cowart sees their presence as an indication of how Morrison "extends and modifies an inherited literary tradition . . . into a fiction of universal humanity and moral authority" (100). *American Literature* 62 (March 1990): 87–100.

5. Lauren Lepow, "Paradise Lost and Found: Dualism and Edenic Myth in Toni Morrison's *Tar Baby*," *Contemporary Literature* 28 (3) (1987): 365.

6. Henry Louis Gates Jr., *"Race," Writing, and Difference* (Chicago: Univ. of Chicago Press, 1986), 5.

7. Lepow, "Paradise Lost and Found," 364.

8. A good introduction to and summary of modern fantasy theory is included in *Critical Terms for Science Fiction and Fantasy*, ed. Gary Wolf (New York: Greenwood Press, 1986), xix–xxv.

9. Kathryn Hume, *Fantasy and Mimesis* (New York: Methuen, 1984), 6. Subsequent references to this work will be made in the text.

10. Theresa Enos, " 'An Eternal Golden Braid': Rhetor as Audience, Audience as Rhetor," in *A Sense of Audience in Written Communication*, ed. Gesa Kirsch and Duane H. Rouen (London: Sage, 1990), 101.

11. Lepow, "Paradise Lost and Found," 370.

12. Ibid., 371.

13. Enos, " 'An Eternal Golden Braid,' " 106.

14. Interview with Jean Strouse, "Toni Morrison's Black Magic," *Newsweek*, 30 March 1981, 54.

15. Ibid., 57.

16. George M. Foster, "Disease Etiologies in Non-Western Medical Systems," *American Anthropologist* 78 (1976): 775.

17. Ibid.

18. Ibid., 779.

19. In *Mules and Men* (Philadelphia: J. B. Lippincott, 1935), Hurston includes three sections in her appendix that deal with healing: "Formulae of Hoodoo Doctors," "Paraphernalia of Conjure," and "Prescriptions of Root Doctor." A cure for syphilis is "ashes of one good cigar, fifteen cents worth of blue ointment. Mix and put on the sores" (340).

20. Foster, "Disease Etiologies," 776.

21. Robert Scholes, *Structuralism in Literature* (New Haven: Yale Univ. Press, 1974), 60.

22. Jack Zipes, "Breaking the Magic Spell: Politics and the Fairy Tale," *New German Critique* 14 (1986): 118–19.

23. De Weever, "Toni Morrison's Use of Fairy Tale," 131.

24. Diane Kim Bowman, "Flying High: The American Icarus in Morrison, Roth, and Updike," *Perspectives on Contemporary Literature* 8 (1982): 10.
25. A. J. Greimas quoted in Scholes, *Structuralism in Literature*, 90.
26. Leslie A. Harris, "Myth as Structure in Toni Morrison's *Song of Solomon*," *MELUS* 7 (Fall 1980): 70.
27. Jane Bakerman, "The Seams Can't Show: An Interview with Toni Morrison," *Black American Literature Forum* 12 (Summer 1978): 56–60.
28. Toni Morrison quoted in the Strouse *Newsweek* interview, 53.
29. Damian Grant, *Realism* (London: Methuen, 1970; rpt., 1978), 9.
30. Ibid., 55.
31. Tzvetan Todorov quoted in Scholes, *Structuralism in Literature*, 101–2.
32. Grant, *Realism*, 59.
33. Grant, *Realism*, 5–6.
34. Susan Willis, "Eruptions of Funk," *Black American Literature Forum* 16 (1982): 41.
35. Allan Gardner Lloyd-Smith, *Uncanny American Fiction* (New York: St. Martin's Press, 1989), 9.
36. Schelling quoted in Lloyd-Smith, *Uncanny American Fiction*, 1.
37. Toni Morrison quoted in Elizabeth Kastor, review of *Beloved*, in *Washington Post*, rpt. *Raleigh News and Observer*, 23 October 1987, D3.
38. Interview with Bonnie Angelo, "The Pain of Being Black," *Time*, 22 May 1989, 120.
39. Lloyd-Smith, *Uncanny American Fiction*, 10.
40. Ibid., 12.
41. Ibid., 8.
42. Angelo, *Time* interview, 120.
43. Lloyd-Smith, *Uncanny American Fiction*, 9.
44. Robert Roth, "Deconstructing Audience: A Post-Structuralist Rereading," in *A Sense of Audience*, 181.
45. Ibid., 181.
46. Bessie W. Jones, "An Interview with Toni Morrison," in *The World of Toni Morrison*, ed. Bessie W. Jones and Audrey L. Vinson (Dubuque, Iowa: Kendall/Hunt, 1985), 135.
47. Toni Morrison, *Playing in the Dark: Whiteness and the Literary Imagination* (Cambridge, Mass: Harvard Univ. Press, 1992), 4.
48. Ibid.
49. Ann Hulbert, review of *Jazz*, by Toni Morrison, in *New Republic*, 18 May 1992, 48.
50. John Keats quoted in Gerald Graff, "Determinancy/Indeterminancy," in *Critical Terms for Literary Study*, ed. Frank Lentricchia and Thomas McLaughlin (Chicago: Univ. of Chicago Press, 1990), 172.

Bibliography

Adams, Hazard. *Critical Theory Since Plato*. New York: Harcourt Brace Jovanovich, 1971.

Angelo, Bonnie. "The Pain of Being Black." *Time*, 22 May 1989, 120–22.

Armstrong, Nancy. *Desire and Domestic Fiction*. New York: Oxford Univ. Press, 1987.

Awkward, Michael. *Inspiriting Influences: Tradition, Revision, and Afro-American Women's Novels*. New York: Columbia Univ. Press, 1989.

Baker, Houston. "Belief, Theory, and Blues: Notes for a Post-Structuralist Criticism of Afro-American Literature." In *Belief Versus Theory in Black American Literary Criticism*. Ed. Joe Weixlmann and Chester J. Fontenat, 5–30. Greenwood, Fla.: Penkevill, 1986.

Bakerman, Jane. "The Seams Can't Show: An Interview with Toni Morrison." *Black American Literature Forum* 12 (Summer 1978): 56–60.

Bambara, Toni Cade. *The Salt-Eaters*. New York: Random House, 1981.

Bank, Eugene. "Why Skin Color No Longer Makes a Difference." *Ebony*, May 1980, 178–82.

Billingsley, Andrew. *Black Families in White America*. Englewood Cliffs, N.J.: Prentice-Hall, 1968.

Blake, Susan. "Folklore and Community in *Song of Solomon*." *MELUS* 7 (Fall 1980): 77–82.

———. "Toni Morrison." In *Dictionary of Literary Biography*. Vol. 33, *Afro-American Fiction Writers After 1955*. Ed. Thadious Davis and Trudier Harris, 187–99. Detroit: Gale Research, 1984.

Bowman, Diane Kim. "Flying High: The American Icarus in Morrison, Roth, and Updike." *Perspectives on Contemporary Literature* 8 (1982): 10–17.

Braxton, Joanne. *Wild Women in the Whirlwind: Afro-American Culture and the Contemporary Literary Renaissance*. New Brunswick, N.J.: Rutgers Univ. Press, 1990.

Chadwell, Faye. Review of *Jazz*, by Toni Morrison. *Library Journal*, 15 April 1992, 122.

Chapman, Audrey. "Male-Female Relations: How the Past Affects the Present." In *Black Families*. Ed. Harriette Pipes McAdoo, 192–95. Beverly Hills, Calif.: Sage, 1988.

Christian, Barbara. *Black Women Novelists: The Development of a Tradition, 1892–1976*. Westport, Conn.: Greenwood Press, 1980.

———. "Community and Nature: The Novels of Toni Morrison." *Journal of Ethnic Studies* 7 (Winter 1980): 65–78.

Chronicle of Higher Education. 22 April 1992, A6.

Clark, Christopher. "Household Economy." *Journal of Social History* 13 (Winter 1979): 169–89.

Clark, Norris. "Flying Black: Toni Morrison's *The Bluest Eye*, *Sula* and *Song of Solomon*." *Minority Voices* 4 (Fall 1980): 51–63.

———. "Gwendolyn Brooks and a Black Aesthetic." In *A Life Distilled: Gwendolyn Brooks, Her Poetry and Fiction*. Ed. Maria K. Mootry and Gary Smith, 81–100. Urbana: Univ. of Illinois Press, 1987.

Clemons, Walter. Review of *Beloved*, by Toni Morrison. *Newsweek*, 28 September 1987, 74–75.

Coleman, James W. "Beyond the Reach of Love and Caring: Black Life in Toni Morrison's *Song of Solomon*." *Obsidian* 2 (Winter 1986): 151–61.

Collins, Patricia. "Learning from the Outsider Within: The Sociological Significance of Black Feminist Thought." *Social Problems* 33 (December 1986): 514–32.

Conant, Jennet. "A Question of Class and Color: Spike Lee Takes a Hard Look at Black College Life." *Newsweek*, 15 February 1988, 62.

Cowart, David. "Faulkner and Joyce in Morrison's *Song of Solomon*." *American Literature* 62 (March 1980): 87–100.

Crouch, Stanley. Review of *Beloved*, by Toni Morrison. *New Republic*, 19 October 1987, 38–43.

Davis, Angela. *Women, Race and Class*. New York: Random House, 1981.

Davis, C. A. "Self, Society and Myth." *Contemporary Literature* 23 (1982): 323–42.

De Weever, Jacqueline. "Toni Morrison's Use of Fairy Tale, Folk Tale and Myth in the *Song of Solomon*." *Southern Folklore Quarterly* 44 (1980): 131–44.

Dodson, Jualynne. "Conceptualizations of Black Families." In *Black Families*. Ed. Harriette Pipes McAdoo, 77–90. Beverly Hills, Calif.: Sage, 1988.

Dorris, Michael. Review of *Beloved*, by Toni Morrison. *Detroit News*, 6 September 1987, L2.

Du Bois, W. E. B. *Souls of Black Folk*. Chicago: A. C. McClurg, 1903.

Eagleton, Terry. *Marxism and Literary Criticism*. Los Angeles: Univ. of California Press, 1976.

Edelberg, Cynthia. "Morrison's Voices: Formal Education, the Work Ethic, and the Bible." *American Literature* 58 (May 1986): 217–37.

Enos, Theresa. " 'An Eternal Golden Braid': Rhetor as Audience, Audience as Rhetor." In *A Sense of Audience in Written Communication*. Ed. Gesa Kirsch and Duane H. Roen, 99–115. London: Sage, 1990.

Farnham, Christie. "Sapphire? The Issue of Dominance in the Slave Family, 1830–1865." In *To Toil the Livelong Day: America's Women at Work, 1780, 1980*. Ed. Carol Groneman and Mary Beth Norton, 68–86. Ithaca, N.Y.: Cornell Univ. Press, 1987.

Foster, George M. "Disease Etiologies in Non-Western Medical Systems." *American Anthropologist* 78 (1976): 773–82.

Frazier, E. Franklin. *The Negro Family in the United States*. 1939. Rpt. Chicago: Univ. of Chicago Press, 1966.

Gates, David. Review of *Jazz*, by Toni Morrison. *Newsweek*, 27 April 1992, 66.

Gates, Henry Louis Jr., ed. *"Race," Writing, and Difference*. Chicago: Univ. of Chicago Press, 1986.

———. *The Signifying Monkey: A Theory of Afro-American Literary Criticism*. New York: Oxford Univ. Press, 1988.

Giddings, Paula. *Where and When I Enter*. New York: William Morrow, 1984.

Gilman, Sander. "Black Bodies, White Bodies: Toward an Iconography of Female Sexuality in Late Nineteenth-Century Art, Medicine, and Literature." In *"Race," Writing, and Difference*. Ed. Henry Louis Gates Jr., 223–61. Chicago: Univ. of Chicago Press, 1986.

Glanton, Dahleen. "Many Shades of Black, and a Caste System, Too?" *Raleigh News and Observer*, 6 September 1989, D3.

Graff, Gerald. "Determinacy/Indeterminacy." In *Critical Terms for Literary Study*. Ed. Frank Lentricchia and Thomas McLaughlin, 163–76. Chicago: Univ. of Chicago Press, 1990.

Grant, Damian. *Realism*. London: Methuen, 1970; rpt. 1978.

Gray, Paul. Review of *Beloved*, by Toni Morrison. *Time*, 21 September 1987, 75.

Gunn, Thom. "William Carlos Williams." *Encounter* 25 (July 1965): 67–74.

Harley, Sharon. "For the Good of Family and Race: Gender, Work, and Domestic Roles in the Black Community, 1880–1930." *Signs* 15 (Winter 1990): 346–49.

Harris, Leslie A. "Myth as Structure in Toni Morrison's *Song of Solomon*." *MELUS* 7 (Fall 1980): 67–76.

Hawkes, Terence. *Structuralism and Semiotics*. Berkeley: Univ. of California Press, 1977.

Hogue, W. Lawrence. "Literary Production: A Silence in Afro-American Critical Practices." In *Belief Versus Theory in Black American Literary Criticism*. Ed. Joe Weixlmann and Chester J. Fontenat, 31–45. Greenwood, Fla.: Pen Kevill, 1986.

Holloway, Karla F. C., and Stephanie A. Demetrakopoulos. *New Dimensions of Spirituality*. New York: Greenwood Press, 1987.

Hooks, Bell. *Ain't I a Woman?* Boston: South End Press, 1981.

Hulbert, Ann. Review of *Jazz*, by Toni Morrison. *New Republic*, 18 May 1992, 43–48.

Hume, Kathryn. *Fantasy and Mimesis*. New York: Methuen, 1984.

Hurston, Zora Neale. *Mules and Men*. Philadelphia: J. B. Lippincott, 1935.

Iannone, Carol. "Toni Morrison's Career." *Commentary* 84 (December 1987): 59–63.

Jewell, K. Sue. *Survival of the Black Family: The Institutional Impact of U.S. Social Policy*. New York: Praeger, 1988.

Jones, Bessie W. "An Interview with Toni Morrison." In *The World of Toni Morrison*. Ed. Bessie W. Jones and Audrey L. Vinson. Dubuque, Iowa: Kendall/Hunt, 1985.

Jones, Jacqueline. *Labor of Love, Labor of Sorrow: Black Women, Work, and the Family from Slavery to the Present*. New York: Basic Books, 1985.

Kakutani, Michiko. Review of *Beloved*, by Toni Morrison. *New York Times*, 2 September 1987, C24.

Kant, Immanuel. "Analytic of the Beautiful." In *Critical Theory Since Plato*. Ed. Hazard Adams, 379–99. New York: Harcourt Brace Jovanovich, 1971.

Kaplan, E. Ann. *Women and Film: Both Sides of the Camera*. New York: Methuen, 1983.

Kastor, Elizabeth. Review of *Beloved*, by Toni Morrison. *Washington Post*. Rpt. *Raleigh News and Observer*, 23 October 1987, D3.

Kubitschek, Missy Dehn. *Claiming the Heritage: African-American Women Novelists and History*. Jackson: Univ. Press of Mississippi, 1991.

Ladner, Joyce. *Tomorrow's Tomorrow: The Black Woman*. Garden City, N.Y.: Doubleday, 1971.

Leonard, John. Review of *Beloved*, by Toni Morrison. *Los Angeles Times Book Review*, 30 August 1987, 1.

Lepow, Lauren, "Paradise Lost and Found: Dualism and Edenic Myth in Toni Morrison's *Tar Baby*." *Contemporary Literature* 28, 3 (1987): 364–77.

"Light vs. Dark: Why Skin Color No Longer Makes a Difference." *Ebony*, May 1980, 178–82.

Lloyd-Smith, Allan Gardner. *Uncanny American Fiction*. New York: St. Martin's Press, 1989.

McAdoo, Harriette Pipes, ed. *Black Families*. Beverly Hills, Calif.: Sage, 1988.

McAdoo, John L. "The Roles of Black Fathers in the Socialization of Black Children." In *Black Families*. Ed. Harriette Pipes McAdoo, 257–69. Beverly Hills, Calif.: Sage, 1988.

McKay, Nellie. "An Interview with Toni Morrison." *Contemporary Literature* 24 (Winter 1983): 413–29.

Malveaux, Julianne. "The Economic Statuses of Black Families." In *Black Families*. Ed. Harriette Pipes McAdoo, 133–47. Beverly Hills, Calif.: Sage, 1988.

Mariani, Paul. *William Carlos Williams: A New World Naked*. New York: McGraw-Hill, 1981.

Marriott, Michel. "Light-Skinned Men: Problems and Privileges." *Essence*, November 1988, 75 (4).

Morrison, Toni. *Beloved*. New York: Knopf, 1987.

——. *The Bluest Eye*. New York: Washington Square Press, 1970.

——. *Jazz*. New York: Knopf, 1992.

——. *Playing in the Dark: Whiteness and the Literary Imagination*. Cambridge: Harvard Univ. Press, 1992.

——. "Rootedness: The Ancestor as Foundation." In *Black Women Writers (1950–1980): A Critical Evaluation*. Ed. Mari Evans. Garden City, N.Y.: Anchor Press/Doubleday, 1984.

——. *Song of Solomon*. New York: New American Library, 1977.

——. *Sula*. New York: New American Library, 1973.

——. *Tar Baby*. New York: New American Library, 1981.

Moynihan, Patrick. *Negro Family: The Case for National Action*. Washington, D.C.: U.S. Department of Labor, Office of Planning and Research, March 1965.

Nielson, David. *Black Ethos: Northern Urban Negro Life and Thought, 1890-1930*. 2d ed. 1977. Rpt. New York: Dial Press, 1982.

Peterson, Walter Scott. *An Approach to Paterson*. New Haven: Yale Univ. Press, 1967.

Pleck, Elizabeth. "The Two-Parent Household: Black Family Structure in Late Nineteenth-Century Boston." In *American Family in Social-Historical Perspective*. Ed. Michael Gordon, 152–70. New York: St. Martin's Press, 1973.

Publishers Weekly. Review of *Beloved*, by Toni Morrison. 17 July 1987, 53.

Reed, Harry. "Toni Morrison, *Song of Solomon* and Black Cultural Nationalism." *Centennial Review* 32 (Winter 1988): 50–64.

Roth, Robert. "Deconstructing Audience: A Post-Structuralist Rereading." In *A Sense of Audience in Written Communication*. Ed. Gesa Kirsch and Duane H. Roen, 175–91. London: Sage, 1990.

Rubin, Merle. Review of *Beloved*, by Toni Morrison. *Christian Science Monitor*, 5 October 1987, 20.

Russ, Joanna. *How to Suppress Women's Writing*. Austin: Univ. of Texas Press, 1983.

Samuels, Wilfrid. "Liminality and the Search for Self in Toni Morrison's *Song of Solomon*." *Minority Voices* 5 (Spring-Fall 1981): 59–68.

Schaef, Anne. *When Society Becomes an Addict*. San Francisco: Harper and Row, 1987.

Scholes, Robert. *Structuralism in Literature*. New Haven: Yale Univ. Press, 1974.

Shimkin, Demitri B., Edith M. Shimkin, and Dennis A. Frate. *The Extended Family in Black Societies*. Paris: Mouton Publishers, 1978.

Somerville, Jane. "Idealized Beauty and the Denial of Love in Toni Morrison's *Bluest Eye*." *Bulletin of the West Virginia Association of College English Teachers* 9 (Spring 1986): 18–23.

Staples, Robert. *The Black Woman in America*. Chicago: Nelson-Hall, 1973.

Stepto, Robert. *From Behind the Veil: A Study of Afro-American Narrative*. Urbana: Univ. of Illinois Press, 1979.

Stetson, Erlene. "Studying Slavery: Some Literary and Pedagogical Considerations on the Black Female Slave." In *All the Women Are White, All the Blacks Are Men, But Some of Us Are Brave*. Ed. Gloria T. Hull, Patricia Bell Scott, and Barbara Smith, 75–79. Old Westbury, N.Y.: Feminist Press, 1982.

Strouse, Jean. "Toni Morrison's Black Magic." *Newsweek*, 30 March 1981, 52–57.

"U.S. Family Has Eroded Steadily Over Past 8 Years, Researchers Say." *Los Angeles Times*. Rpt. *Raleigh News and Observer*, 21 July 1988, A16.

Walker, Alice. *In Search of Our Mother's Gardens*. San Diego: Harcourt Brace Jovanovich, 1983.

Wallace, Michele. *Black Macho and the Myth of the Superwoman*. New York: Dial Press, 1979.

Wallis, Roy. "Institutions." In *The Social Science Encyclopedia*. Ed. Adam Kuper and Jessica Kuper, 399–400. Boston: Routledge Kegan Paul, 1985.

Washington, Elsie. "The Bluest Eye." *Essence*, January 1988, 114.

Weber, Max. *The Protestant Ethic and the Spirit of Capitalism*. 1904. Rpt. New York: Scribner, 1956.

Welter, Barbara. "The Cult of True Womanhood: 1820–1860." In *American Family in Social-Historical Perspective*. Ed. Michael Gordon, 225–42. New York: St. Martin's Press, 1973.

Werner, Craig. "The Briar Patch as Modernist Myth: Morrison, Barthes and *Tar Baby* As-Is." In *Critical Essays on Toni Morrison*. Ed. Nellie McKay, 150–67. Boston: G. K. Hall, 1988.

White, Deborah. *Ar'n't I a Woman?: Female Slaves in the Plantation South*. New York: Norton, 1985.

Willhelm, Sidney. *Black in a White America*. Cambridge, Mass.: Schenkman, 1983.

Williams, William Carlos. *The Autobiography of William Carlos Williams*. New York: New Directions Books, 1951.

———. *Paterson*. New York: New Directions Books, 1963.

Willis, Susan. "Eruptions of Funk." *Black American Literature Forum* 16 (1982): 34–42.

Wolf, Gary, ed. *Critical Terms for Science Fiction and Fantasy*. New York: Greenwood Press, 1986.

Woodson, Carter Godwin. *A Century of Negro Migration*. Washington, D.C.: Association for the Study of Negro Life and History, 1918.

Zipes, Jack. "Breaking the Magic Spell: Politics and the Fairy Tale." *New German Critique* 14 (1986): 117–35.

Index